IMAGES
of America

NEWPORT REVISITED

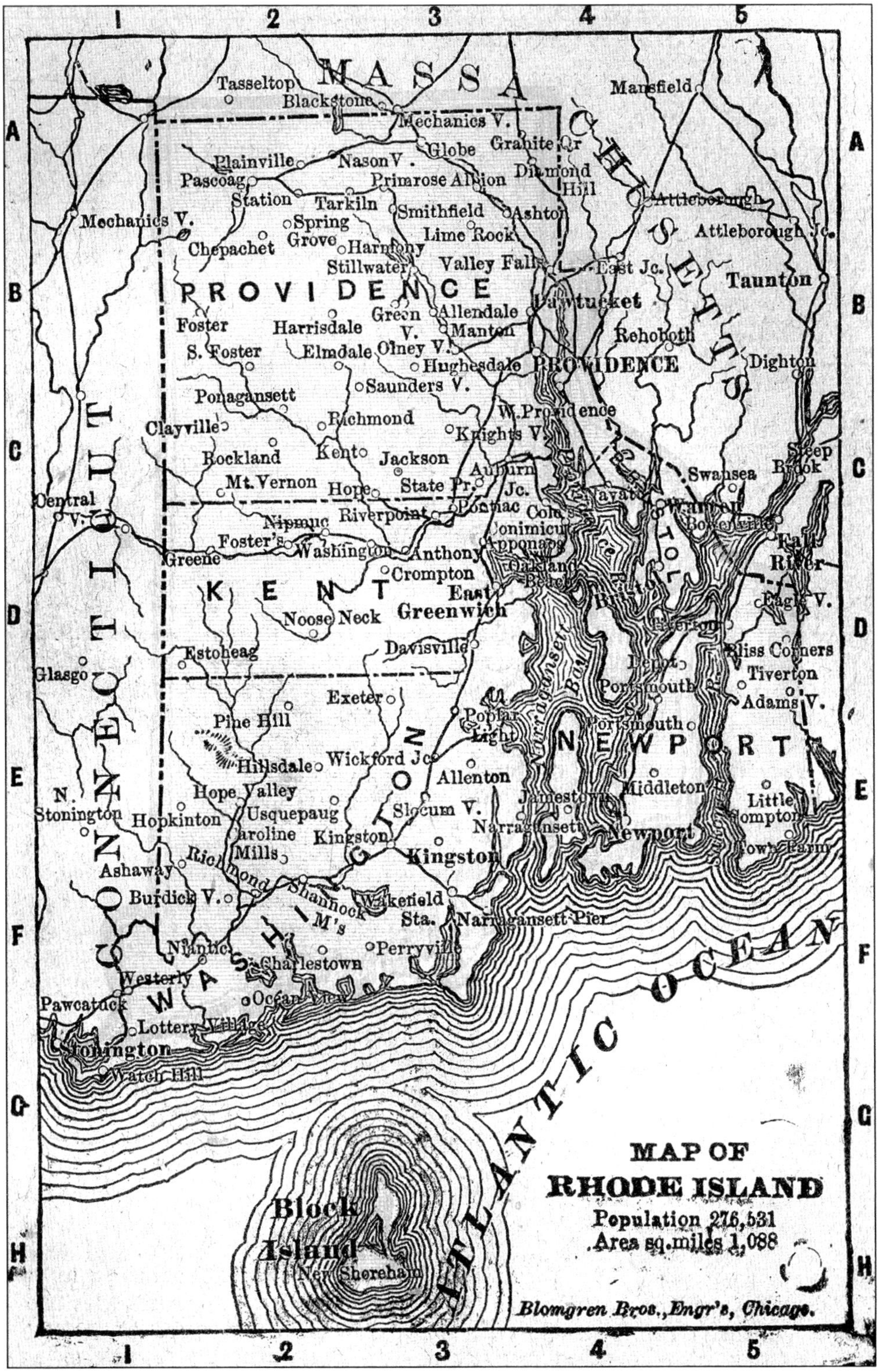

This map of Rhode Island dates from the late 1800s.

IMAGES
of America

NEWPORT REVISITED

Rob Lewis and Ryan A. Young

ARCADIA
PUBLISHING

ISBN 978-0-7385-0924-2

Published by Arcadia Publishing
Charleston, South Carolina

Printed in the United States of America

Library of Congress Catalog Card Number: 2001091063

For all general information contact Arcadia Publishing at:
Telephone 843-853-2070
Fax 843-853-0044
E-mail sales@arcadiapublishing.com
For customer service and orders:
Toll-Free 1-888-313-2665

Visit us on the Internet at www.arcadiapublishing.com

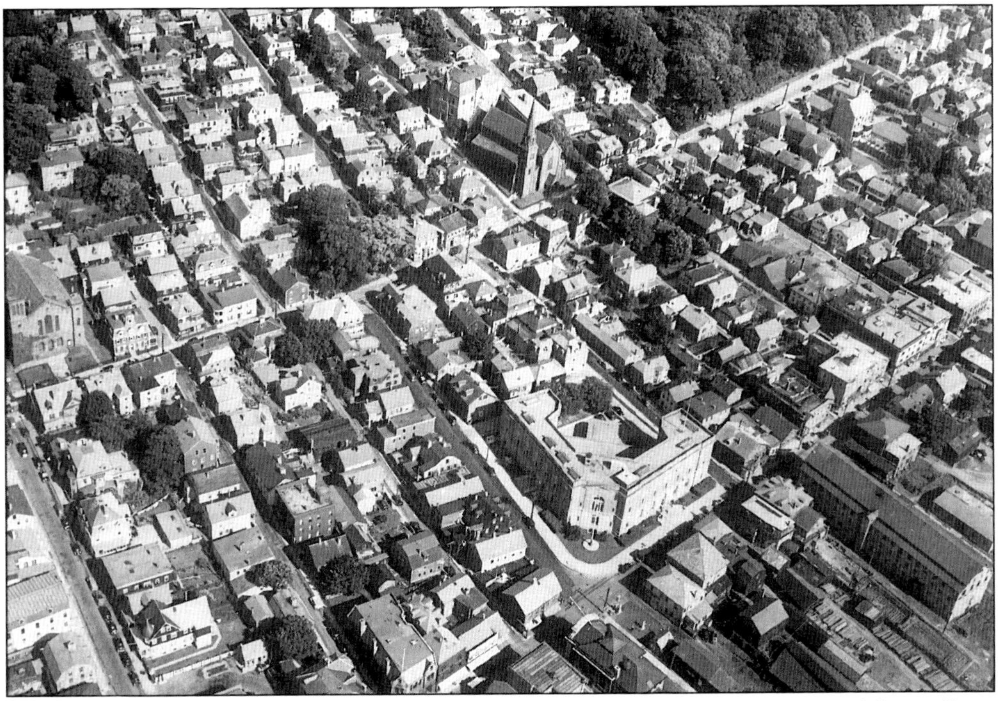

Downtown Newport is shown in a bird's-eye view taken in July 1938. (Courtesy of the William Bachus collection.)

Contents

Introduction 7

1. Around Town 9

2. Historic Homes and Buildings 35

3. The Bridges of Newport County 55

4. Along the Water's Edge 63

5. Times to Remember 81

6. Castles by the Sea 97

7. The Navy in Newport 119

Acknowledgments 128

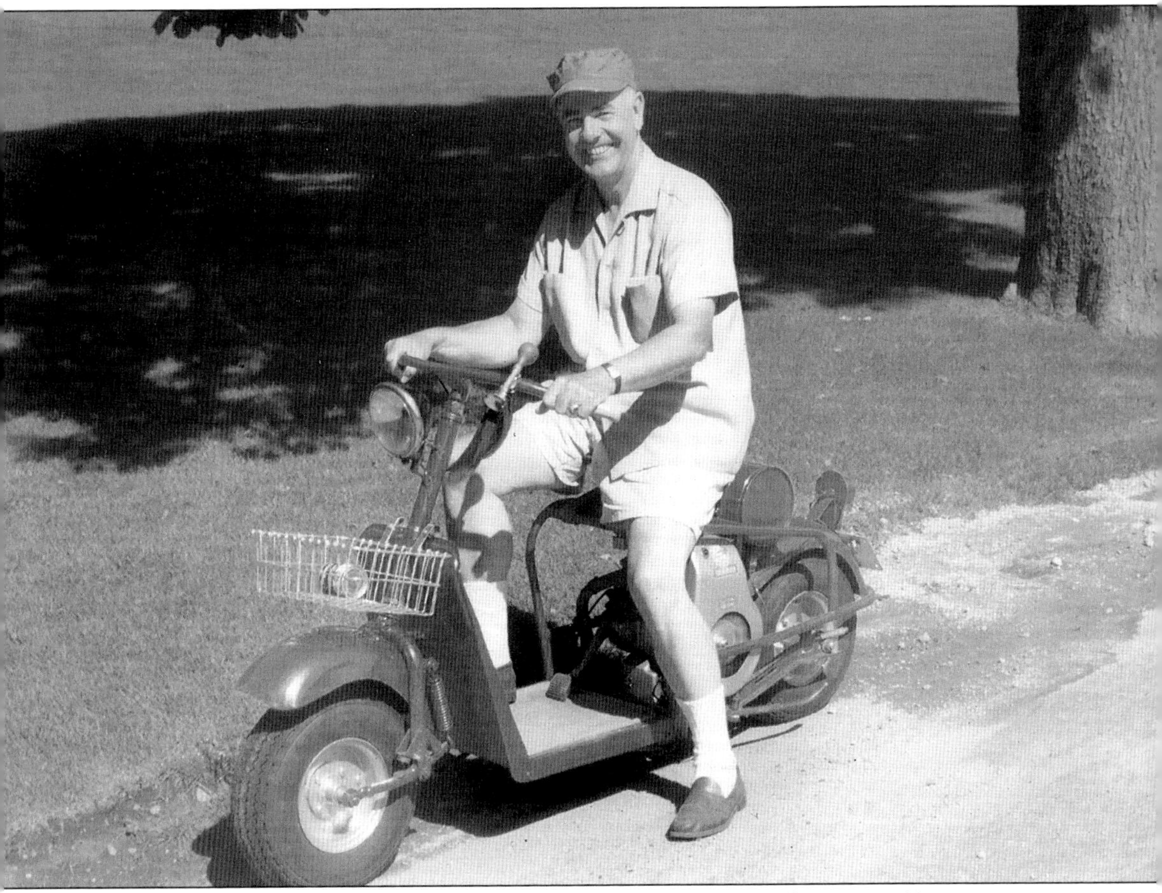

This book is dedicated to Essig Remington "Doc" Young, shown here in 1962.

INTRODUCTION

Since the mid-1600s, Newport's temperate climate and natural harbor have made it an ideal place to settle. The Aquidneck Island soil was fertile, and the proximity to the ocean made seafood bountiful. The natural formation of the land made the inner harbor almost wakeless, an ideal port that rivaled Boston and New York in its day. Newport today can boast hundreds of 18th- and 19th-century dwellings, with outstanding examples such as the Colony House and Brick Market. In trying to cover the mansions, we chose some that remain today and some that are long gone, victims to acts of God, man, and progress.

People travel from all parts of the world to get a taste of what Newport has to offer. They come to visit Newport every summer not only to see the mansions (or rather, "castles by the sea") but also to enjoy the wide array of activities, such as sailing, fishing, golfing, hiking, and the beach and wildlife areas.

Ryan A. Young's grandfather Essig Remington "Doc" Young was not only the skipper of his 19-foot Rhodes sailboat but also the skipper of this book. His love of sailing and his interest in photography has enabled us to put together a fine collection of images regarding local points of interest. He documented Newport's renaissance in the 1960s as it progressed from a run-down seaport to one of the East Coast's brightest gems. Doc not only photographed Newport but also collected Newport-related ephemera, which was a wonderful aid to our research.

One

AROUND TOWN

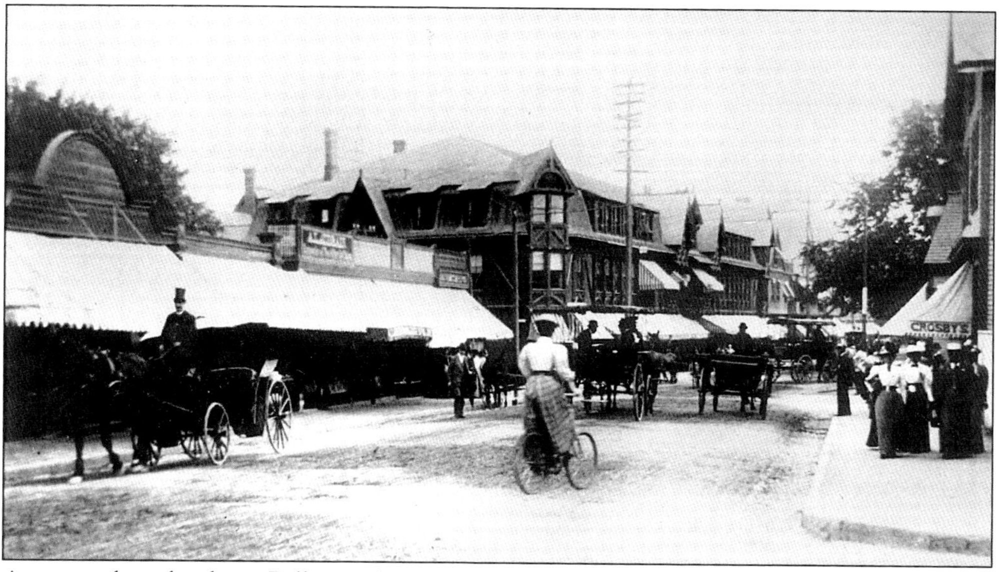

A woman bicycles down Bellevue Avenue *c.* 1900. In the center is the Travers Block, located on the corner of Bath Road. Designed by Richard Morris Hunt, the block was built *c.* 1875. The opening of the block marked the beginning of a new upscale shopping area for Newport's summer elite.

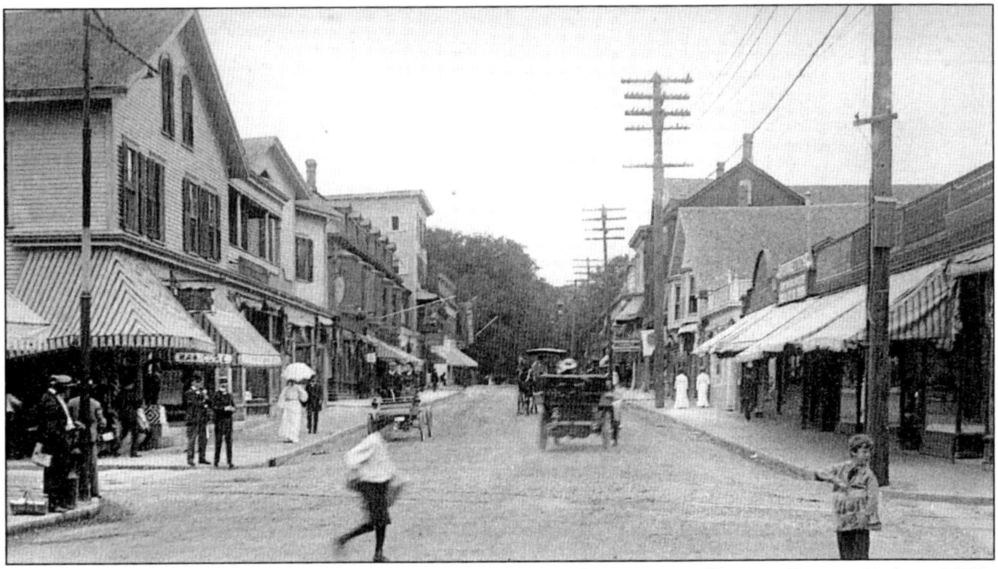

This c. 1910 view looks north on Bellevue Avenue at the corner of Levin Street. Before 1852, Bellevue Avenue ended at Narragansett Avenue. In 1852, a road was cut through farmland that extended the avenue to Bailey's Beach.

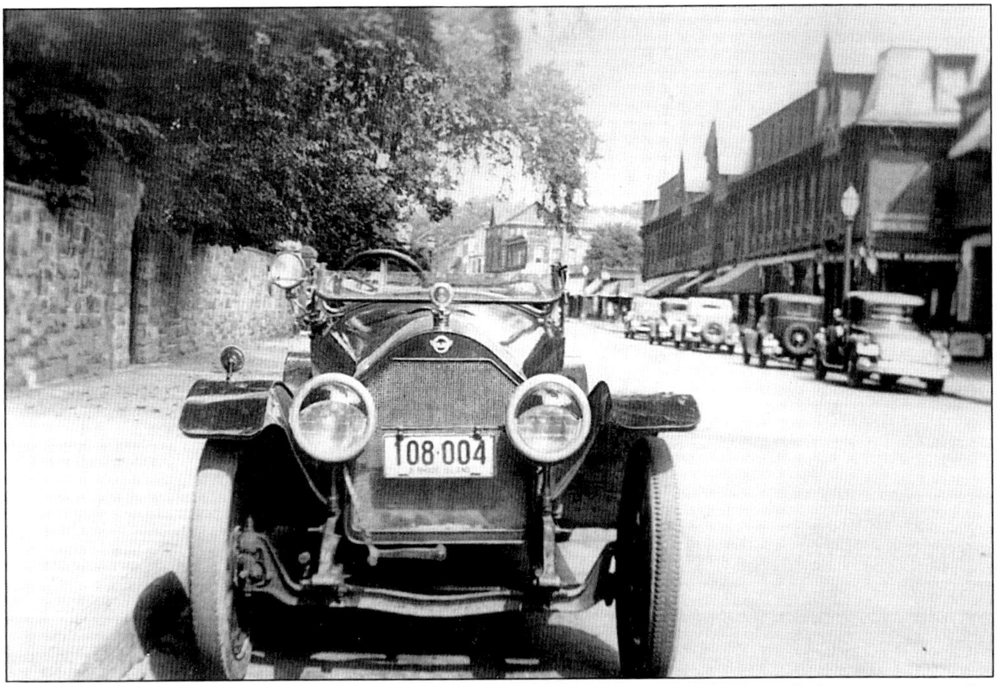

Looking north on Bellevue Avenue, this view shows the Travers Block and the casino on the right. By 1860, Ocean Drive was extended to Brenton Point, completing the circuit.

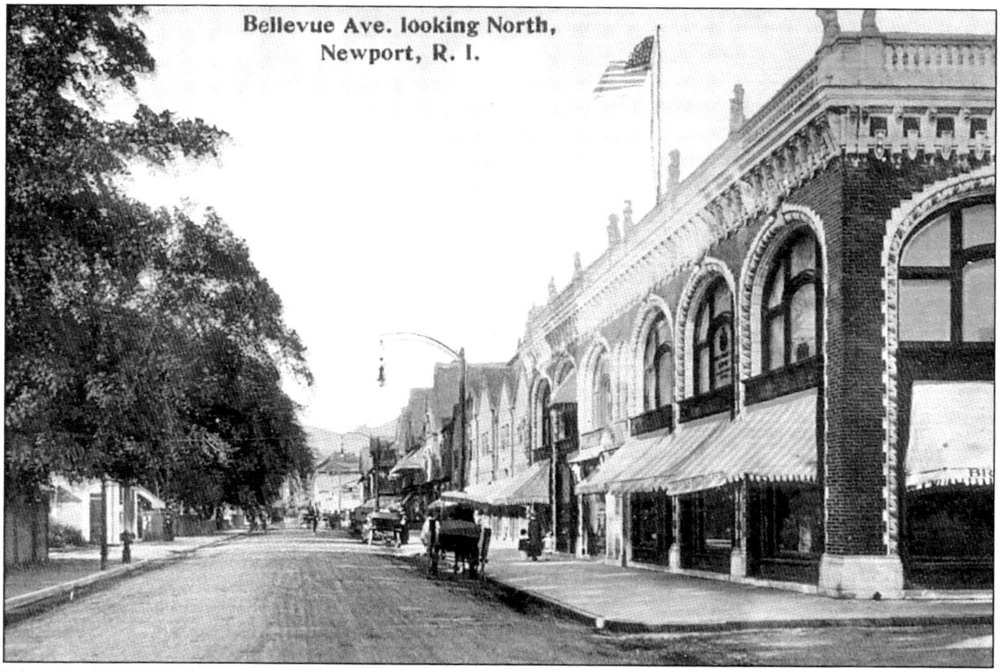

The Audrain Building was designed by Bruce Price after a fire in 1899 consumed the second Ocean House. It was completed in 1901.

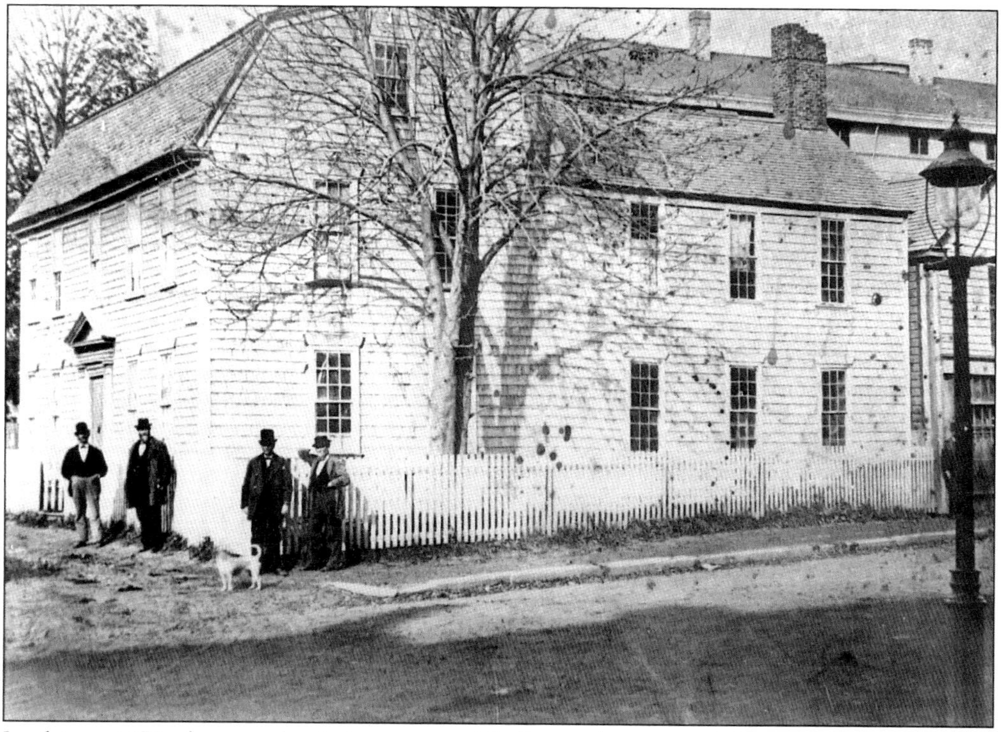

In this *c.* 1870 photograph of the corner of Bellevue Avenue and Prospect Hill Street, the Atlantic House can be seen in the background.

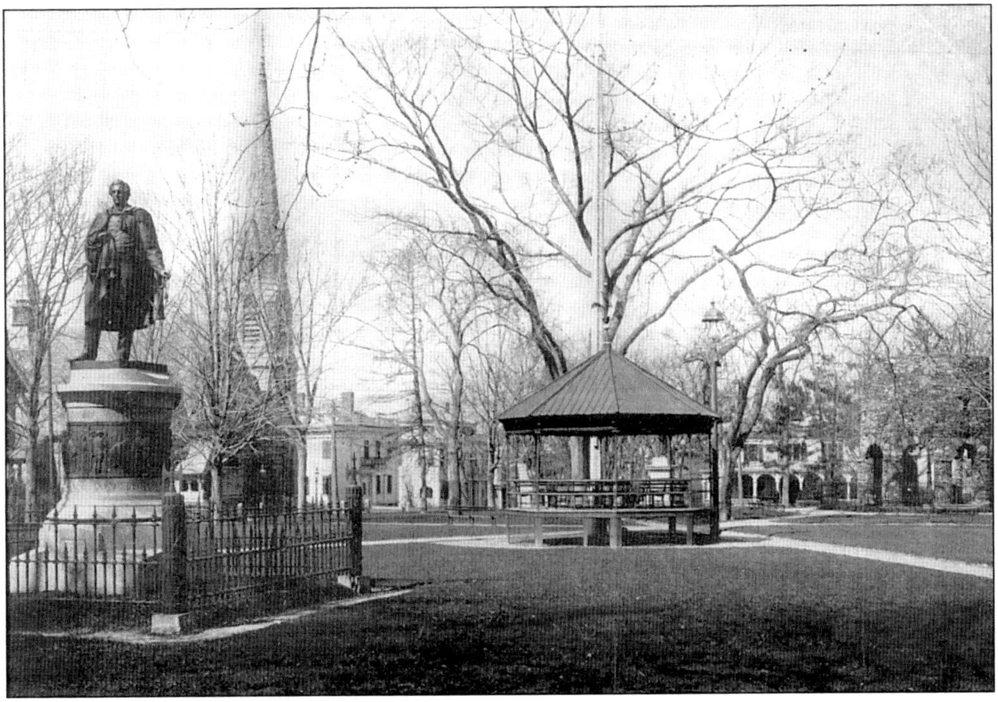
Touro Park is shown here *c.* 1895.

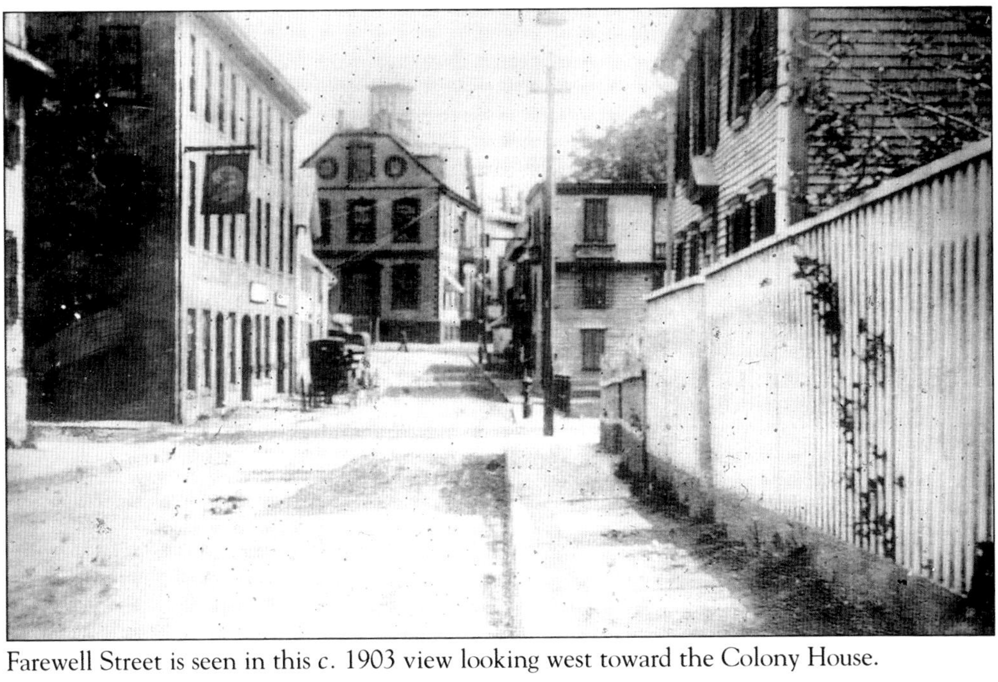
Farewell Street is seen in this *c.* 1903 view looking west toward the Colony House.

In the mid-1840s, this Clarke Street building served as the Second Congregational Church. By 1885, it became the Central Baptist Church. In this photograph, the church and street are "dressed" for the movie *Amistad*. (Photograph by Dorothy Burnette.)

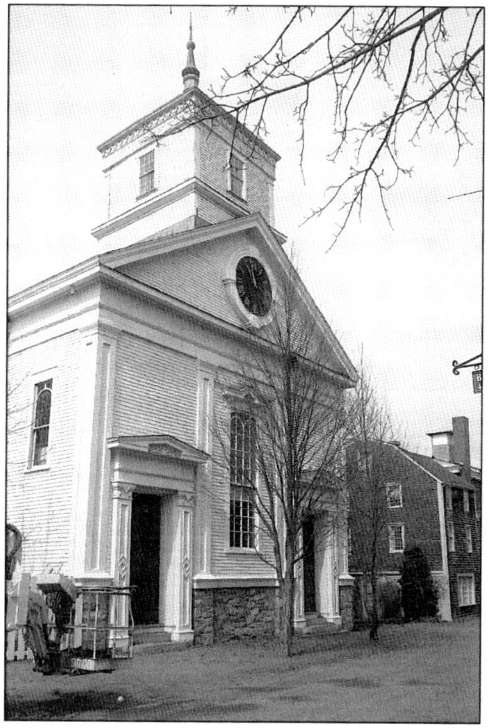

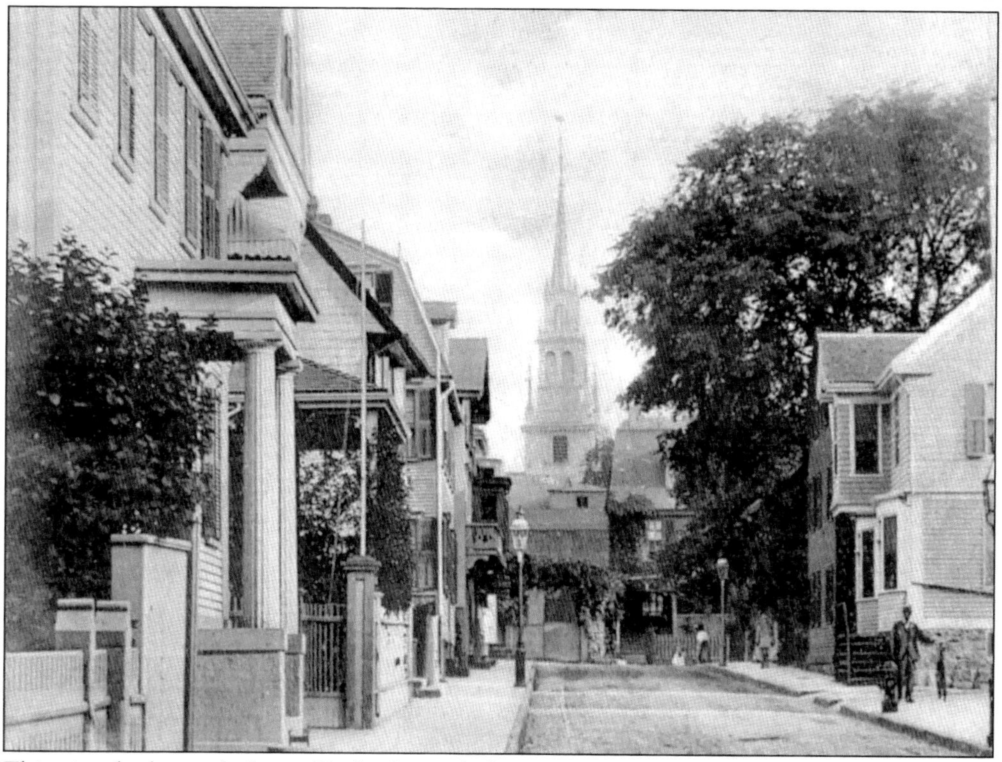

This view looks south down Clarke Street before 1908. Because of the number and caliber of historic structures on this street, it has always been a target for preservation.

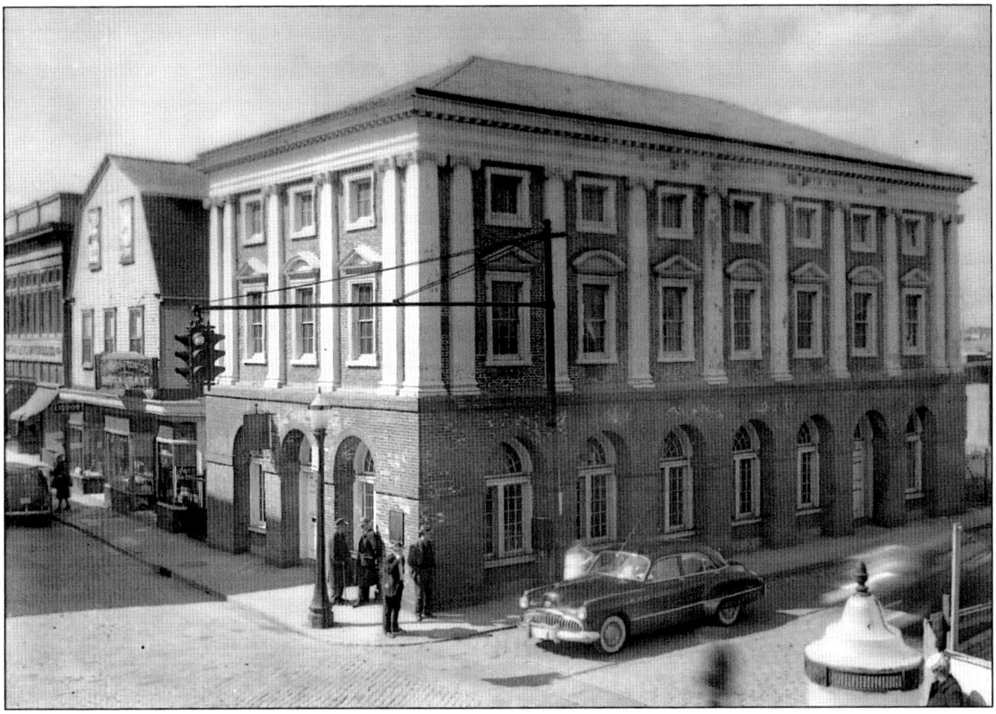

The Brick Market was built in the 1760s on a Peter Harrison design. It was used as a dry goods storage on the second floor and a market house on the first. The Isaac Gould House is visible on the left.

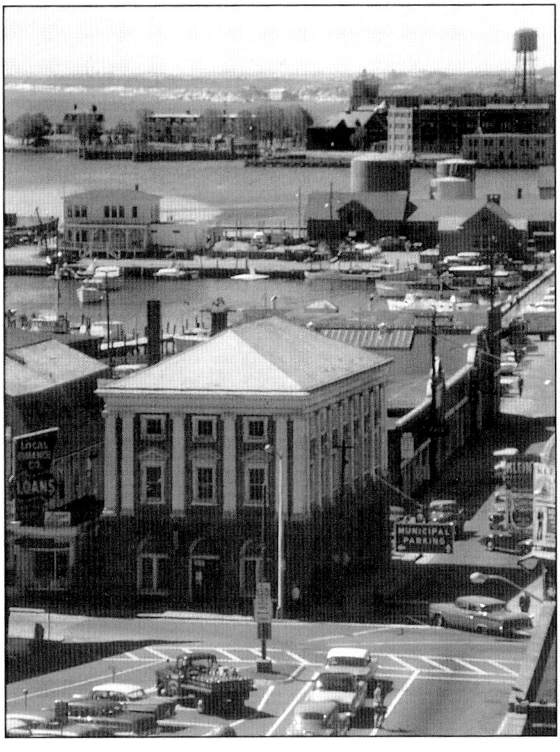

This late-1960s view from the U.S. Navy YMCA roof shows the Brick Market and the waterworks building just behind it. In the distance is Goat Island and the defunct torpedo station.

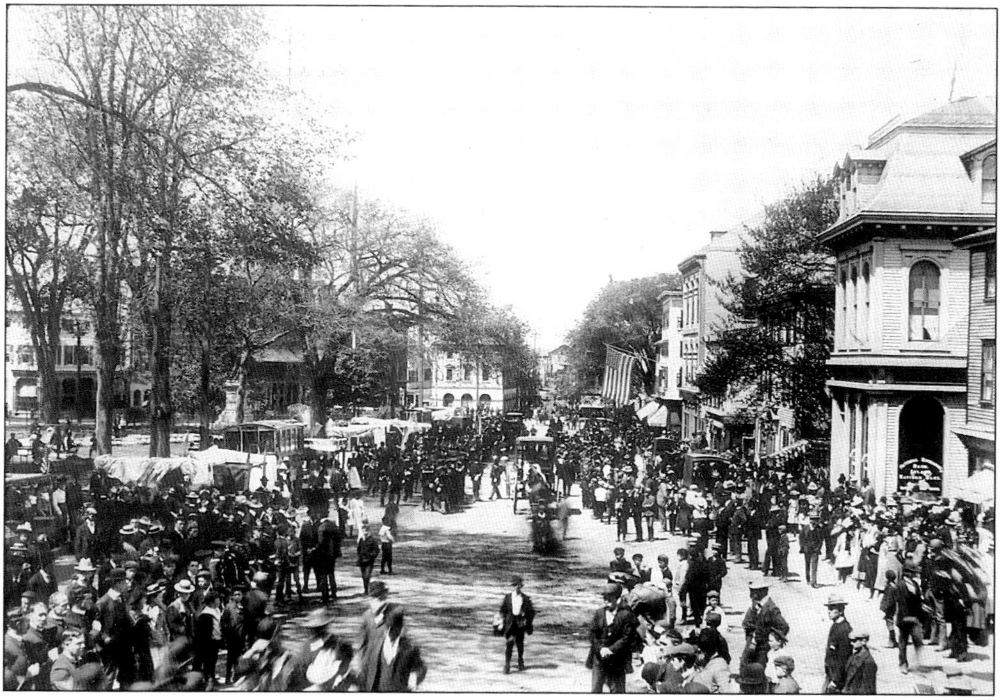

In the early years of the city, the open space around the town spring was called the Parade. After George Washington's death in 1799, the square was renamed in his honor.

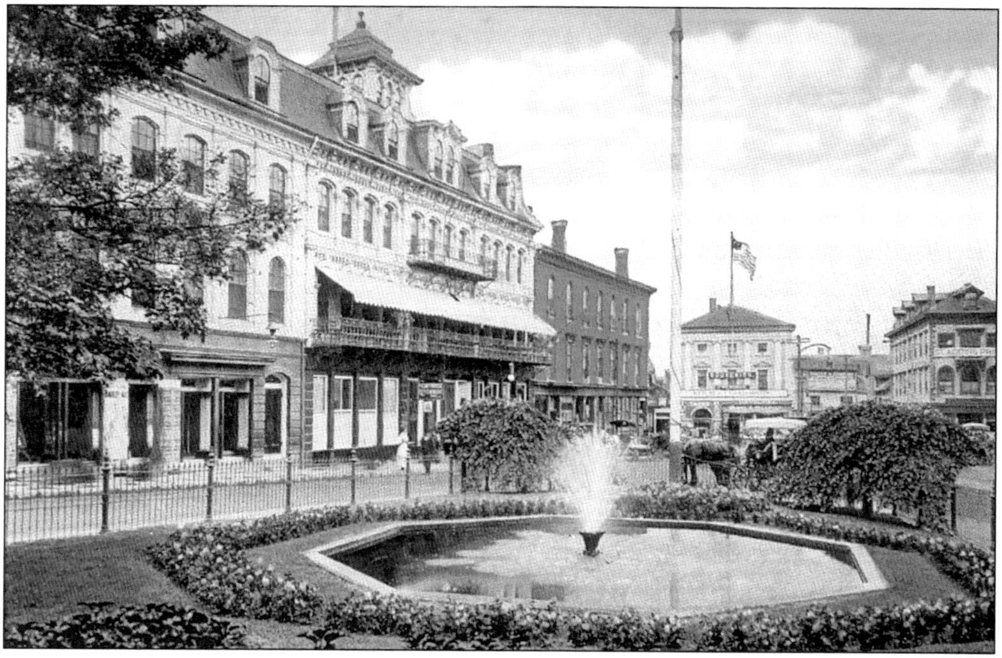

Newport was first settled around a natural spring. In 1802, the water was diverted to Washington Square. This fountain was installed in the park in 1928. The Opera House and the Perry House are visible to the left.

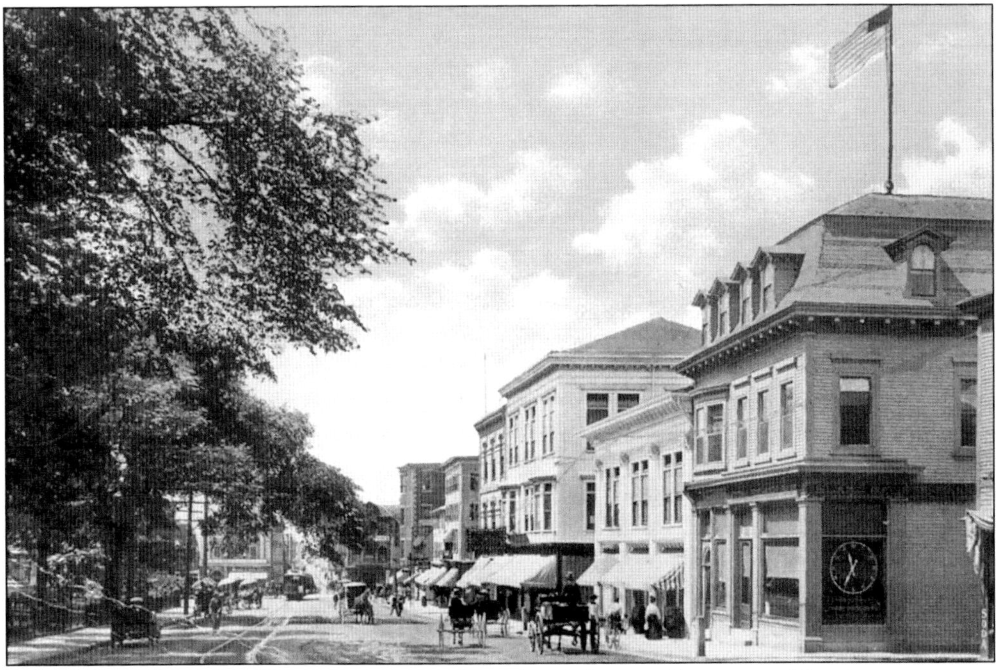

The Island Savings Bank can be seen to the right while a trolley enters Washington Square from Long Wharf.

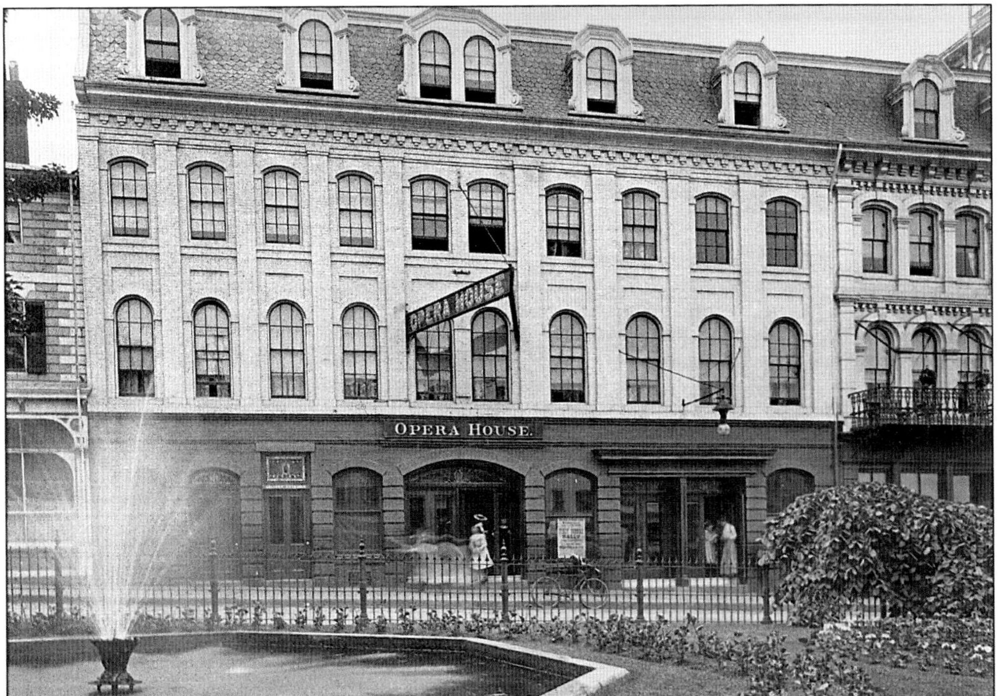

Newport's Opera House was erected in 1867. The four-story building has gone through many renovations through the years. Today, it functions as a theater.

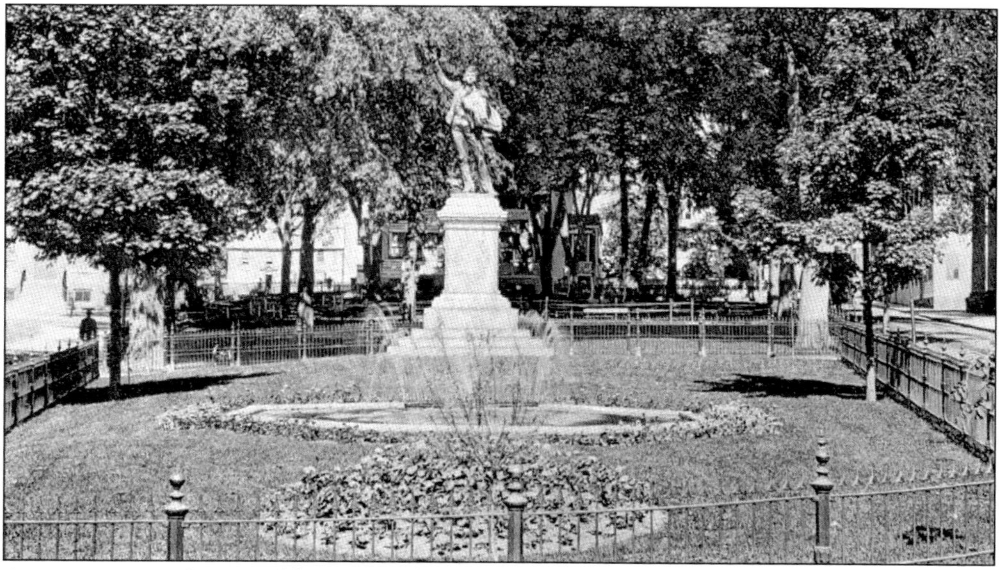

A monument to Commo. Oliver Hazard Perry was erected at the base of Washington Square on September 10, 1885. The sculptor was William G. Turner, who had the statue cast in Florence, Italy. The statue was dedicated on the first anniversary of the Battle of Lake Erie.

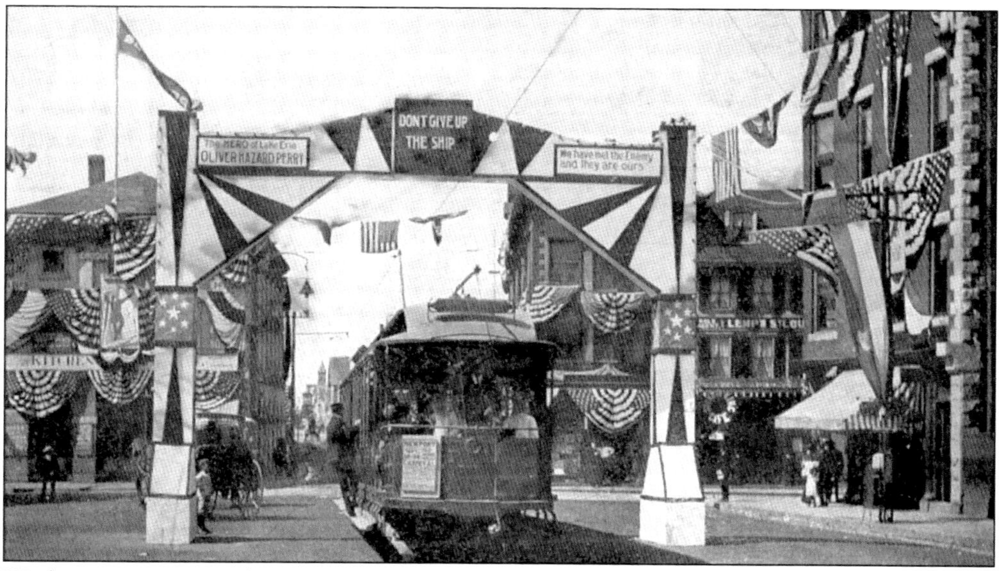

Washington Square is shown dressed up for Old Home Week. Trolley service began in 1889. By the early 1890s, service had expanded throughout the city.

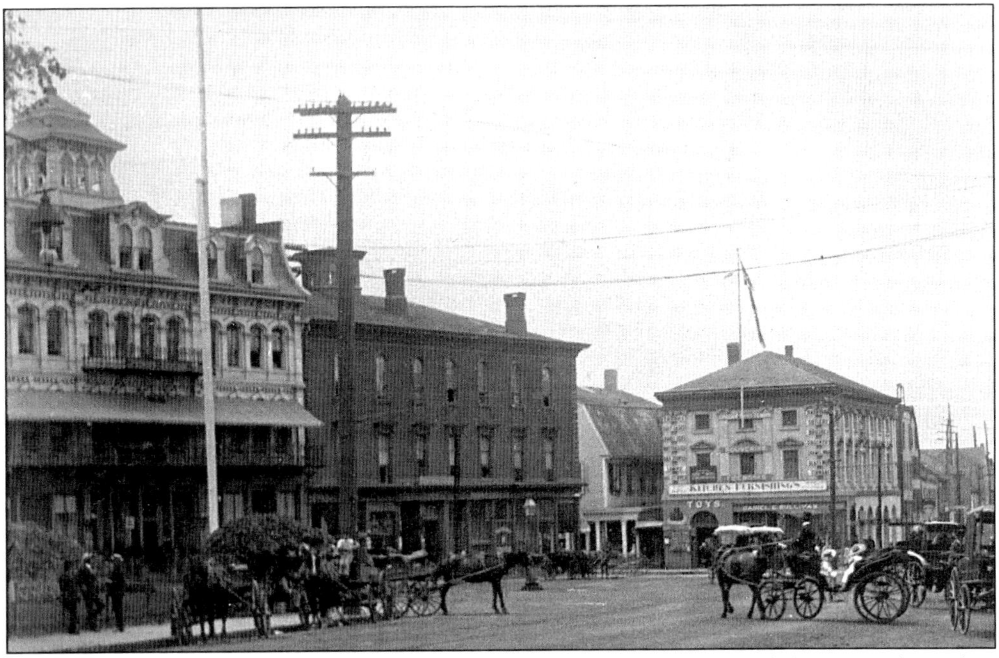

Washington Square is shown in the early 1900s. Brick Market (right) received its first restoration in 1928. Today, it is a museum dedicated to Newport's history, operated by the Newport Historical Society.

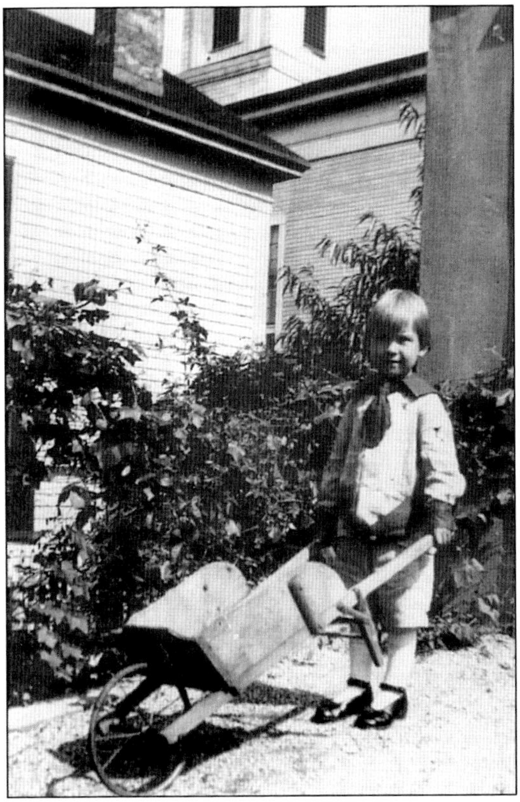

Roy Richardson is hard at work in his backyard c. 1915. The spire of the United Baptist Church can be seen in the distance.

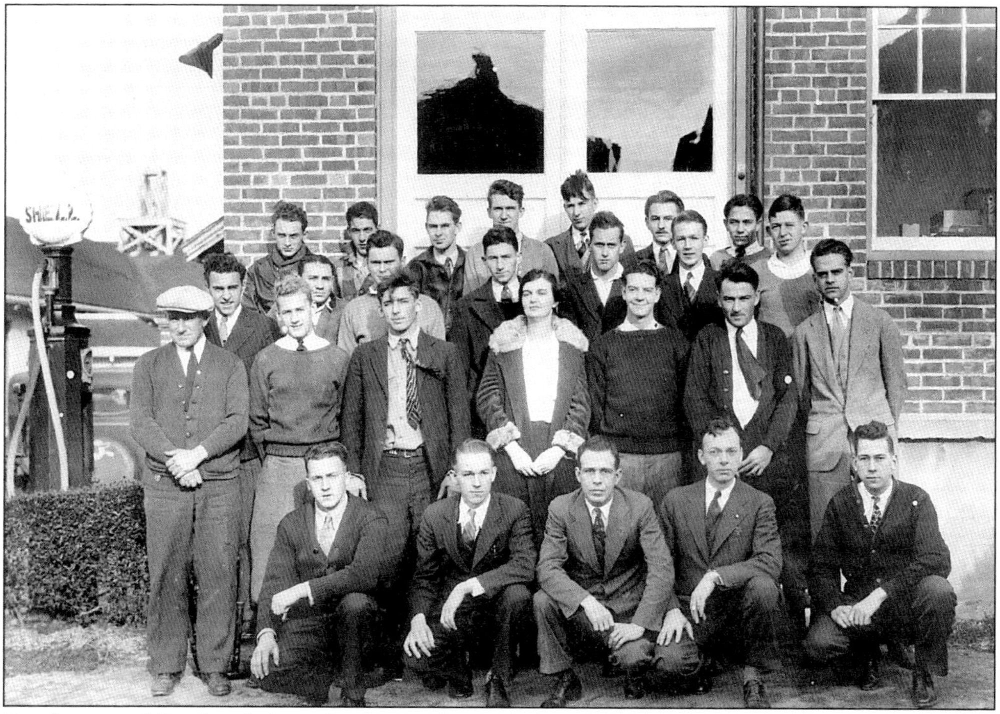

Employees of Eppley Labs, which was located on Sheffield Avenue, line up for a group photograph c. 1935.

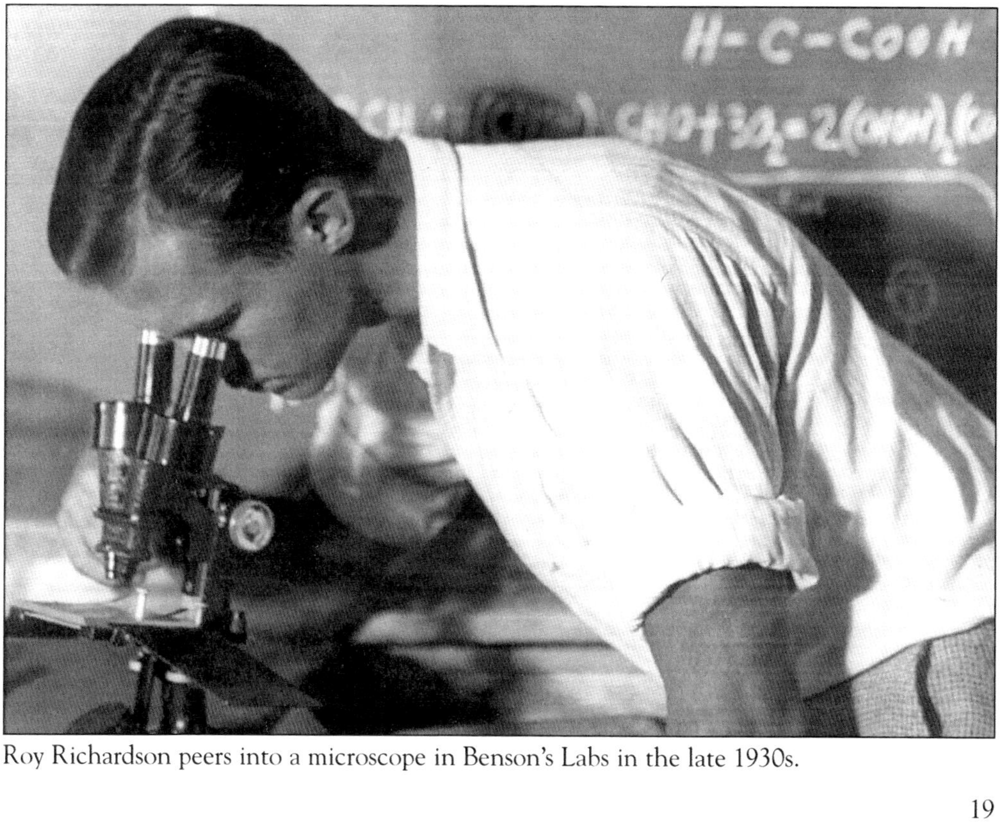

Roy Richardson peers into a microscope in Benson's Labs in the late 1930s.

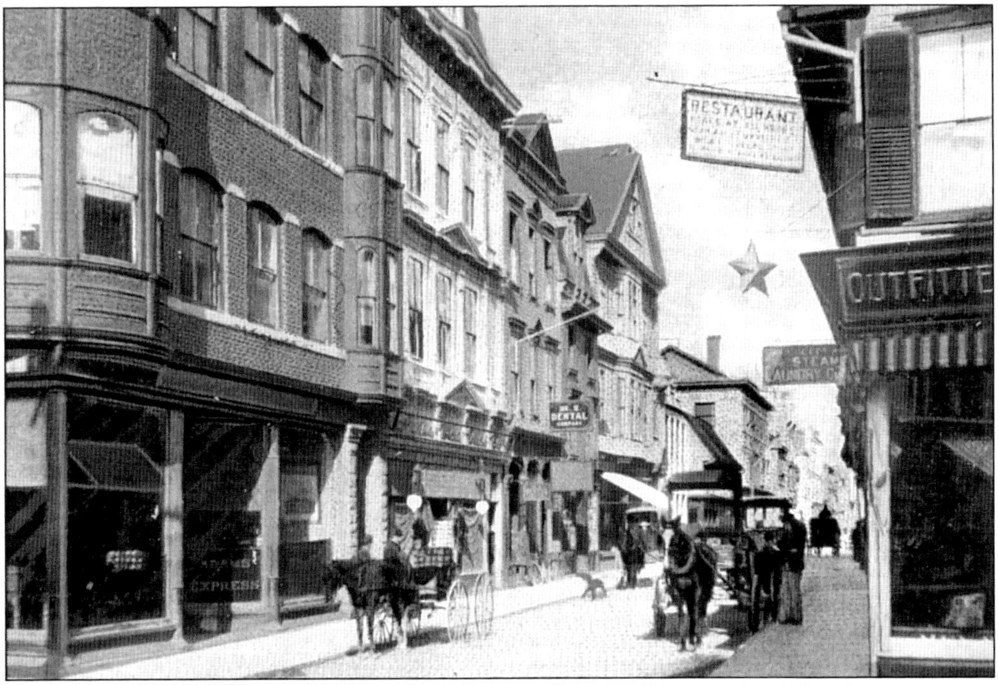

This c. 1910 view looks north along Thames Street from Mill Street. By 1923, the increase in automobile traffic necessitated making Spring and Thames Streets one-way.

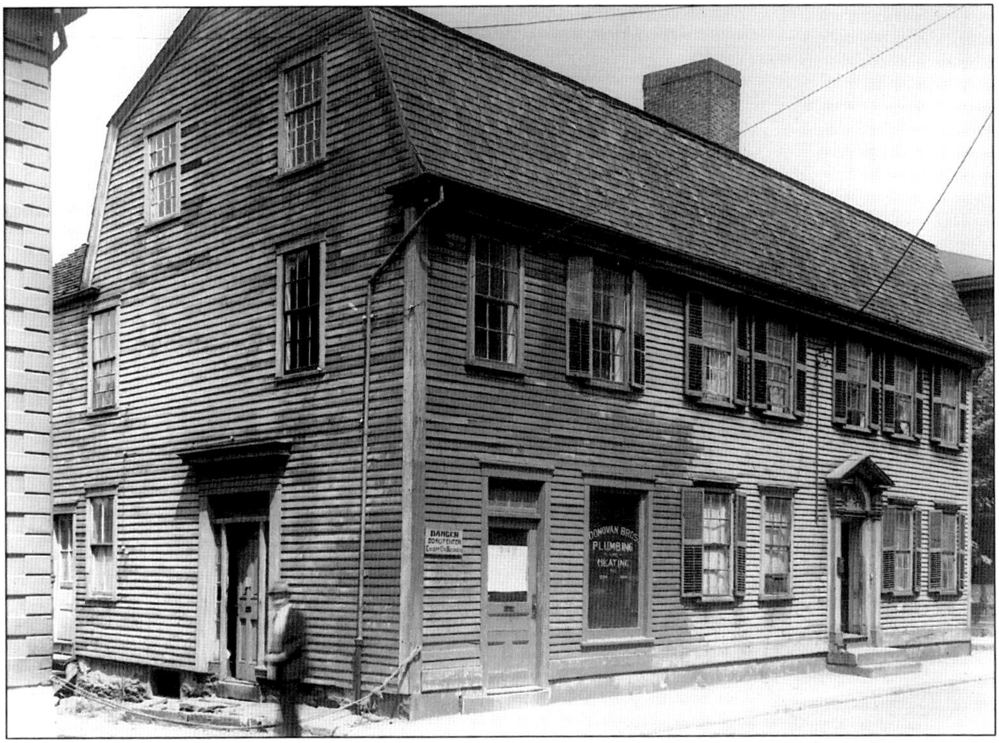

The Hammond House was built c. 1800 on what was part of the Abraham Redwood estate. The house rested on the west side of Thames Street between Fair and Gidley Streets.

This fire barn was designed by Col. James Fludder and built in 1877. This photograph dates from 1902. The building is still standing and has been converted to a private residence.

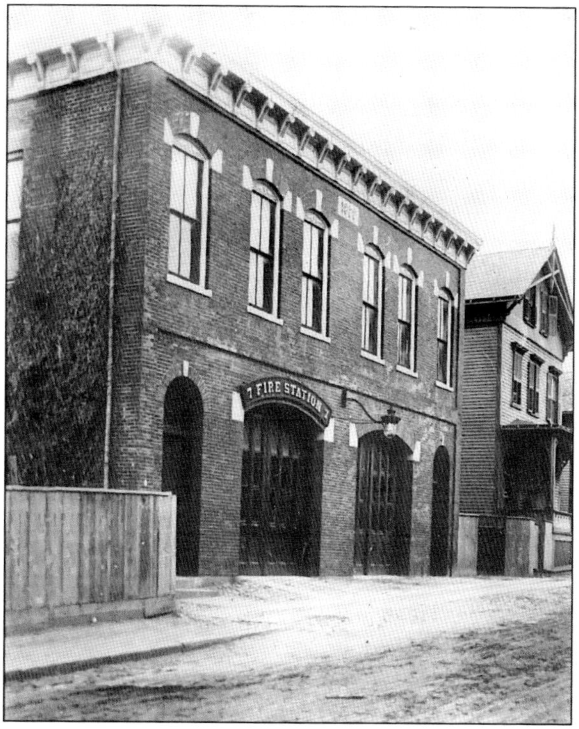

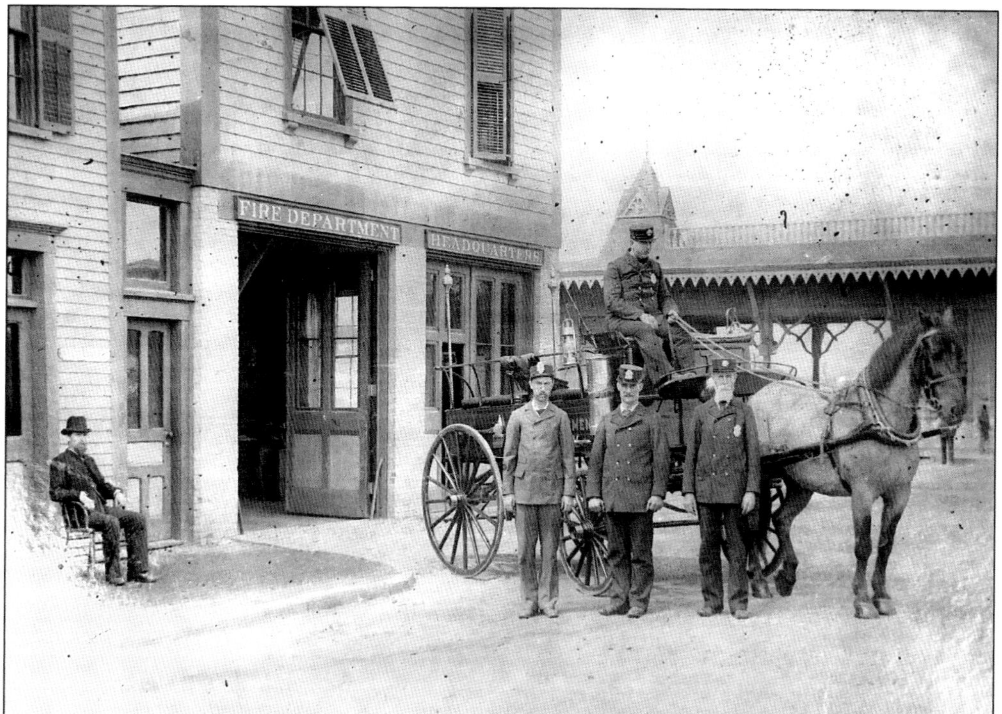

Station 1 was built at the bottom of West Marlborough Street. By 1888, Newport had four steamers, seven hose carriages, and one hook-and-ladder vehicle—all drawn by horse. The payroll had 124 paid firemen.

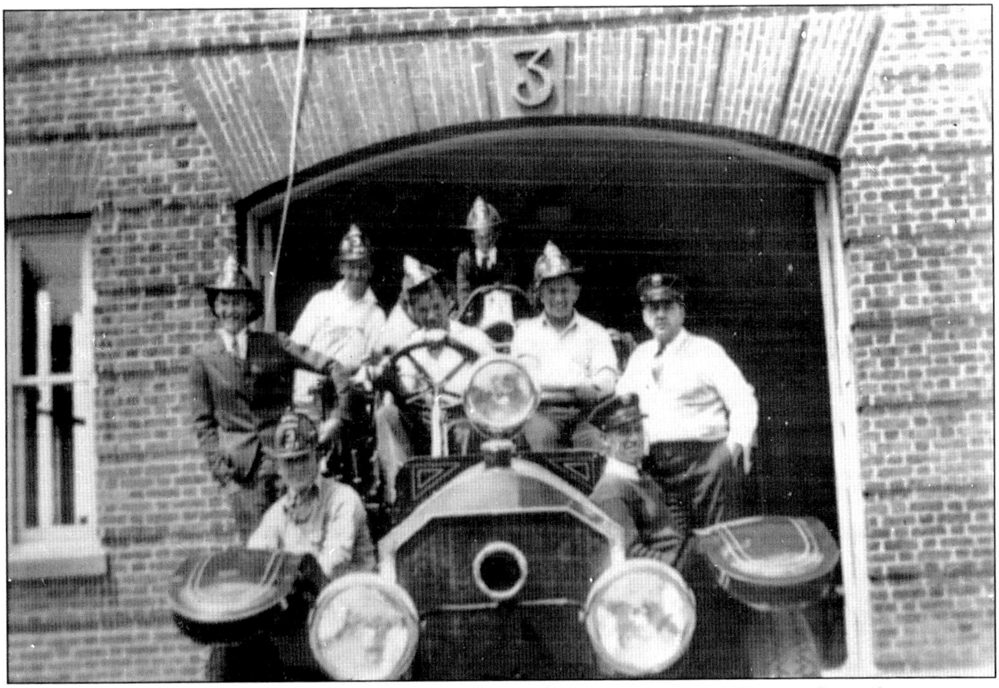

Station 3 was built on Coggshall Avenue in the early 1900s to cover the southward expansion of the city.

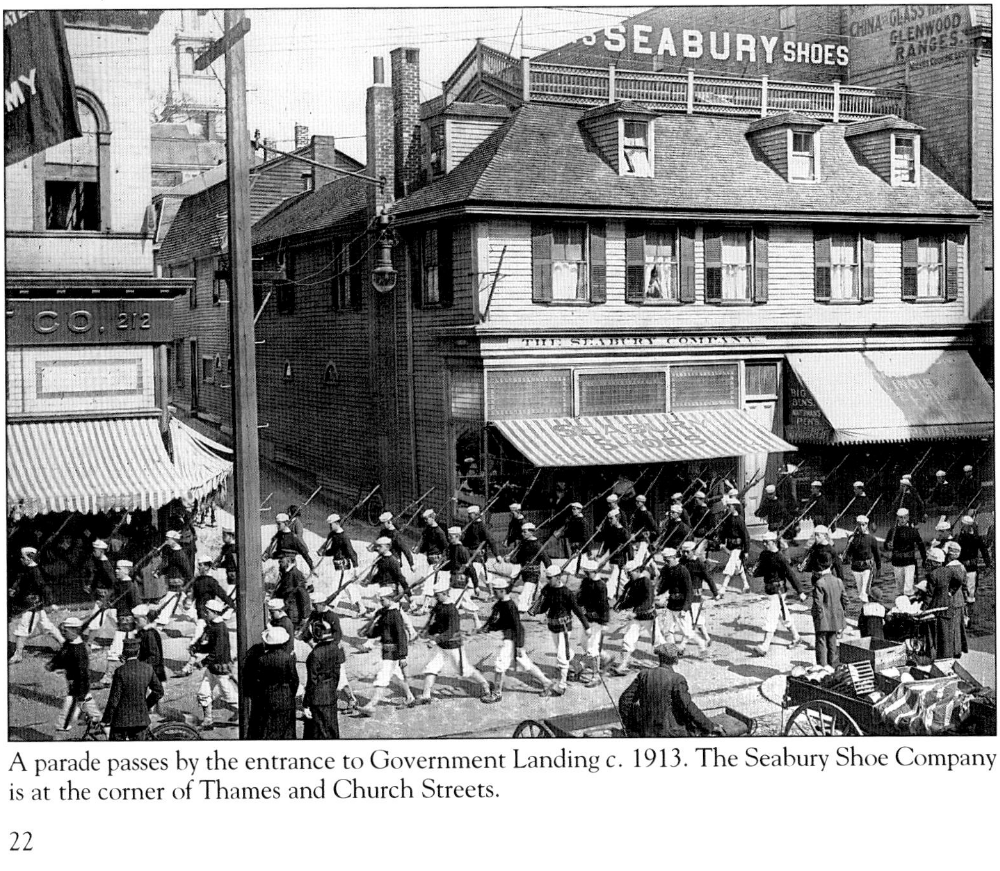

A parade passes by the entrance to Government Landing *c.* 1913. The Seabury Shoe Company is at the corner of Thames and Church Streets.

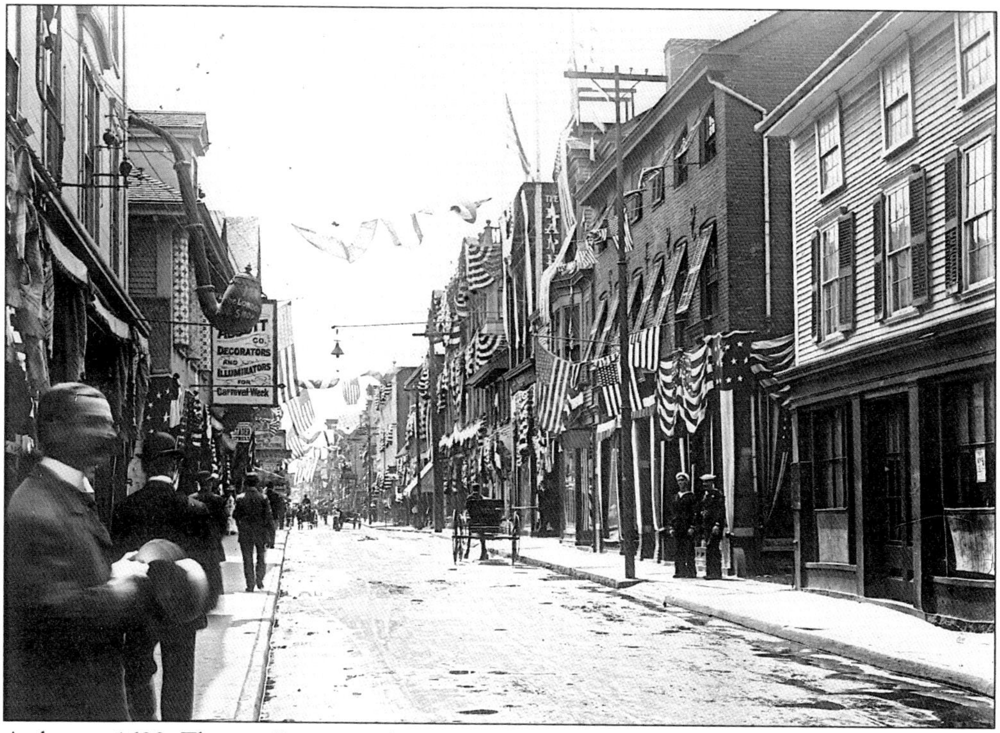

As late as 1690, Thames Street was known as the Strand, a name for the waterfront. Thames Street is listed on the 1712 Mumford map. This 1906 photograph shows Thames Street decorated to celebrate the Newport Carnival.

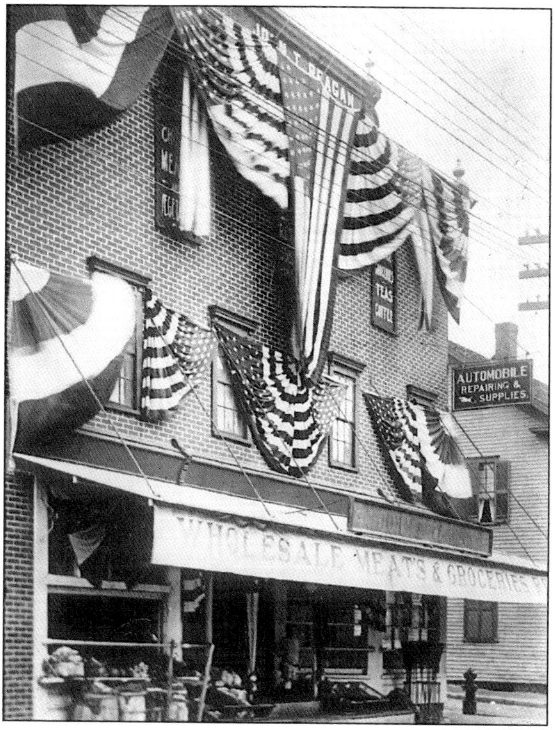

The J.T. Reagan building shows its colors for the Newport Carnival.

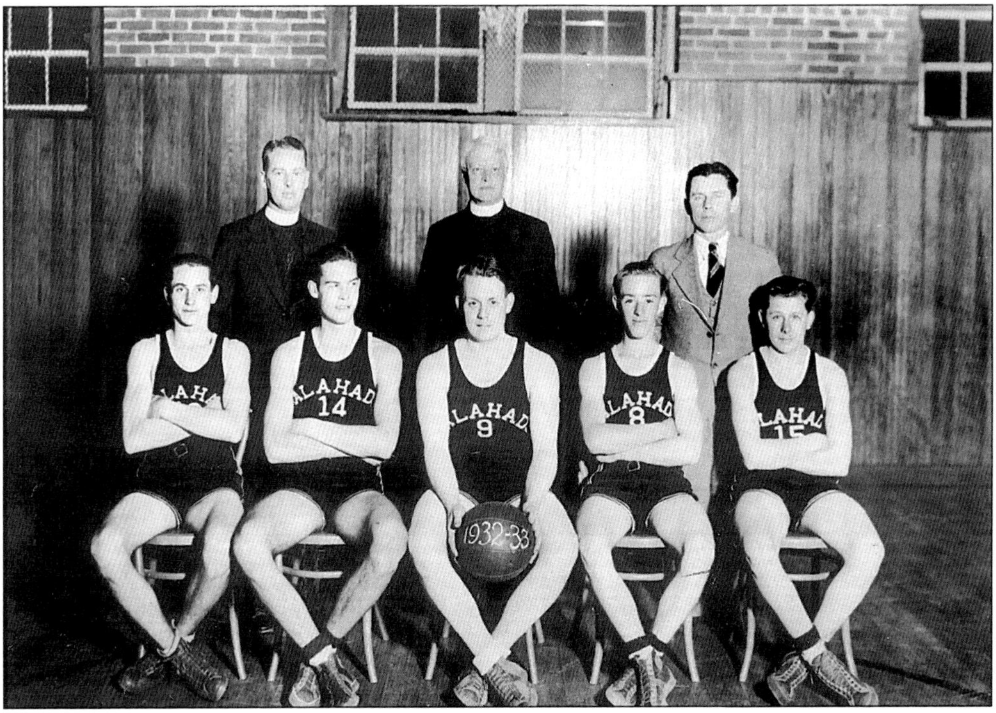

The St. Gallahad Society was organized in the early 20th century by Trinty Church as a social club for boys. Shown in this photograph of the 1932 basketball team are, from left to right, the following: (front row) Jack Smith, Roy Richardson, Roger Thomas, Daffy Hughes, and Mike Capuchiano; (back row) Rev. James Green, Rev. Stan Hughes, and manager John Smith.

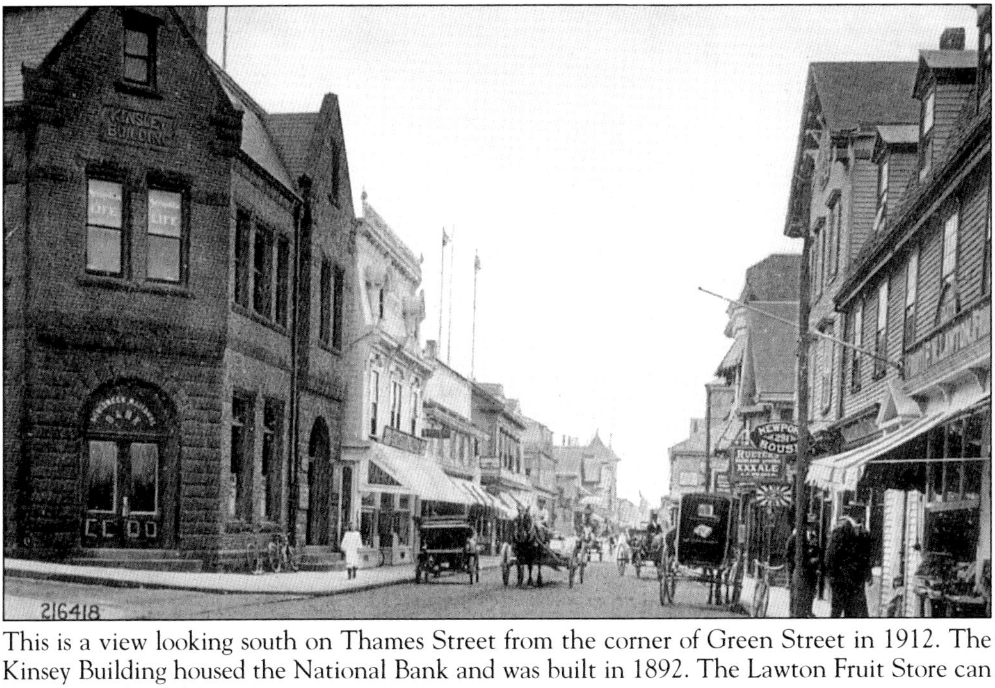

This is a view looking south on Thames Street from the corner of Green Street in 1912. The Kinsey Building housed the National Bank and was built in 1892. The Lawton Fruit Store can be seen to the right.

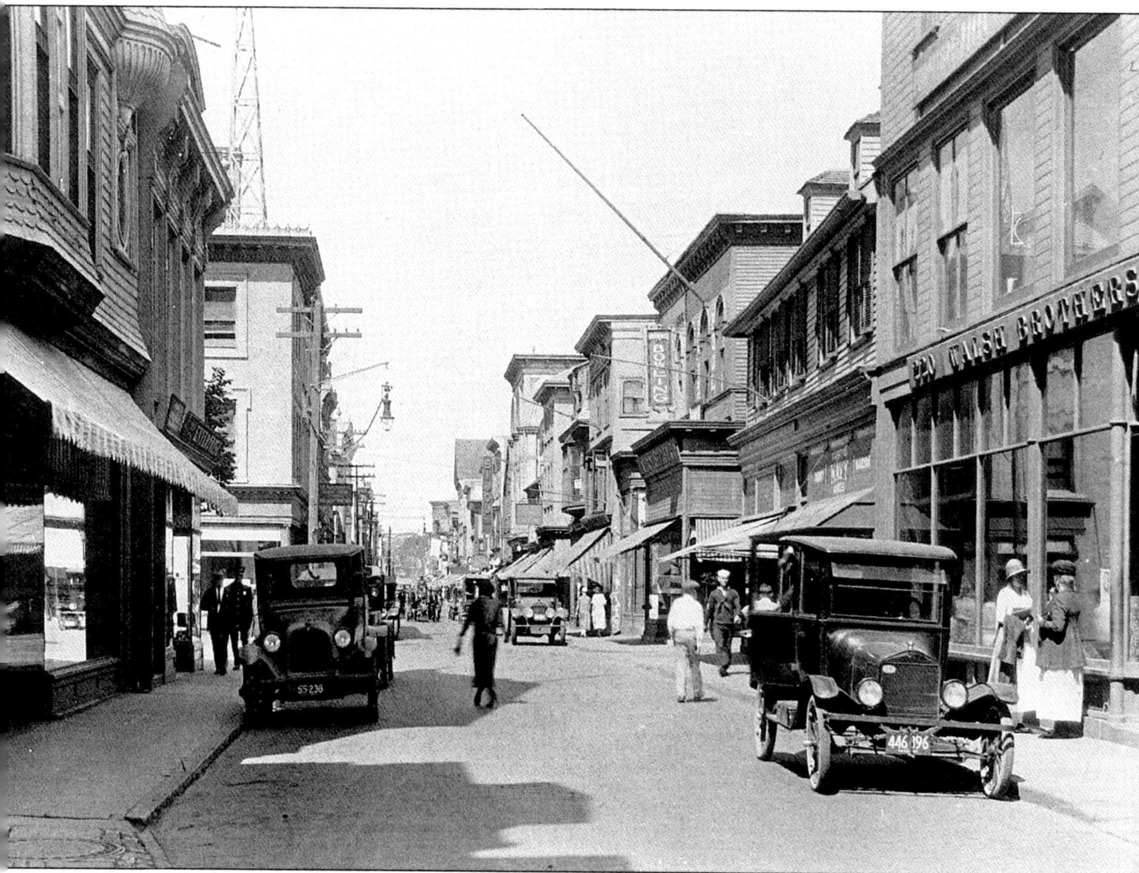

Thames Street was always considered the main street of Newport. The street was busy both from the land and waterside. A town crier was walking Thames Street as early as 1681. His name was Richard Barnes. The last town crier was Henry Lincoln, who held the post in 1885.

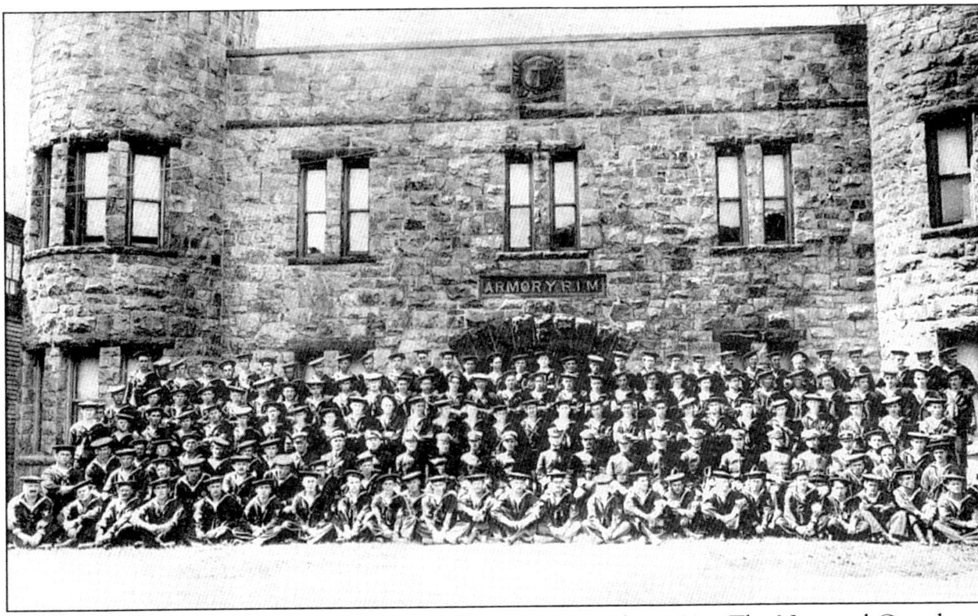

The state armory, designed by William Gosling, was opened in 1894. The National Guard and the naval reserve shared quarters in the building. This 1925 photograph shows cadets posing in front of the armory.

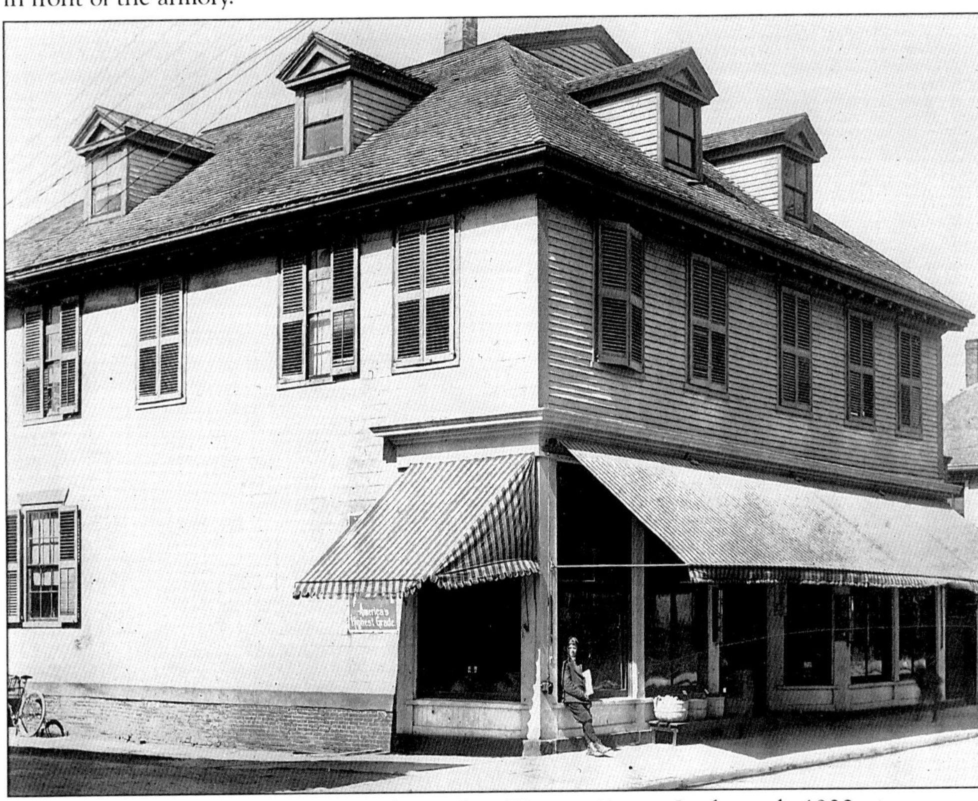

The Kaull and Anthony Market was located on Thames Street. In the early 1900s, it was torn down and the land became part of the Newport shipyard.

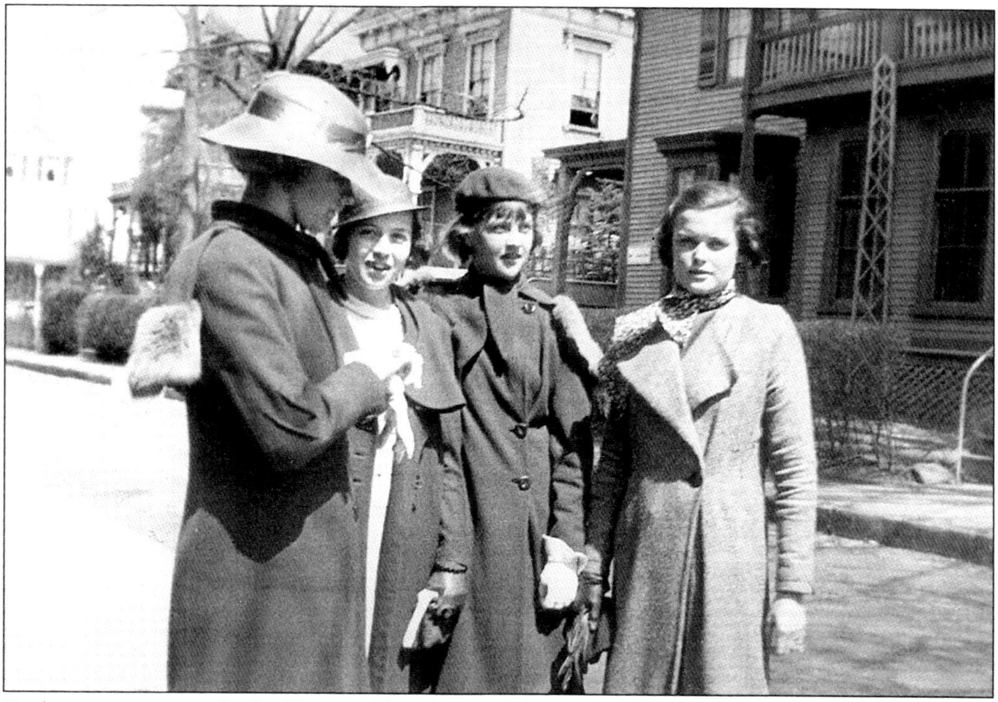

Striking a pose outside the Trinity Church parish house in 1935 are, from left to right, Victoria Christionsen, Gert Gibson, Mary Christionsen, and Nellie Leary.

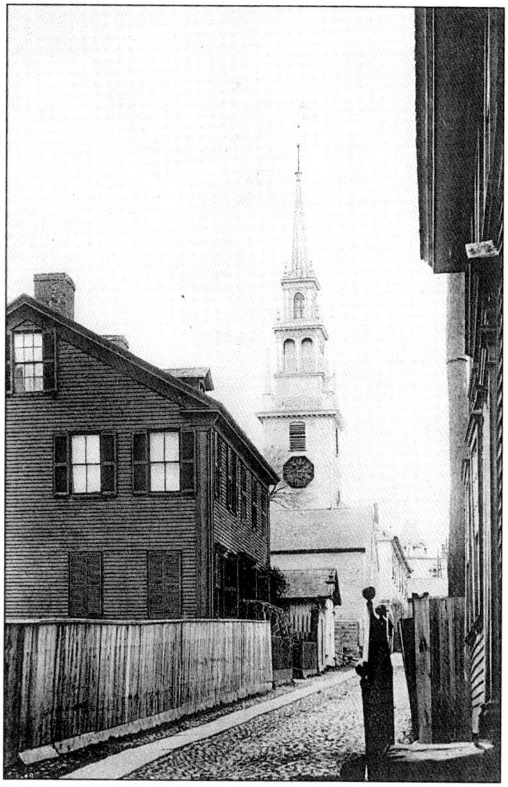

This early-1900s view looks east up Frank Street toward Trinity Church. The Newport Restoration Foundation, founded by Doris Duke, cleared the houses on both sides to make Queen Anne Square.

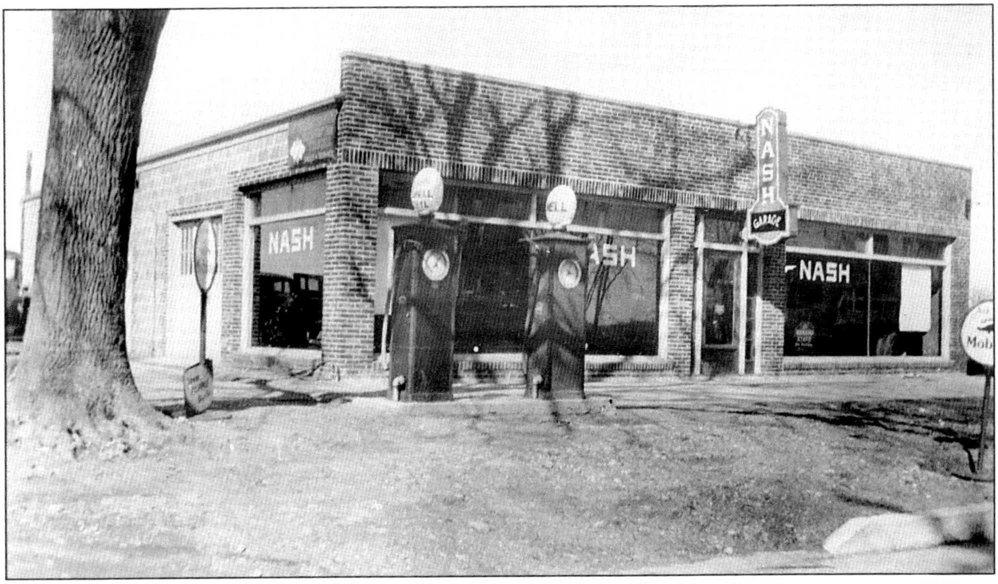

This garage on Deblois Street was Newport's first Nash dealership. It is shown here in 1932.

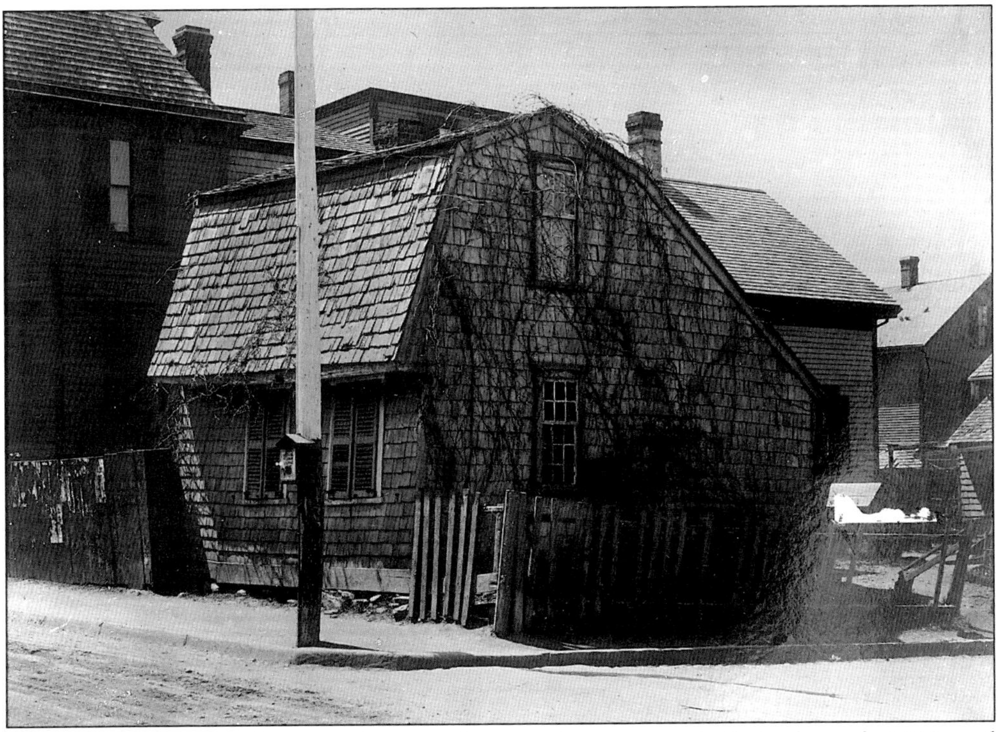

Located at the corner of Pope and Spring Streets, this house was built in the early 1800s and was razed in the early 1900s. It is shown here c. 1875.

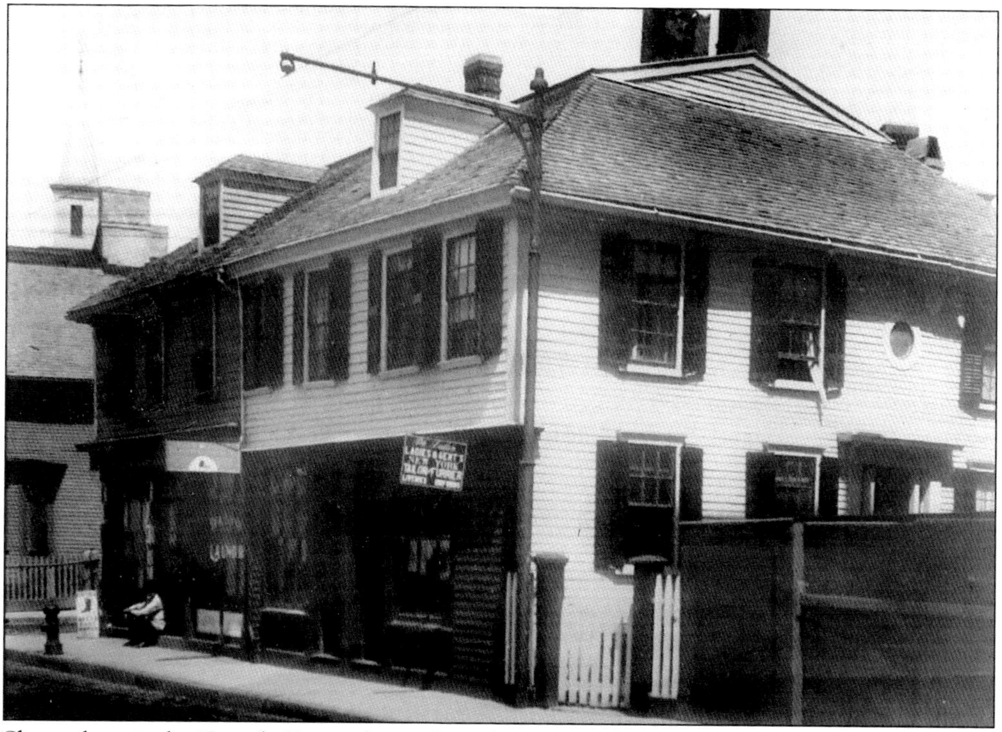

Shown here is the Tweedy House, located on the corner of Spring and Touro Streets. The land sale was recorded in 1709 between Walter Clarke and Elizabeth Newby. The house stayed in the Newby family until almost 1800.

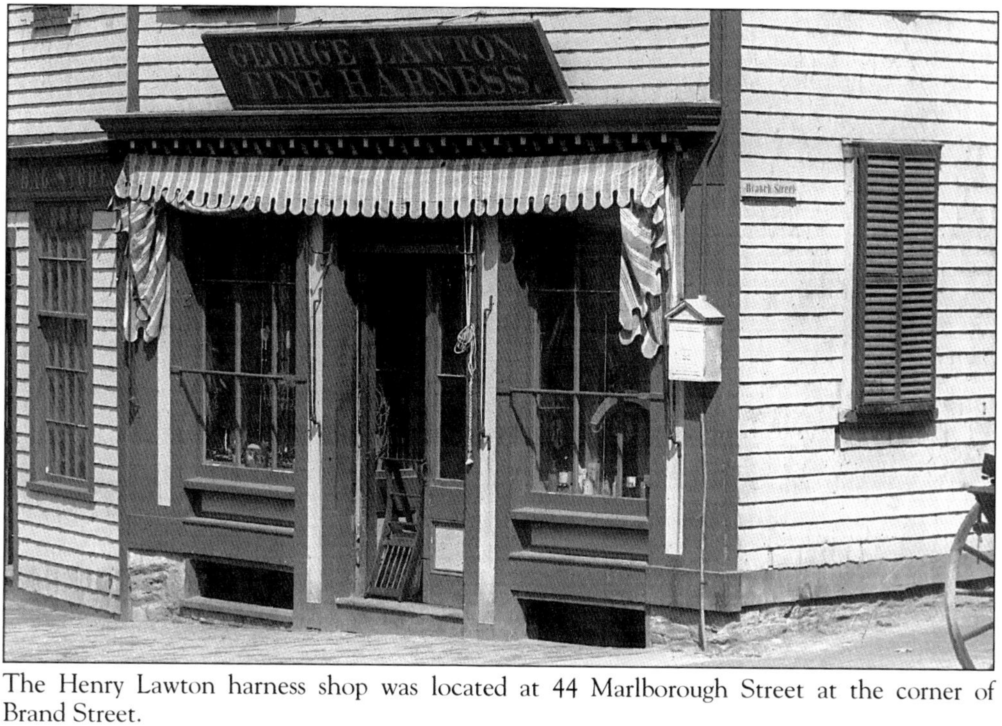

The Henry Lawton harness shop was located at 44 Marlborough Street at the corner of Brand Street.

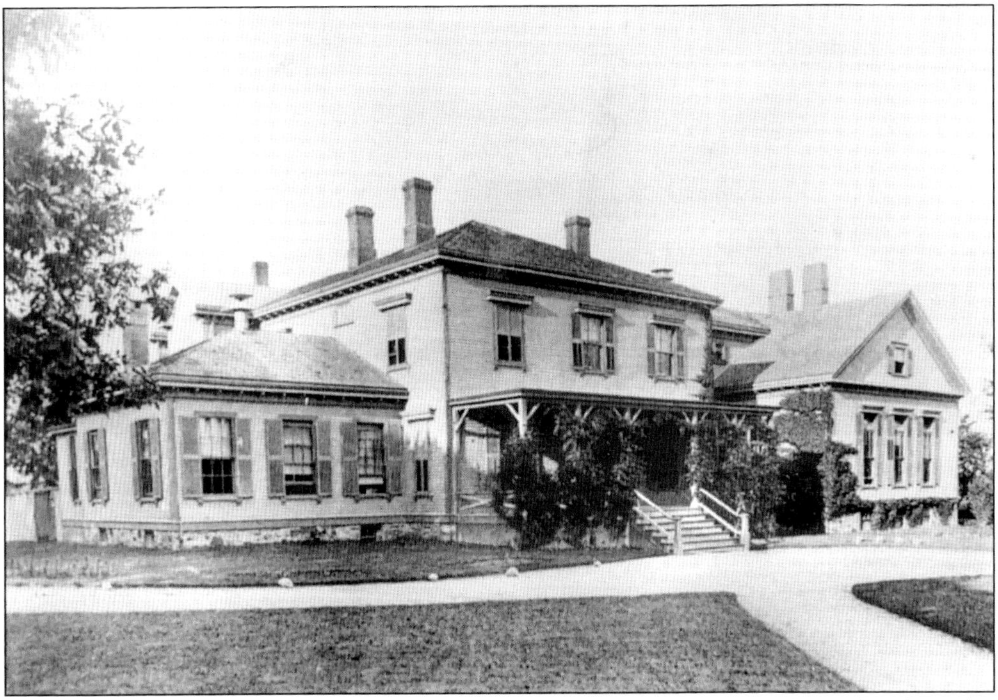

The Newport Hospital was founded in 1873. In this 1890s photograph, the Ledyard ward is located to the left and the 1893 Littlefield ward is to the right.

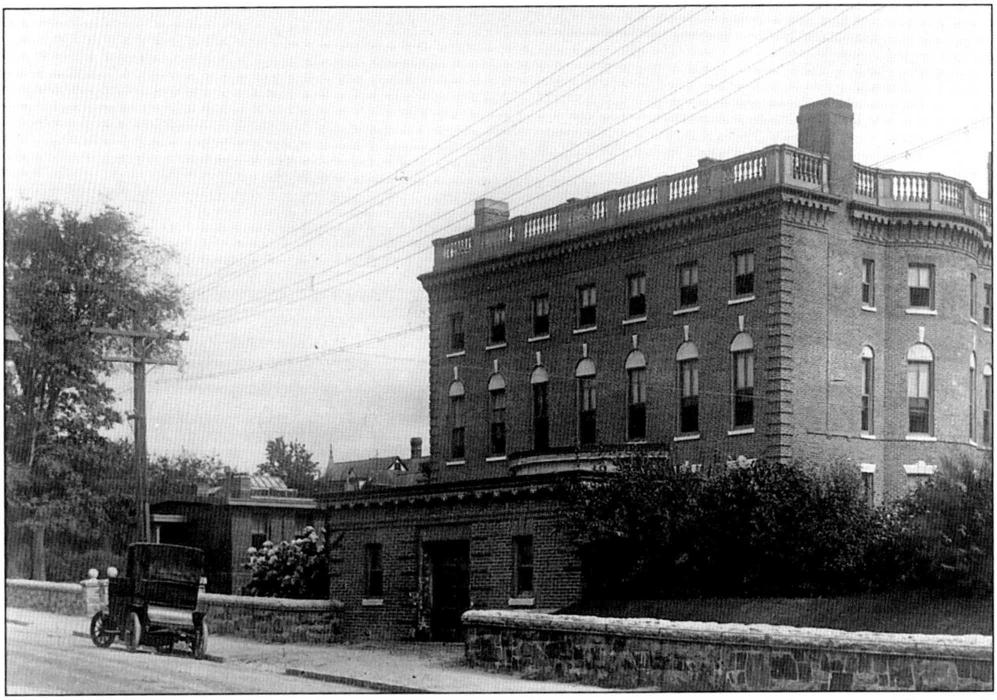

The Hazard Administration Building was completed in 1903 on the site of the original hospital. It was erected with funds provided by John Alfred Hazard's estate. During this same year, the hospital purchased its first x-ray equipment. (See page 104.)

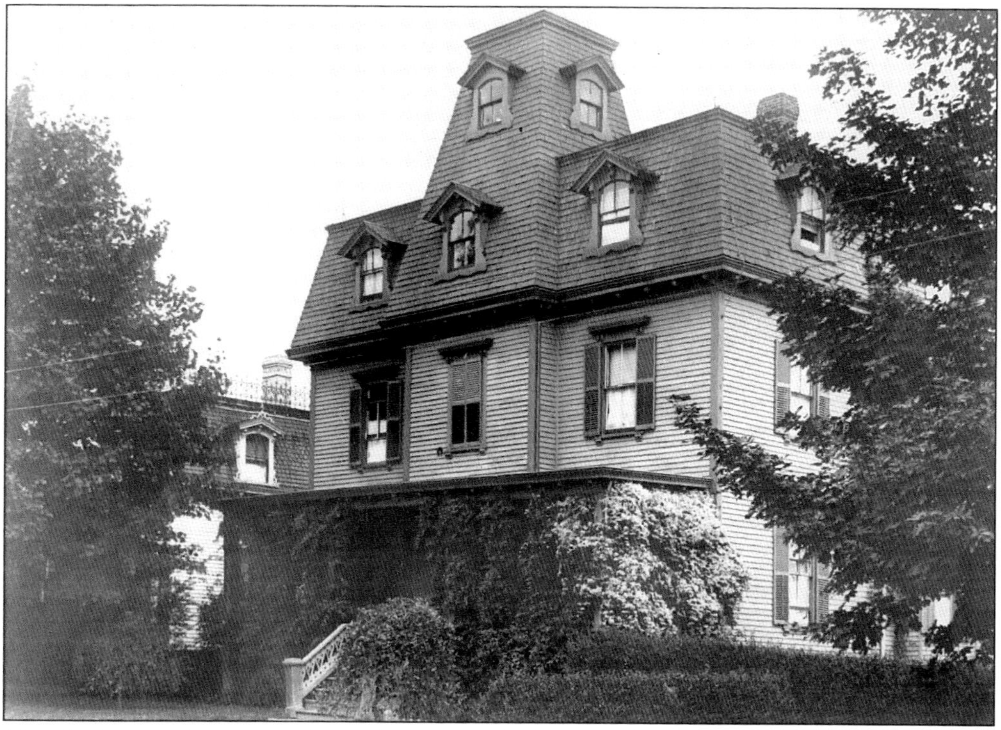

The Peckham House was located on Powel Avenue. In 1874, the hospital purchased the property.

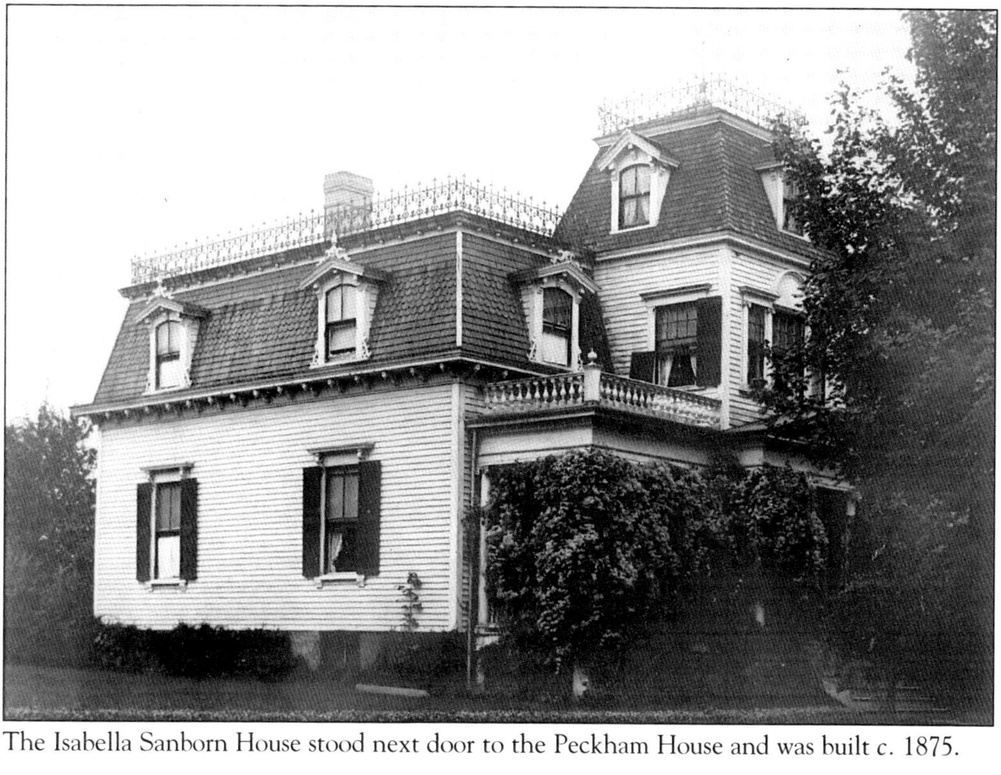

The Isabella Sanborn House stood next door to the Peckham House and was built c. 1875.

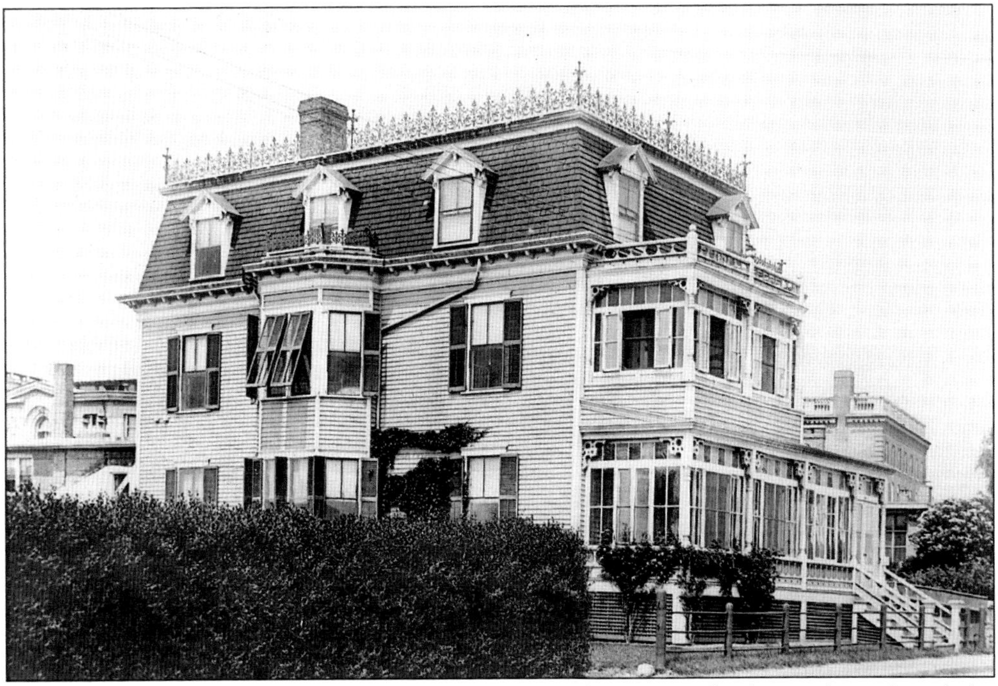

The Carolina C. Wilson House was built in the early 1880s. The hospital purchased the property in the 1920s and razed the building in the 1930s. The Hazard and Vanderbilt Buildings are seen in the distance.

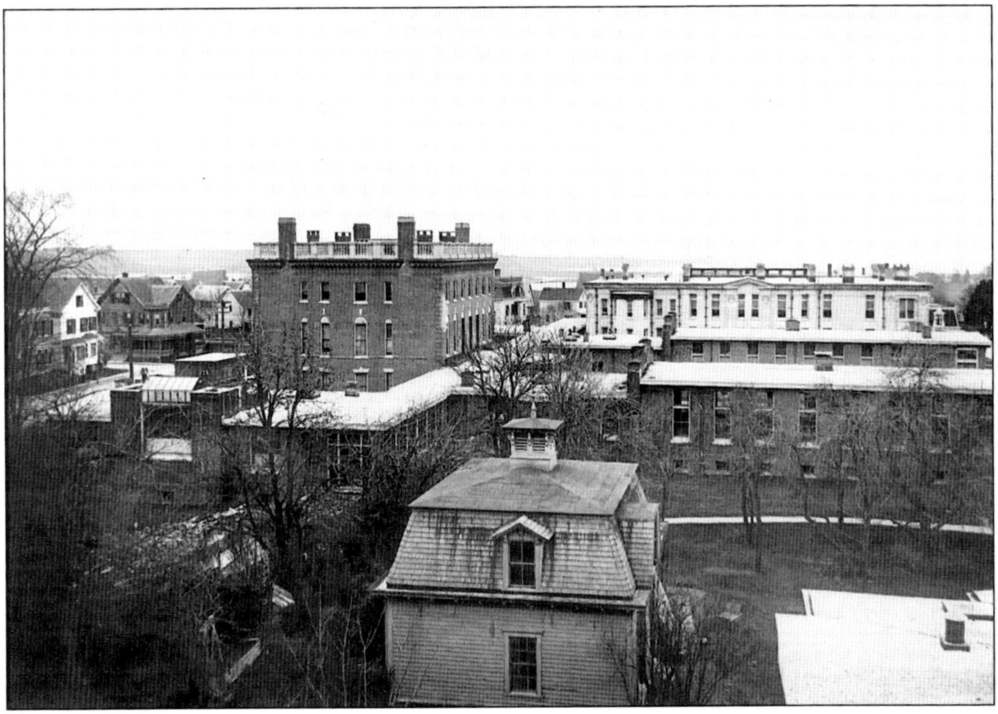

This view of the hospital campus shows the connecting corridor that joined the buildings. The Vanderbilt surgical suite can be seen to the left with its huge skylight.

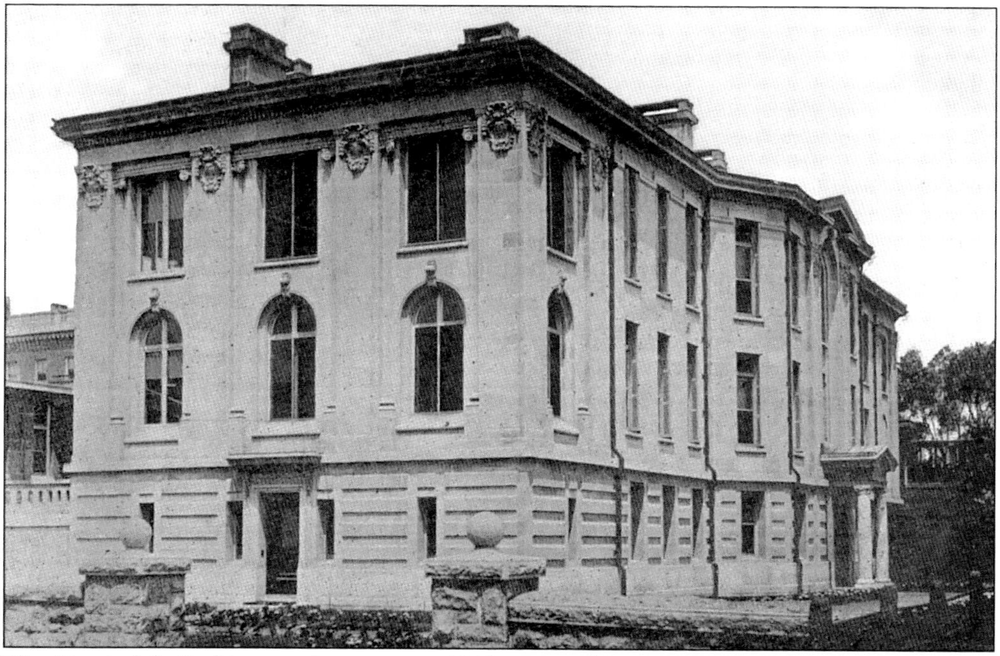

The Vanderbilt Building is shown on a 1910 postcard. In 1901, Mrs. Cornelius Vanderbilt donated the funds to build the Vanderbilt Pavilion. The building was designed by William Atkinson and cost $100,000. It opened in 1903 and added 34 new beds.

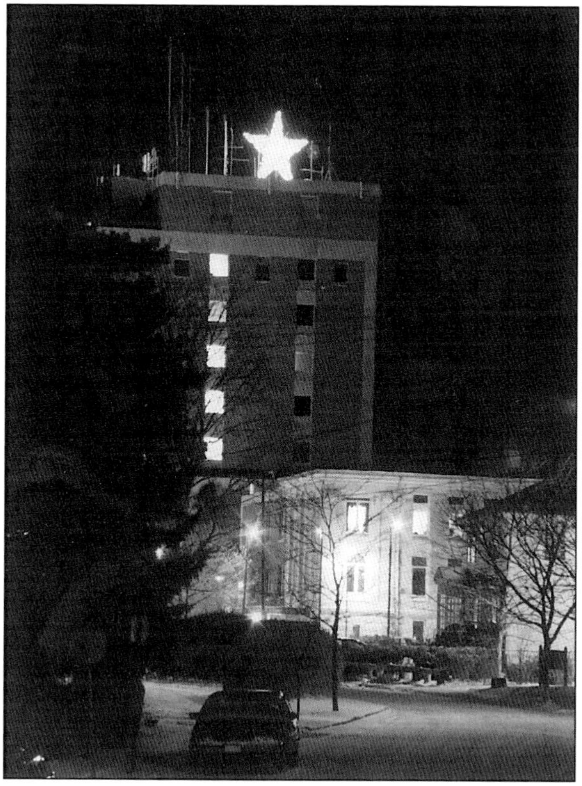

A Christmas star appears over the Vanderbilt Pavilion. Every year, members of the engineering department erect the stars to mark the holiday season. The building to the right was moved to Friendship Street to make room for the east wing. (Photograph by Rob Lewis.)

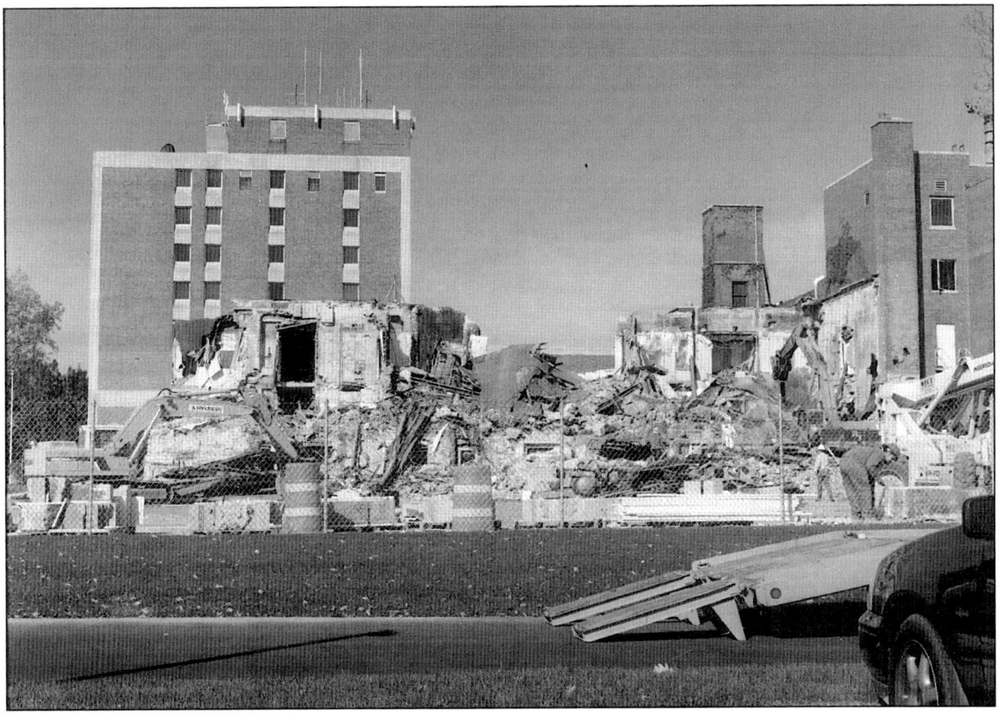

The Vanderbilt Building was razed in 1998. The 1968 Tower Building, now named after William K. Turner, stands above the debris. (Photograph by Ryan Young.)

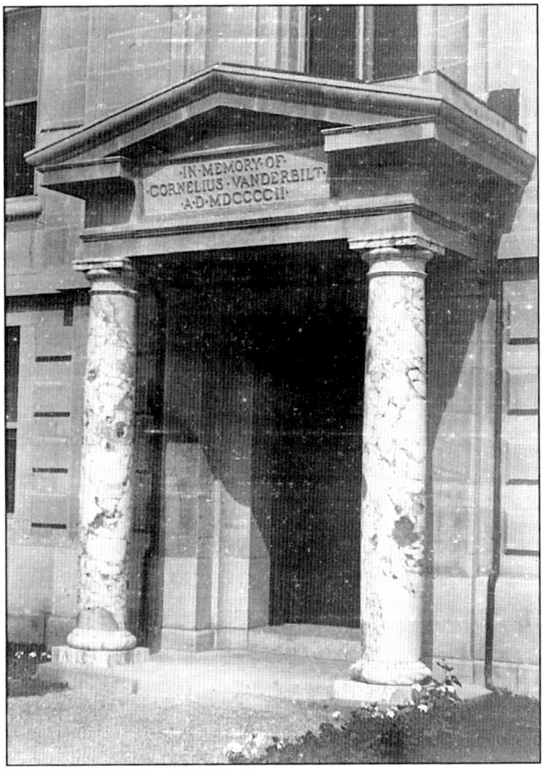

The entrance to the Vanderbilt Pavilion is shown in 1903. The entrance and some of the stones were salvaged to build a facade in the east wing connecting structure.

Two

Historic Homes and Buildings

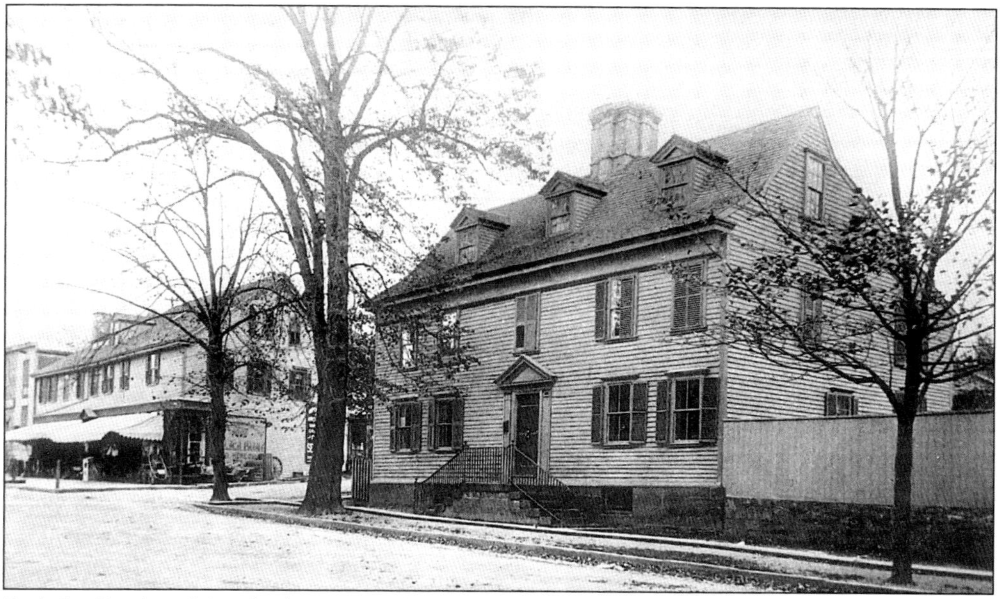

Built by Stephen Mumford in 1675, the Wonton-Lyman-Hazard House has the distinction of being Newport's oldest house. It was purchased and restored by the Newport Historical Society in 1927. The three rooftop dormers were removed during the restoration. The first George Weaver hardware store was on the opposite corner.

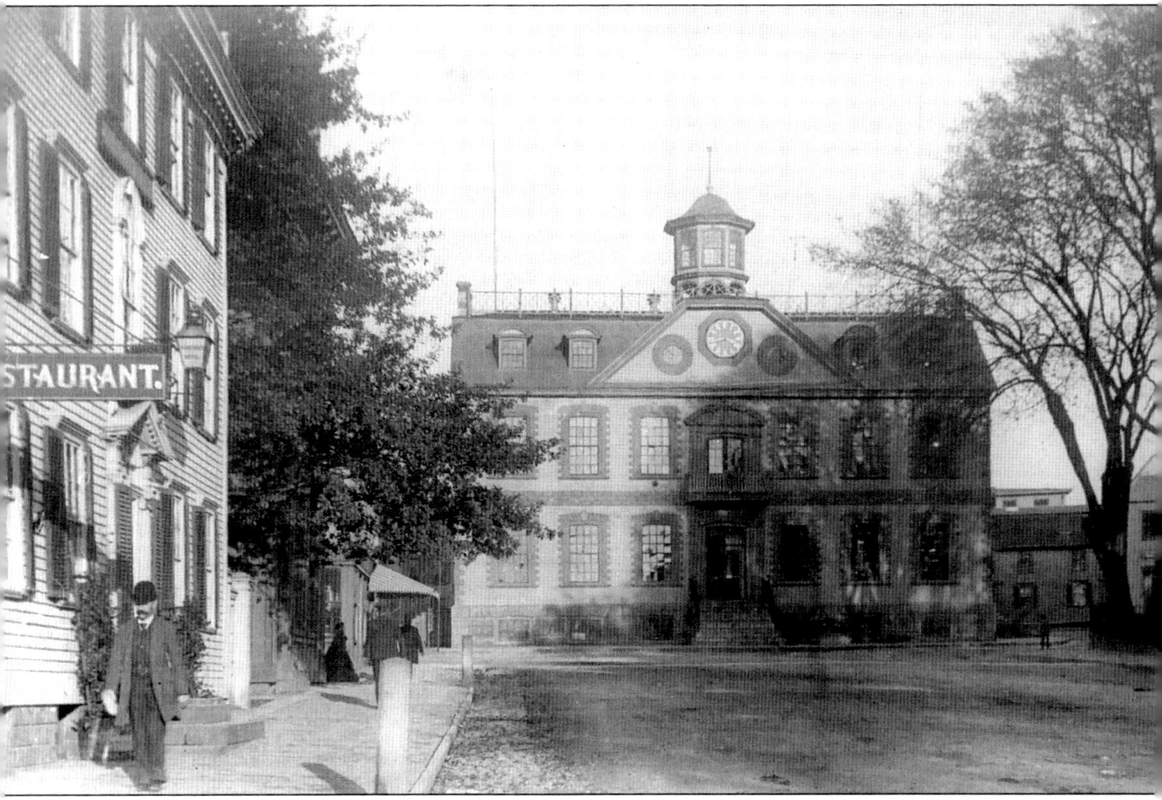

The Colony House was designed by Richard Mundy in 1739. The plans called for brick construction on a rusticated foundation. It was to replace an earlier building from 1687. Over the years, the building has seen many uses. During the British occupation, it was used as a barracks and later as a hospital by the French. From the balcony, many events in our history have been announced. George Washington was entertained in its great hall and, for many years, the basement space was rented out for shops and storage.

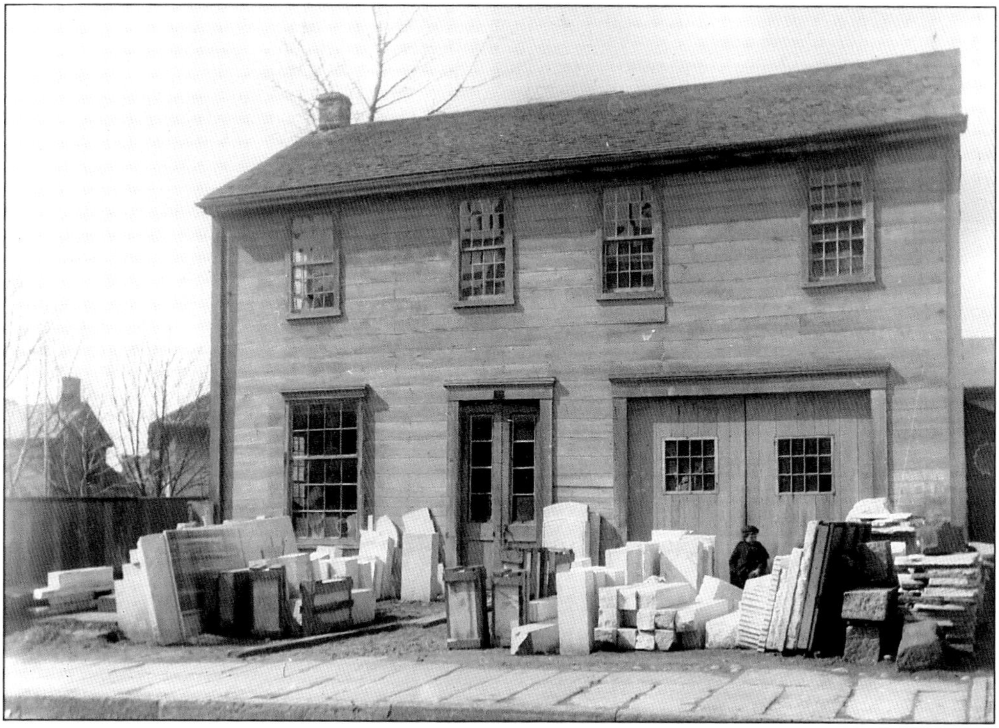

The first John Stevens set up his stone-cutting shop in 1705. In 1757, his grandson of the same name purchased this Thames Street lot and building for the business. In the 1920s, John Benson purchased the business.

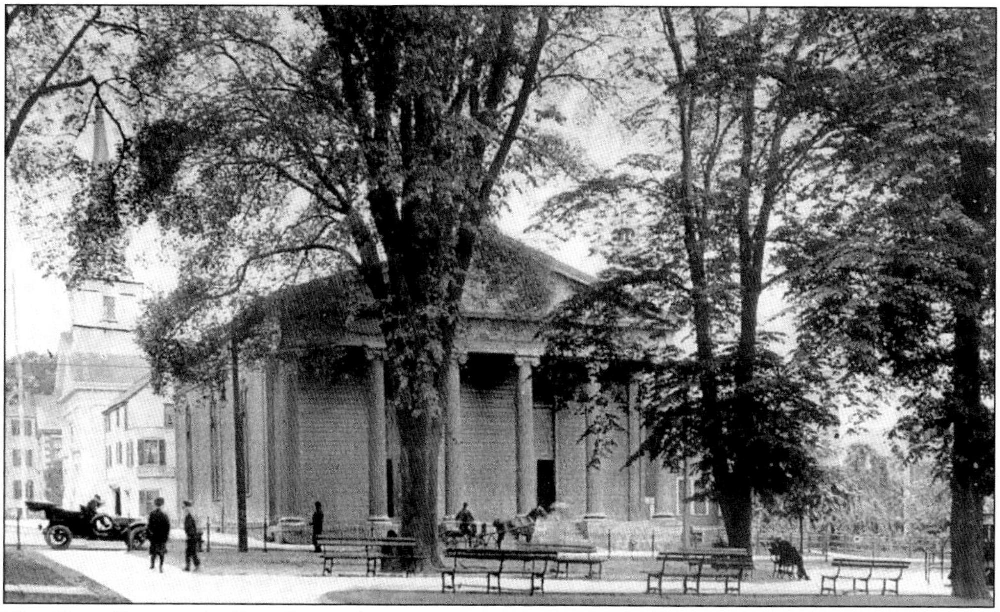

The Zion Episcopal Church was built on the corner of Clarke and Touro Streets in 1831. It was designed by Russell Warren and was one of Newport's first Greek Revival edifices. On September 6, 1886, Bishop Hendricken dedicated the new St. Joseph's. The building later became the Strand Theater and now houses the Jane Pickens Theater.

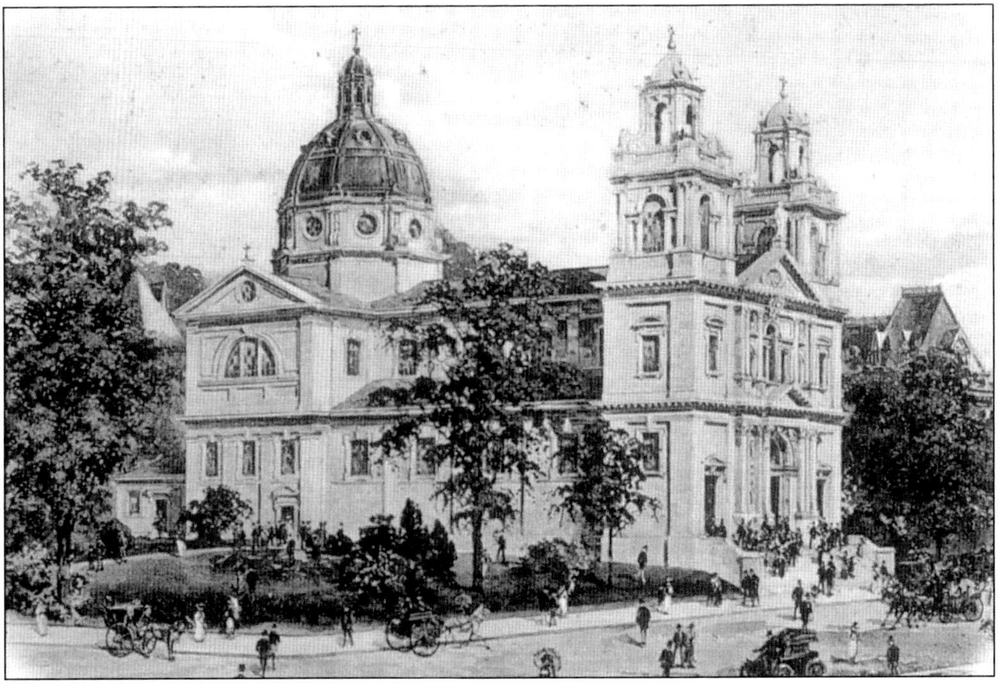

This 1906 postcard depicts what the new St. Joseph's on Broadway would look like. Note the dome on the rear of the church and the twin towers. After several financial setbacks, the plans switched from granite walls to brick and a scaled-back exterior.

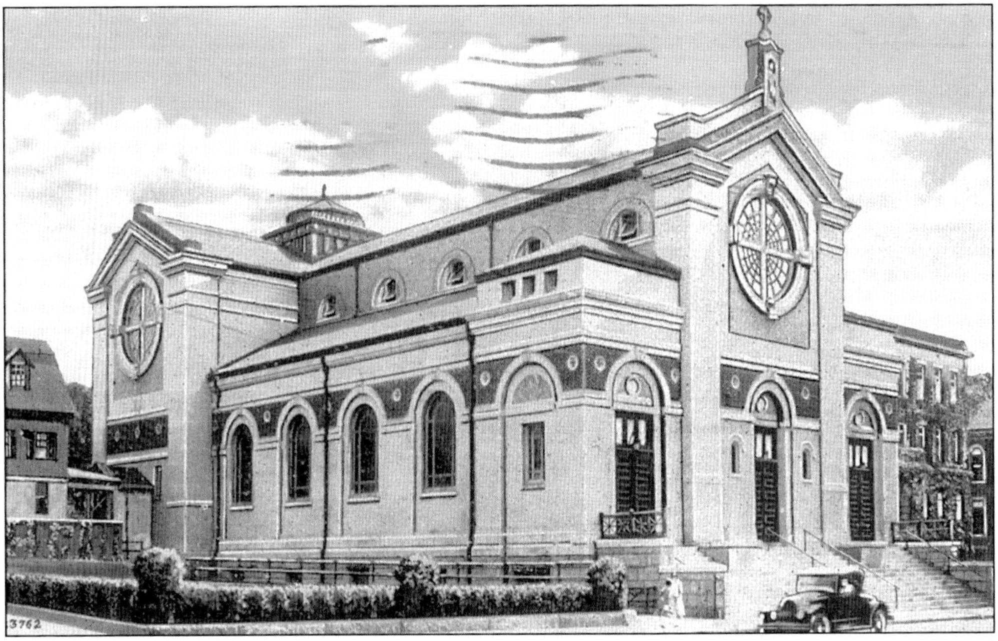

As the church expanded, the Kimber Estate on Broadway and Mann Avenue was purchased for $17,500. The cornerstone was laid in 1911. On September 8, 1912, Bishop Harkins had the honor of dedicating the new church.

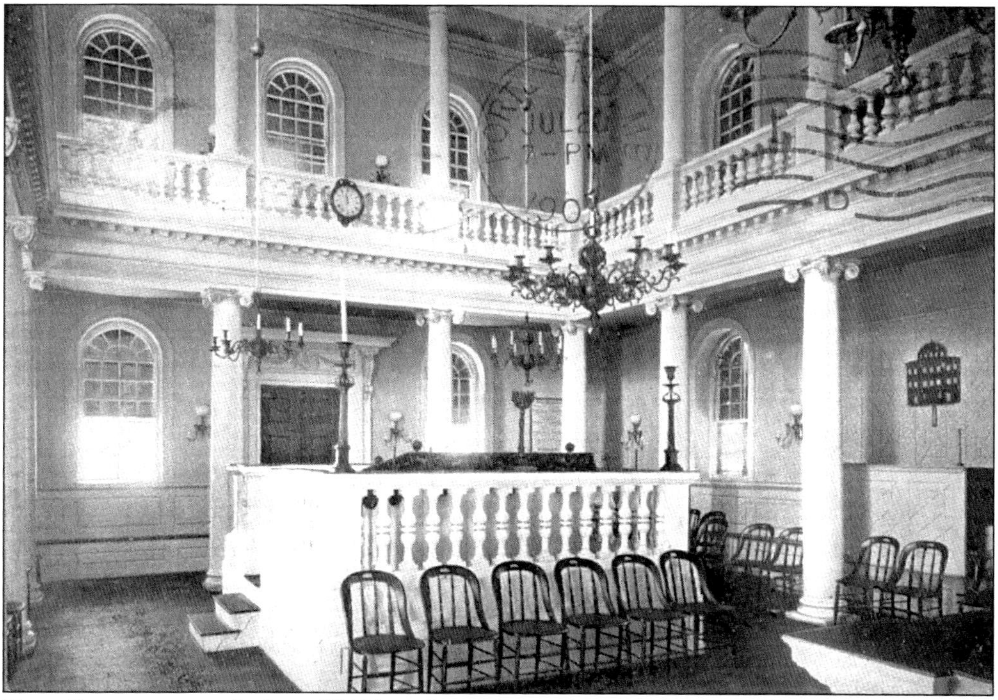

Touro Synagogue was built in 1763 based on a Peter Harrison design. It closed during the years of the Revolutionary War and was reopened in 1883. It is the oldest synagogue in America.

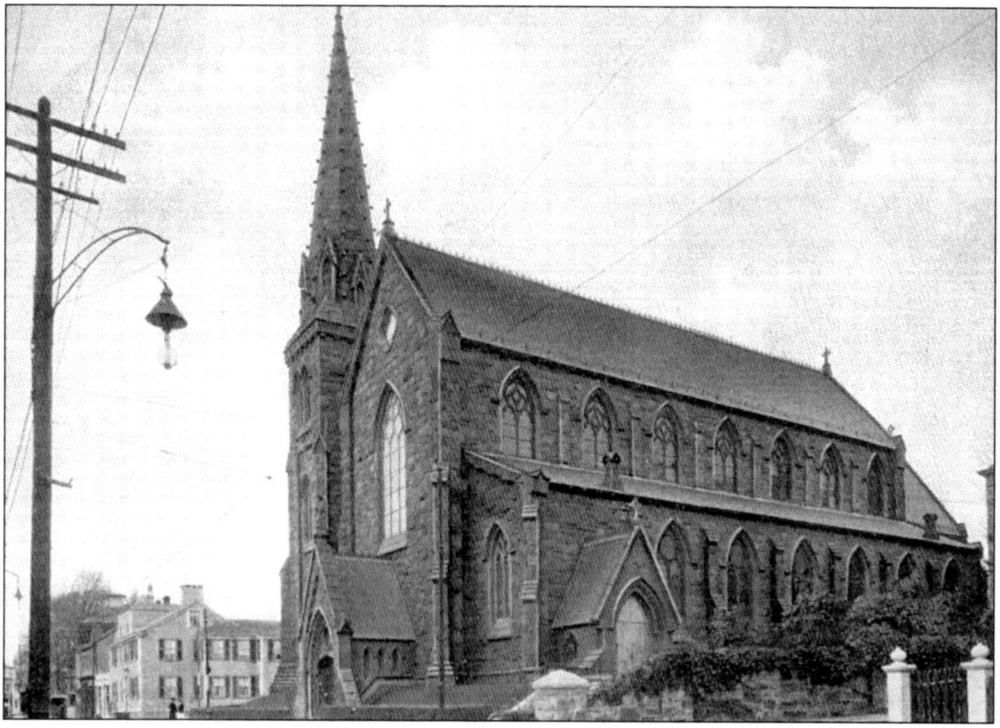

In 1848, Patrick C. Keely designed this church to be built on the corner of Spring and Levin Streets. On July 25, 1852, it was dedicated as St. Mary's, Lady of the Isle.

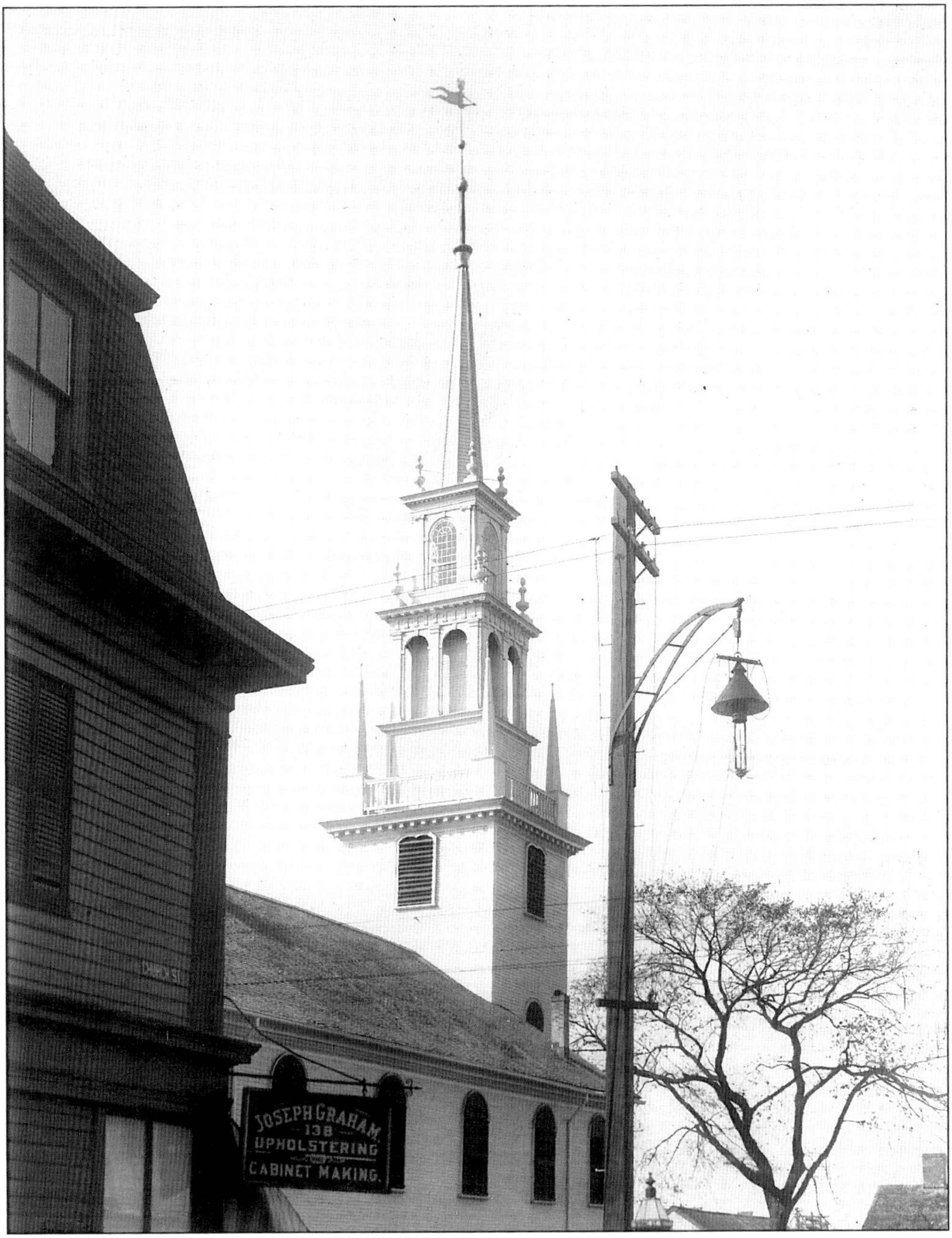

This building was the second home of Trinity Church. The first church was erected in 1702 and, by 1725, it had outgrown its quarters. This church was built shortly after. The spire was designed in 1725 but was not added until 1741. Note the electric streetlight. The first streetlights were installed in 1882 on Bellevue Avenue and Thames Street.

Seen in this view is Trinity Church from Queen Anne Square after a light dusting of snow. The tower was rebuilt after a severe gale damaged it in 1768. (Photograph by Rob Lewis.)

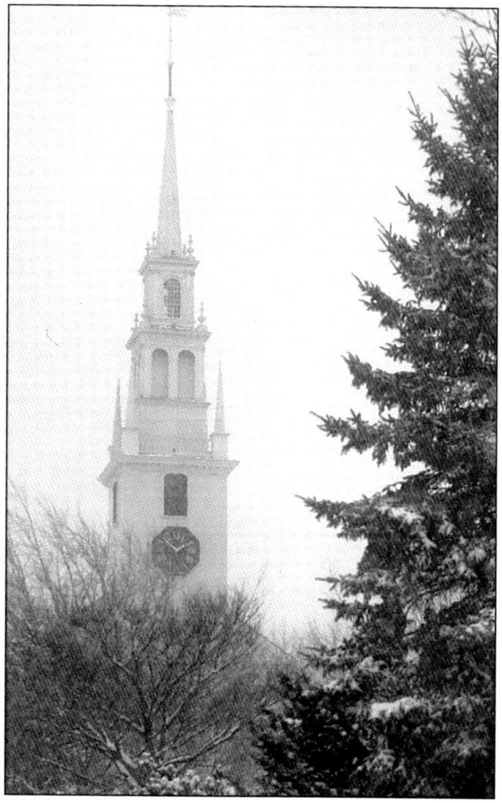

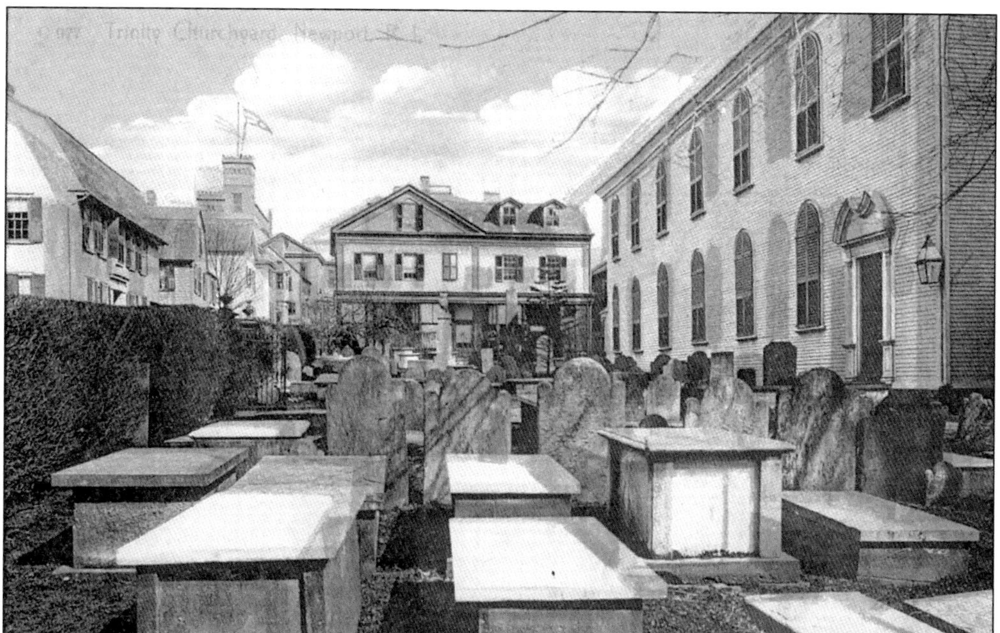

Trinity's churchyard serves as the final resting place for many of Newport's early families.

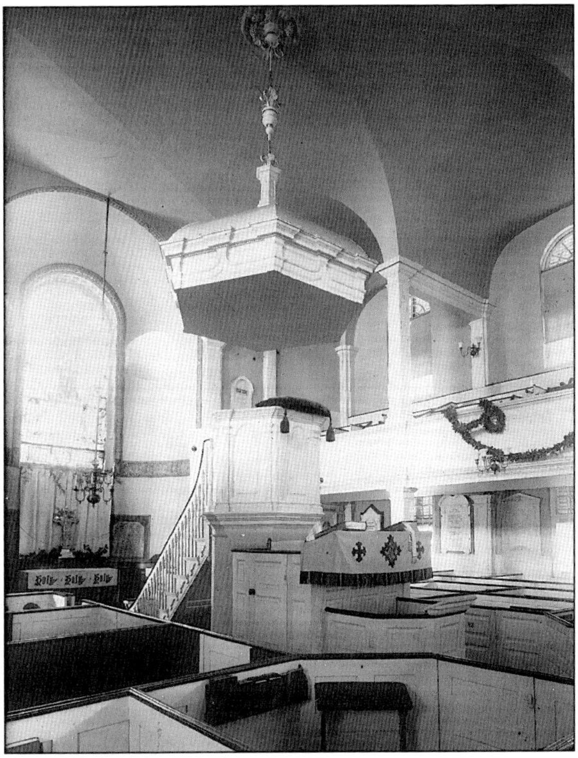

One of Trinity Church's most unique features is the triple-deck wine glass pulpit. It has a preacher's desk, a reading desk, a clerk's desk, and a sounding board above it.

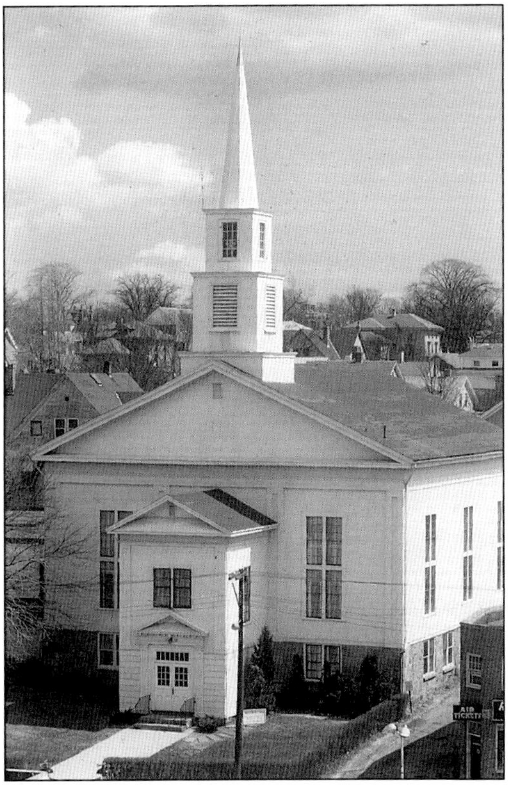

The United Baptist Church on Spring Street was built in 1846 and rests on the site that the 1738 meetinghouse was built on. This is the fourth church the Baptists have worshiped at since forming here in 1638. The first pastor was Dr. John Clarke.

The Masonic Lodge sits on the corner of Church and School Streets. There is a great hall on the first floor, which was used for exhibitions and other amusements.

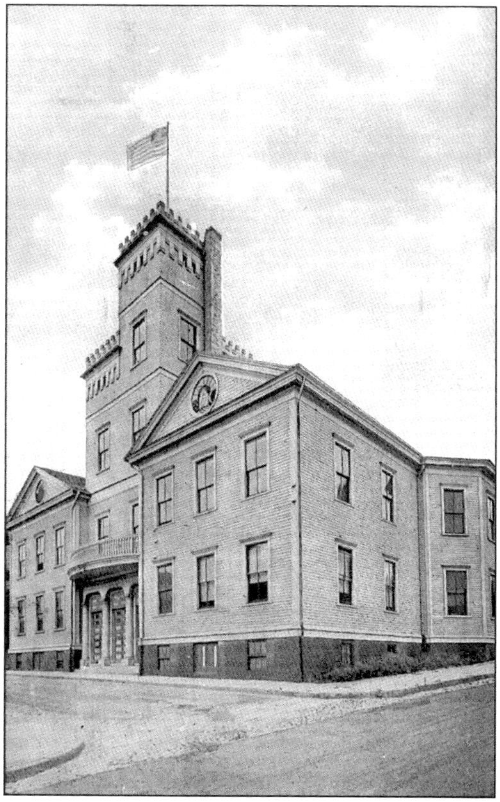

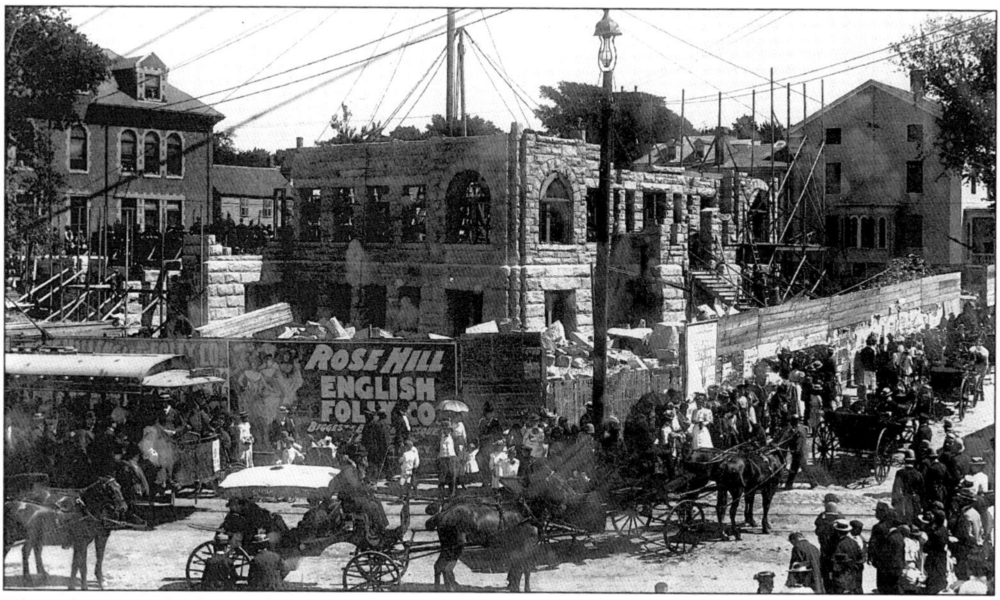

This photograph shows the cornerstone-laying ceremony for the new city hall in 1899 at the corner of Broadway and Bull Street.

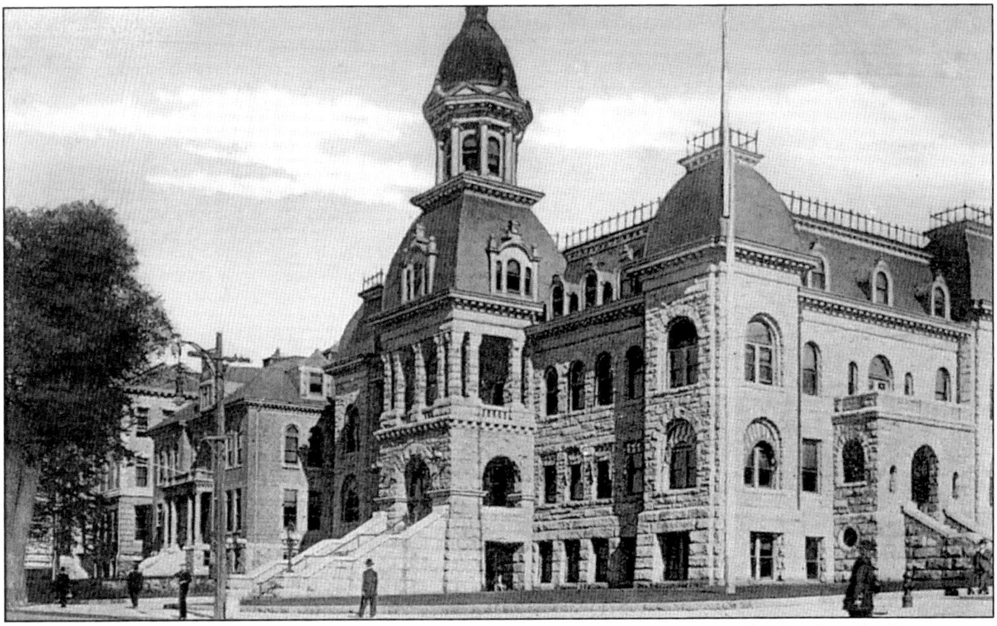

The city hall was completed in 1900. Note the cupola and the mansard-like fourth floor.

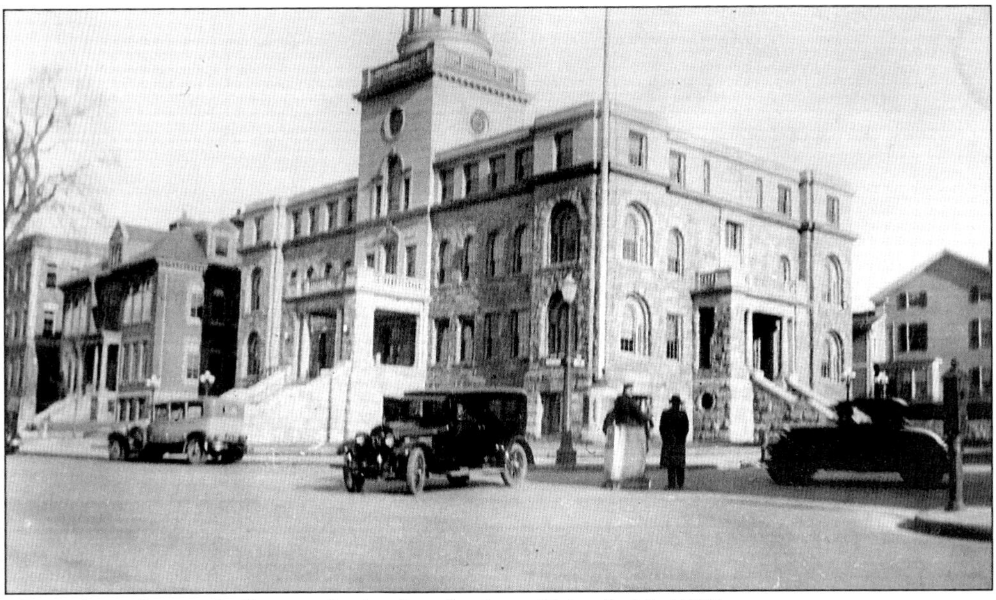

This is how the city hall was rebuilt after the fire of March 24, 1925.

The Rhode Island Lunch was located on the corner of Broadway and Spring Street. It operated until 1970, and what everybody remembers about it was the special "hot cheese everything sandwich."

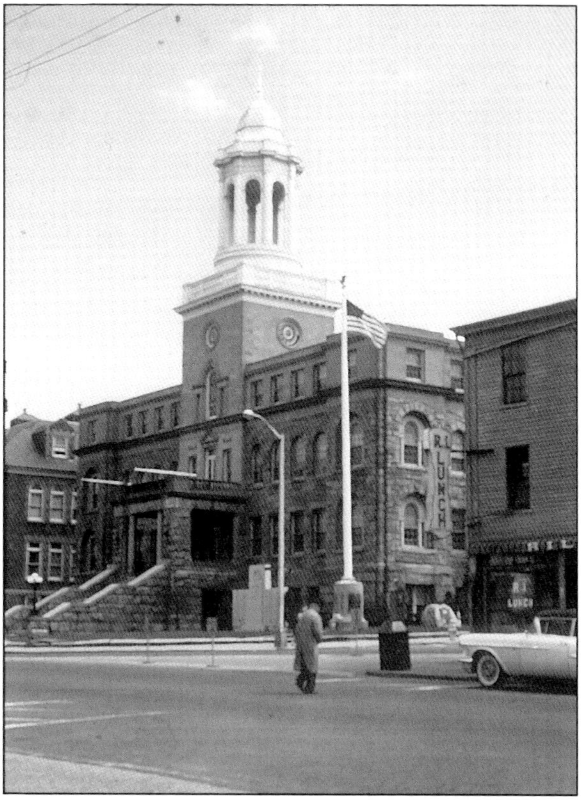

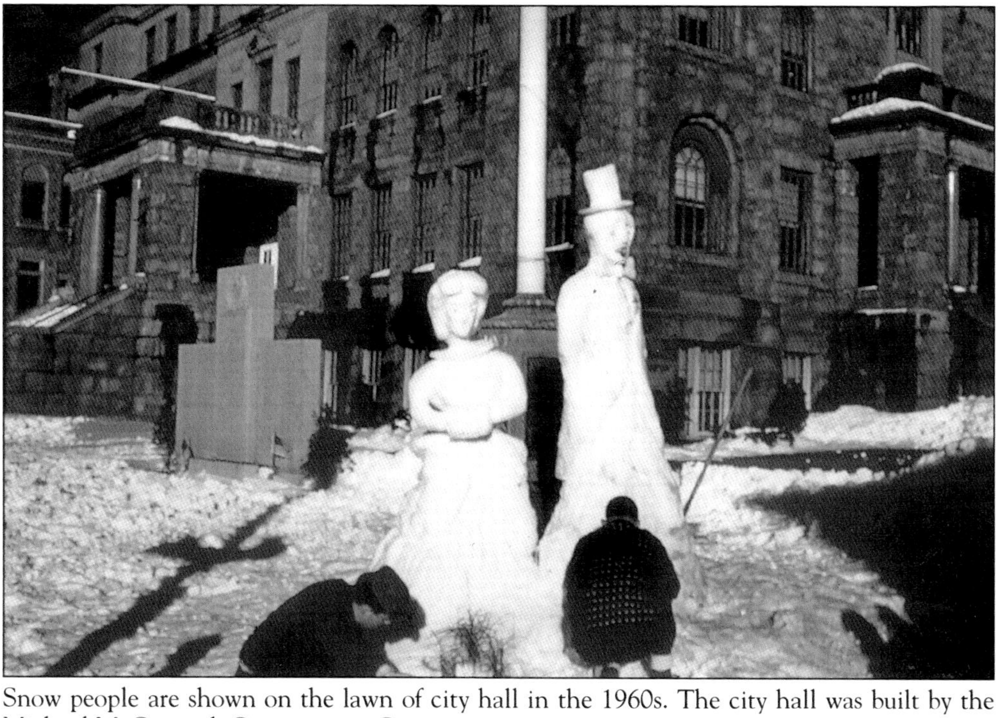

Snow people are shown on the lawn of city hall in the 1960s. The city hall was built by the Michael McCormick Construction Company.

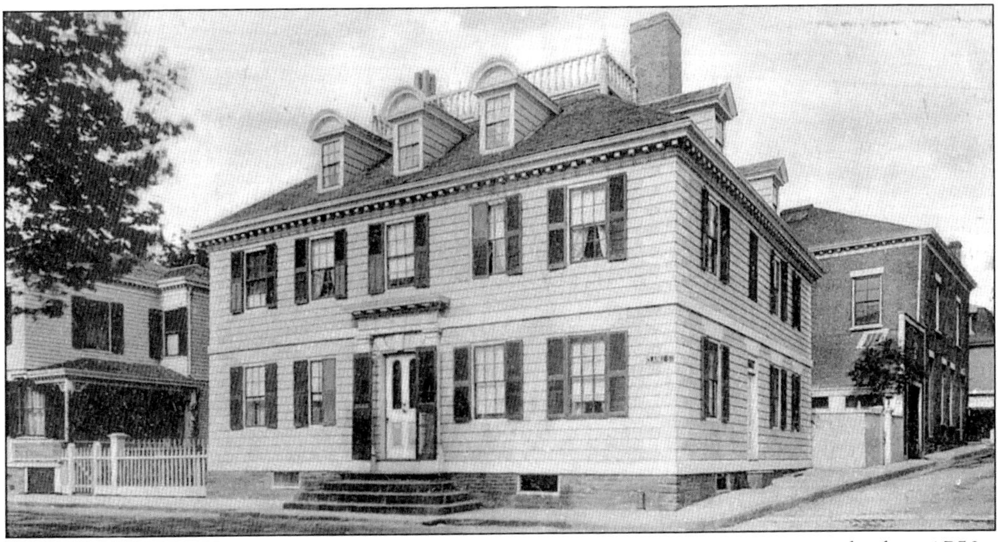

The Vernon House was built on Clarke Street at the corner of Mary Street in the late 1750s. General Rochembeau used the house as his headquarters during the American Revolution.

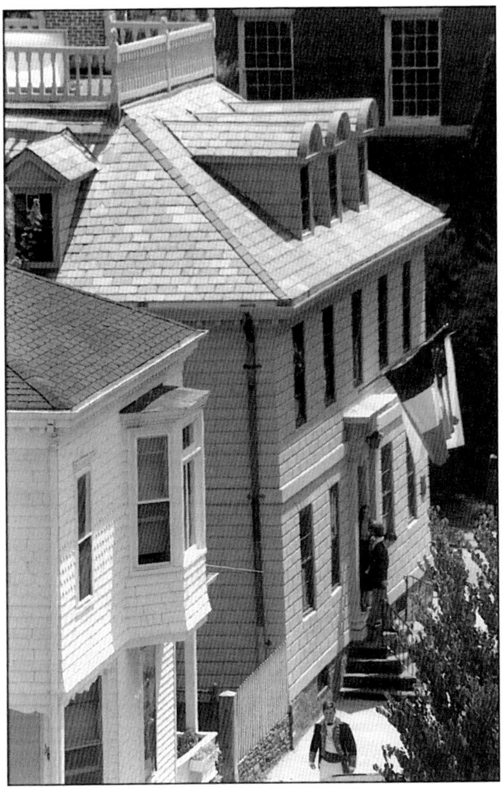

This view of the Vernon House was taken from the steeple of the Second Congregational Church. (Photograph by Rob Lewis.)

French Sailors march along West Broadway on October 27, 1931. The parade was organized to celebrate the 150th anniversary of the landing of the French under General Rochambeau.

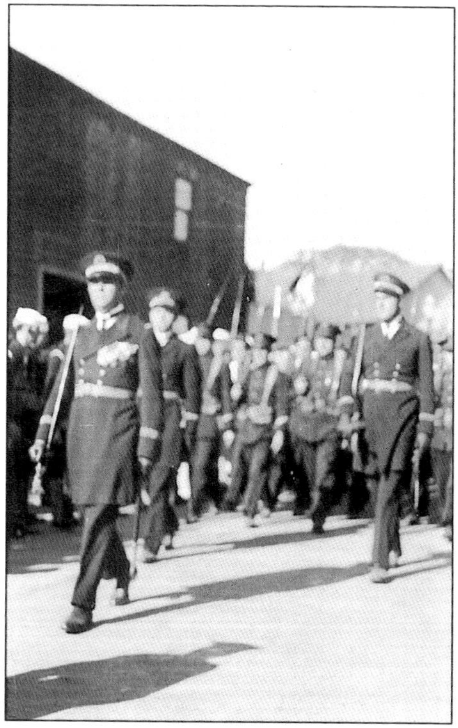

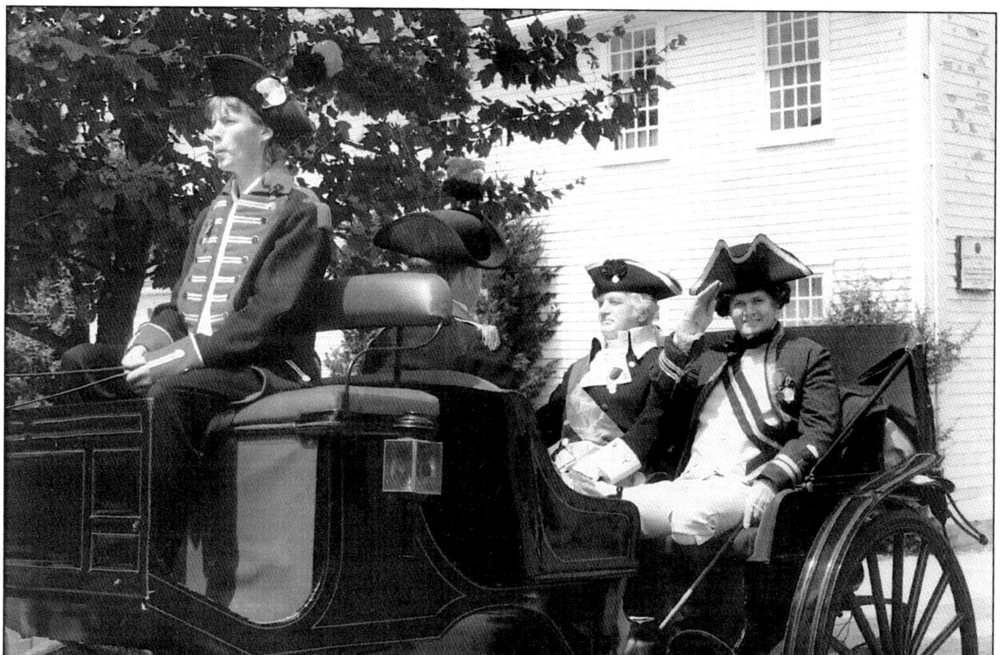

The Artillery Company staged a reenactment of the meeting between Gen. George Washington and General Rochambeau. Here, they are coaching down Clarke Street toward the Vernon House.

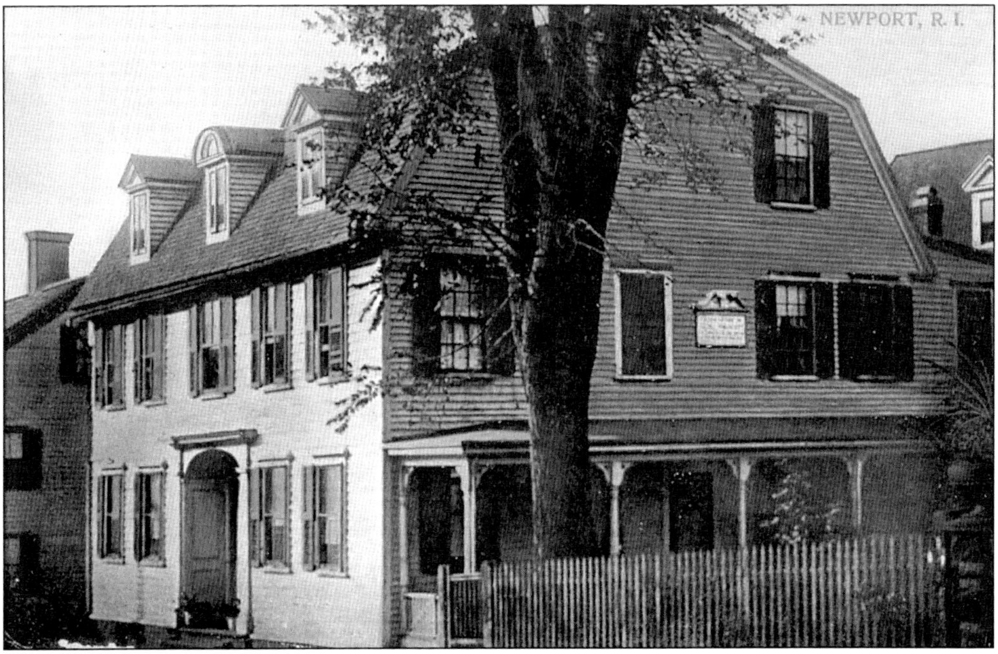

John Bannister was a prominent Newport merchant who built this house on the corner of Spring and Pelham Streets in 1751. During the British occupation, Gen. Richard Prescott used the house as his headquarters. Today, the house serves as a bed-and-breakfast.

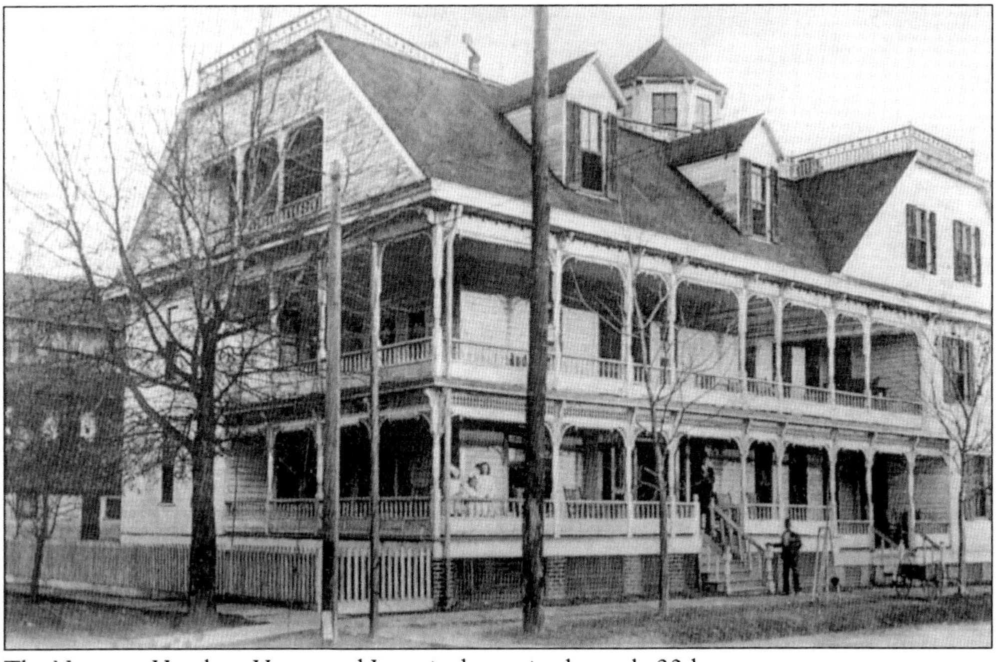

The Newport Hotel on Hammond Lane is shown in the early 20th century.

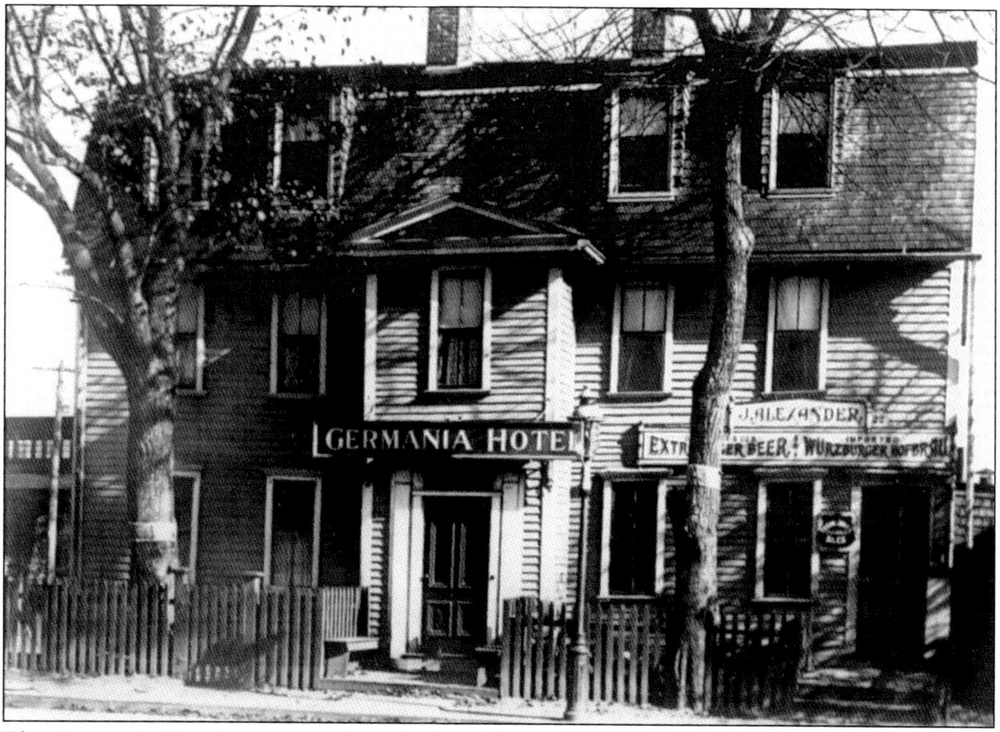

The Germania Hotel was opened in the late 1880s on State Street.

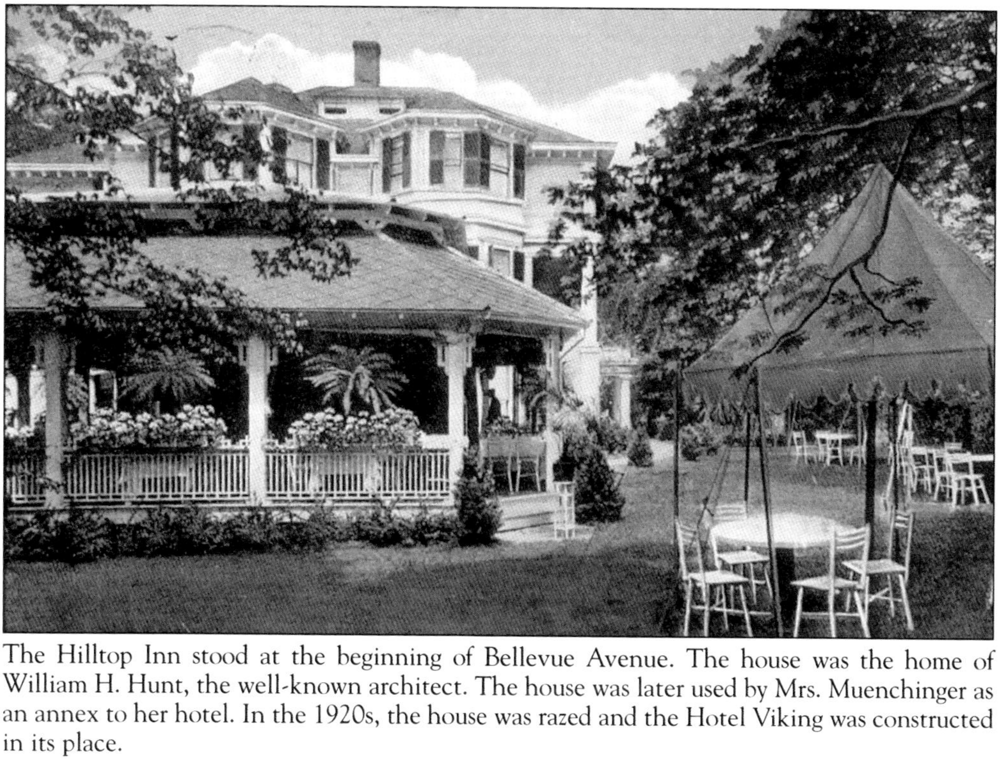

The Hilltop Inn stood at the beginning of Bellevue Avenue. The house was the home of William H. Hunt, the well-known architect. The house was later used by Mrs. Muenchinger as an annex to her hotel. In the 1920s, the house was razed and the Hotel Viking was constructed in its place.

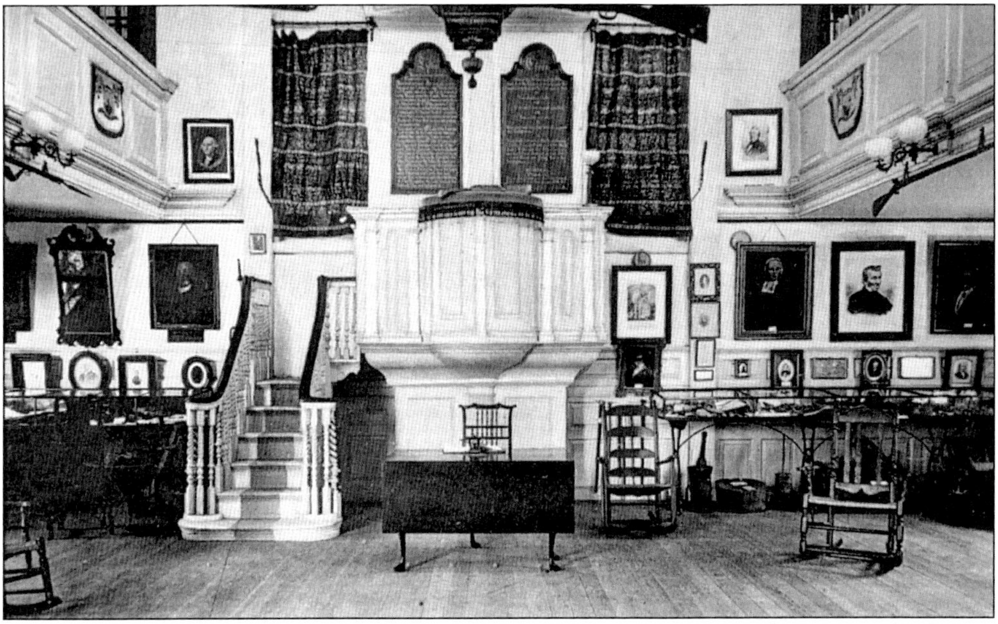

A view of the stairs and pulpit inside of the Sabbatarian Meeting House. The stairway leading to the pulpit was one of the first to have the twisted balusters, which were to be found throughout some of the finest houses built in Newport.

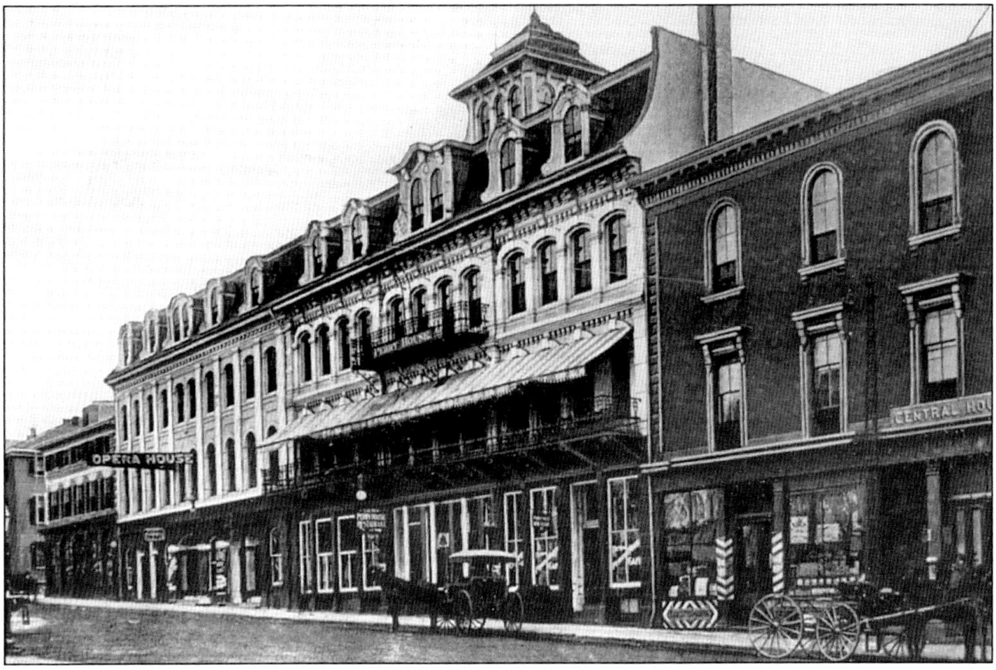

This late-1890s photograph shows the Perry House Hotel on Washington Square. The building was erected by P.C. Shanahan in 1865. It was replaced by the Horgan Building in the late 1920s.

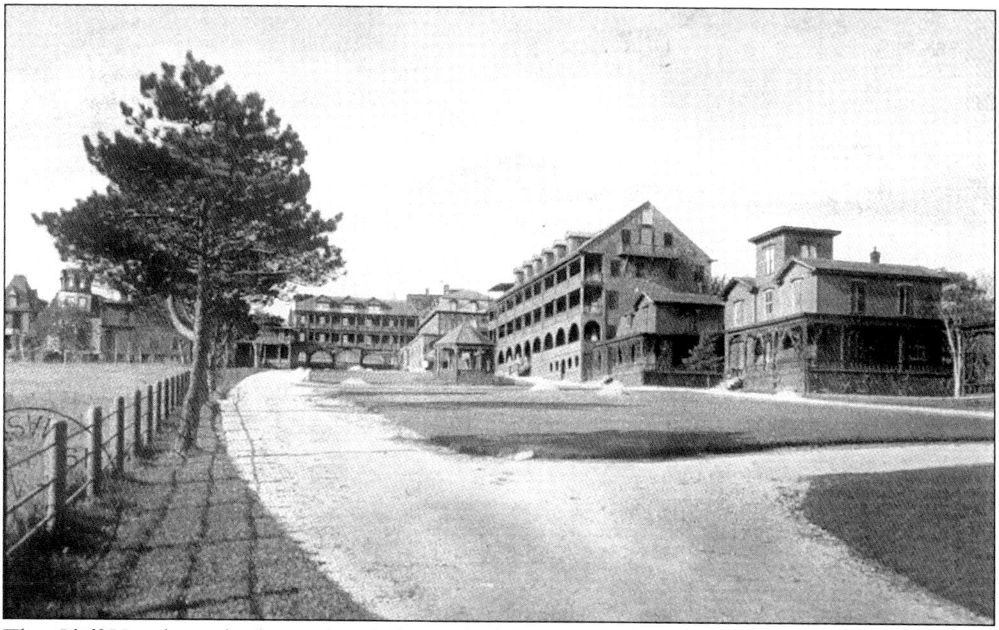

The Cliff Hotel was built on the cliffs overlooking Easton's Beach in 1899. On June 8, 1908, the building burned to the ground.

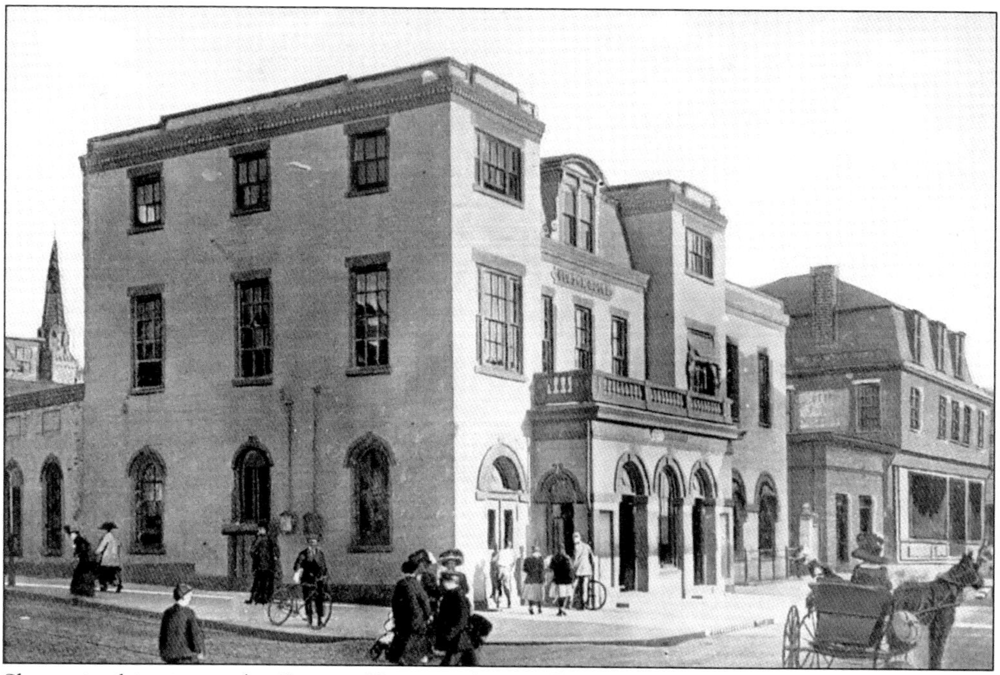

Shown in this view is the Custom House and post office at the corner of Franklin and Thames Streets. The building was erected in 1829 and served Newport until 1916, when it was razed for the new post office.

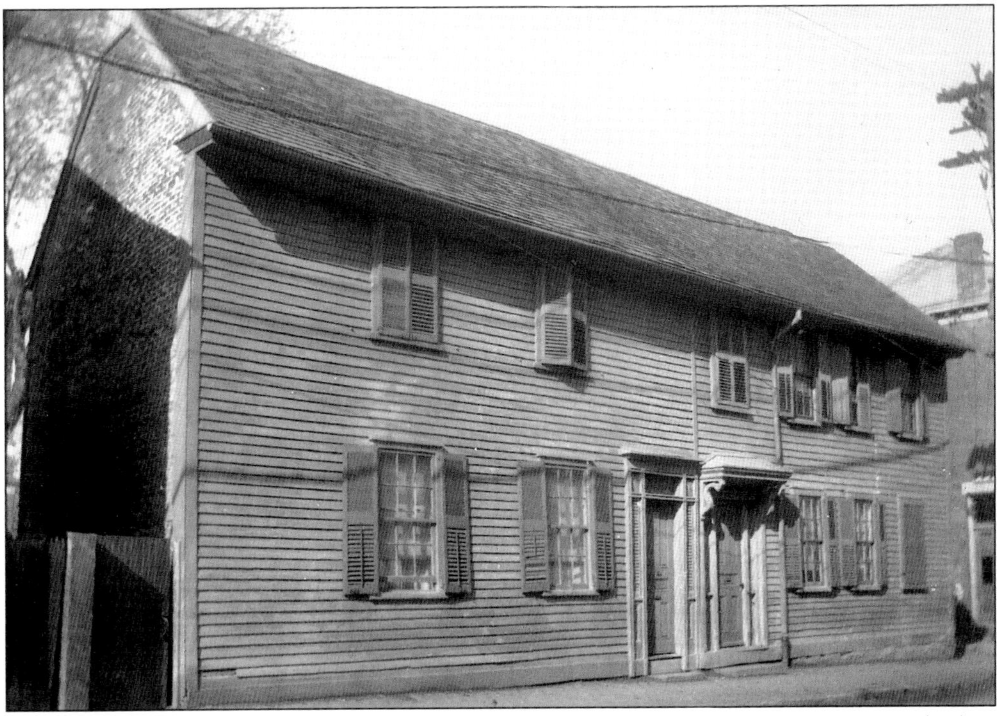

The Odlin-Otis House was built on the corner of Spring and Mary Streets in 1705. In the late 1700s, it was a Quaker school for boys. As can be seen here, the house is a stone-ender.

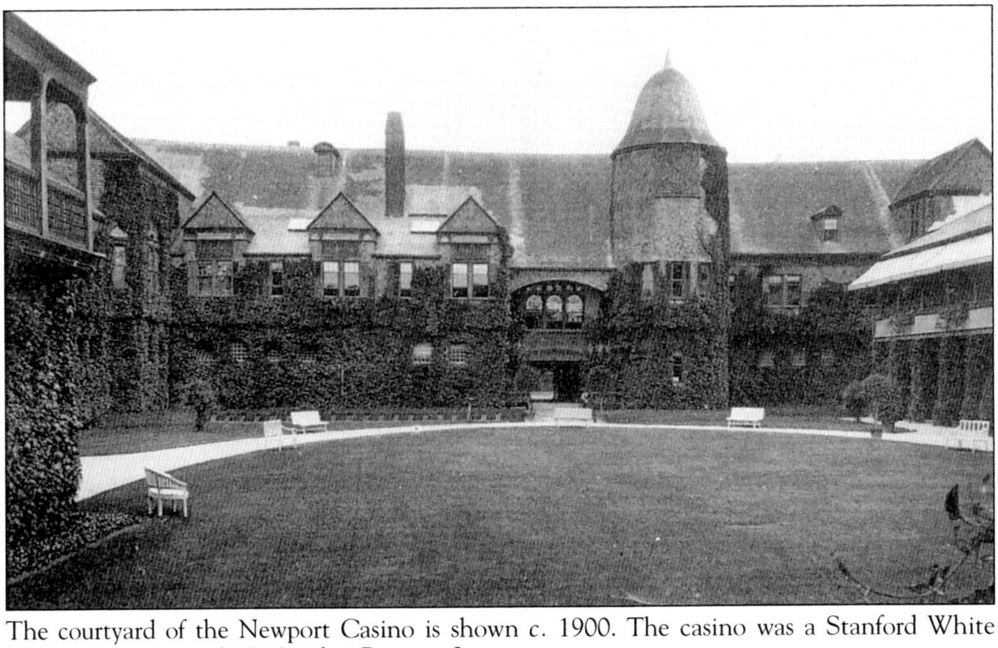

The courtyard of the Newport Casino is shown c. 1900. The casino was a Stanford White design built in 1880 by J. Gordon Bennett Jr.

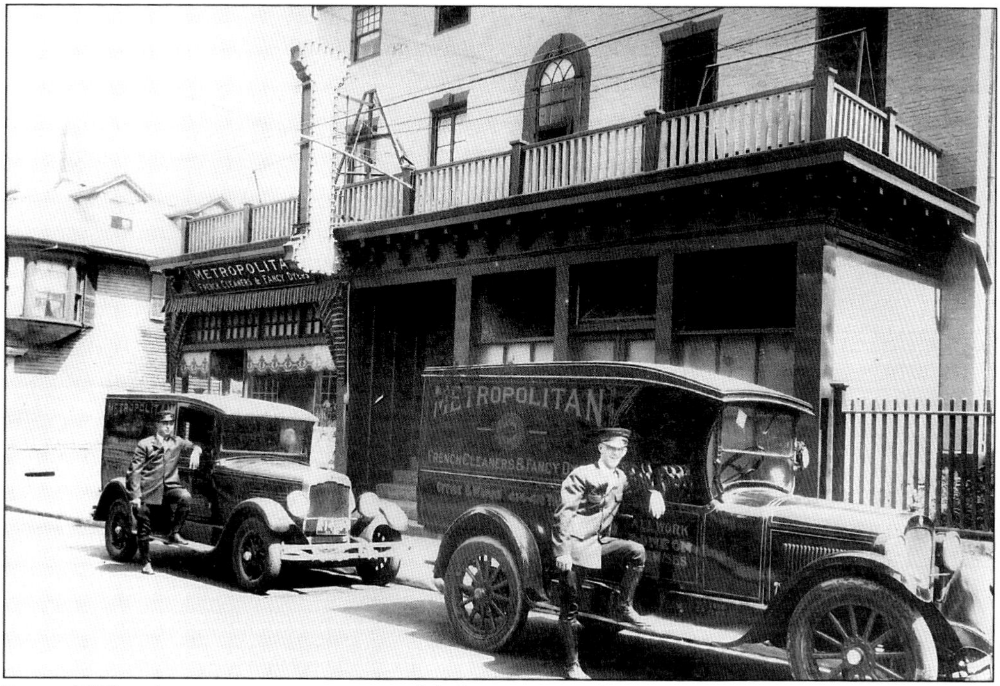

Samuel Whitehorne was a very successful shipping merchant who built this house on Thames Street in 1811. This 1910 photograph shows the building adapted for commercial use as the Metropolitan Cleaners. The house was restored in 1968 by the Newport Restoration Foundation and opened as a museum.

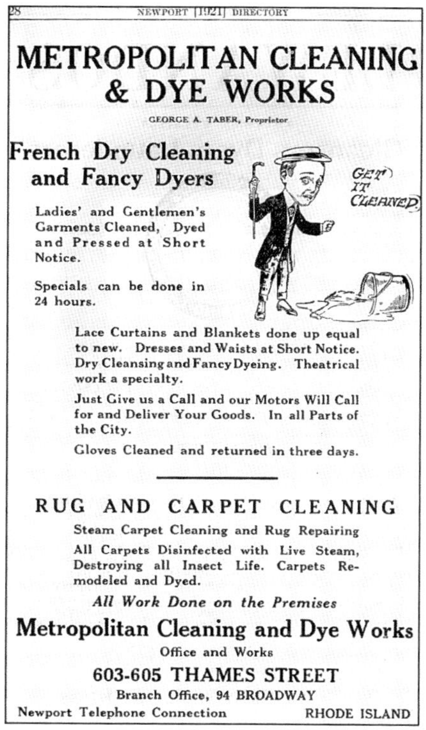

This advertisement for Metropolitan Cleaners appeared in the 1921 Newport telephone directory.

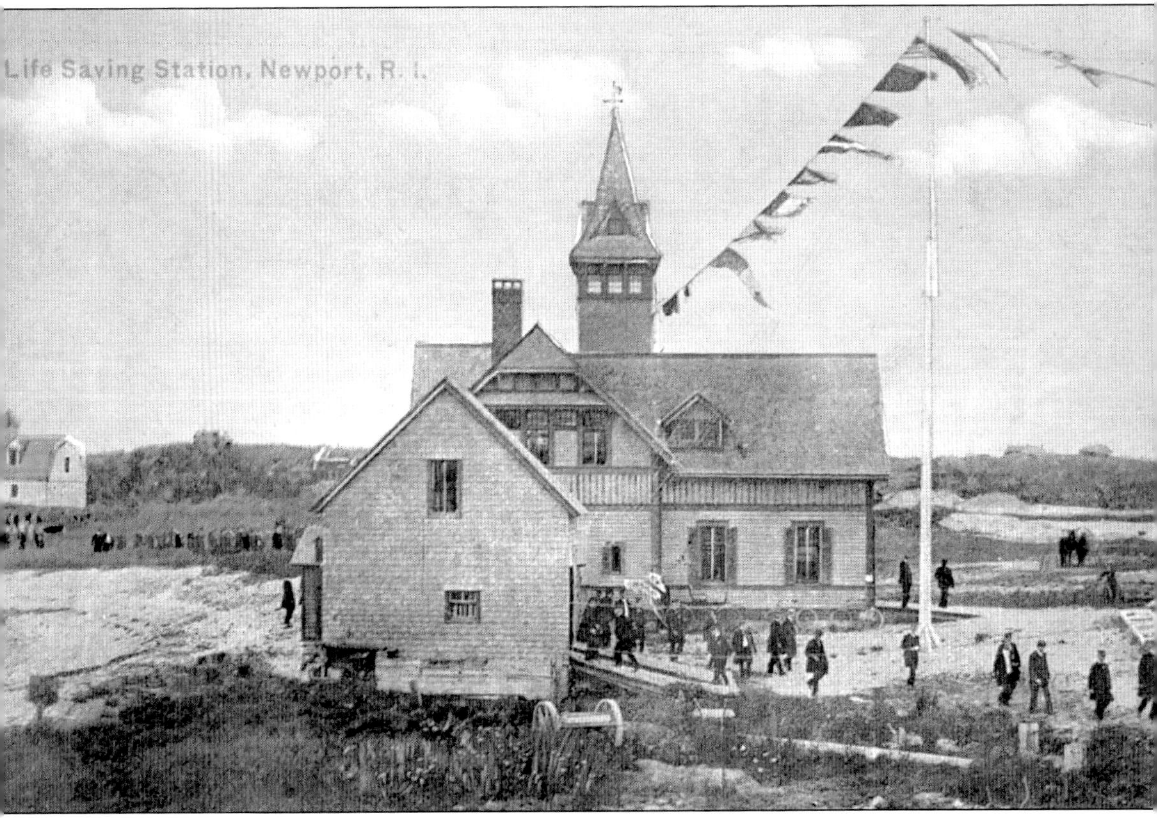

Price's Neck was included in the parcel of land owned by Governor Brenton in the 1600s. It was named after a bootmaker whose name was Price. Brenton brought Price here from England. A 1905 book mentions this lifesaving station at the tip of Price's Neck in view of Mr. Olmsted's house. In the Hurricane of 1938, the building sustained extensive damage. Temporary headquarters were set up at the Seamen's Church Institute and, by 1940, the new Coast Guard station was opened on Castle Hill.

Three

The Bridges of Newport County

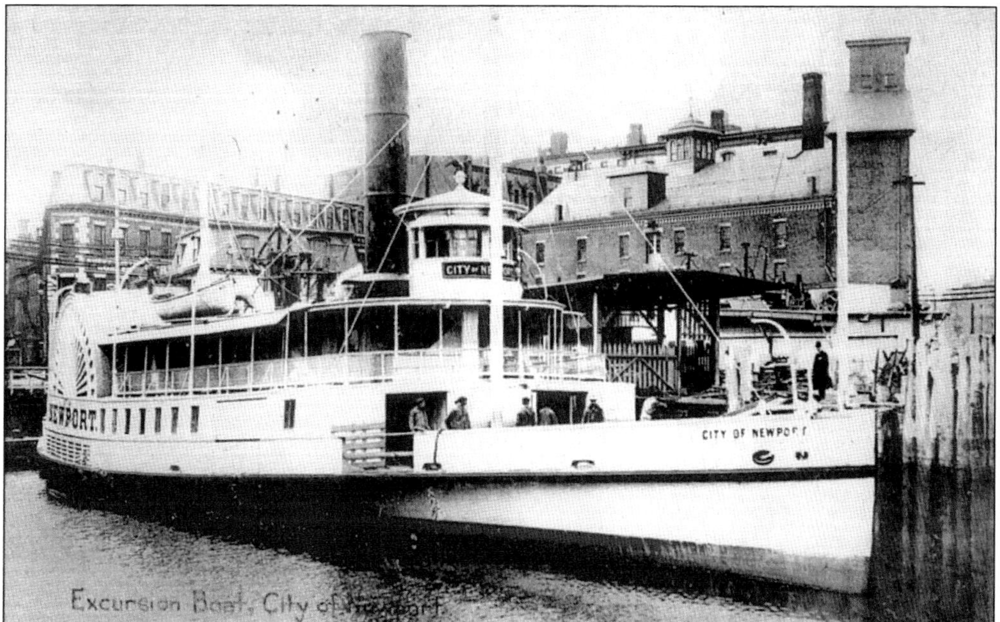

The *City of Newport*, which was built in 1863, was an excursion boat that ferried passengers between Newport, Providence, and Rocky Point. It was owned by the Continental Steamboat Company and was one of four ships.

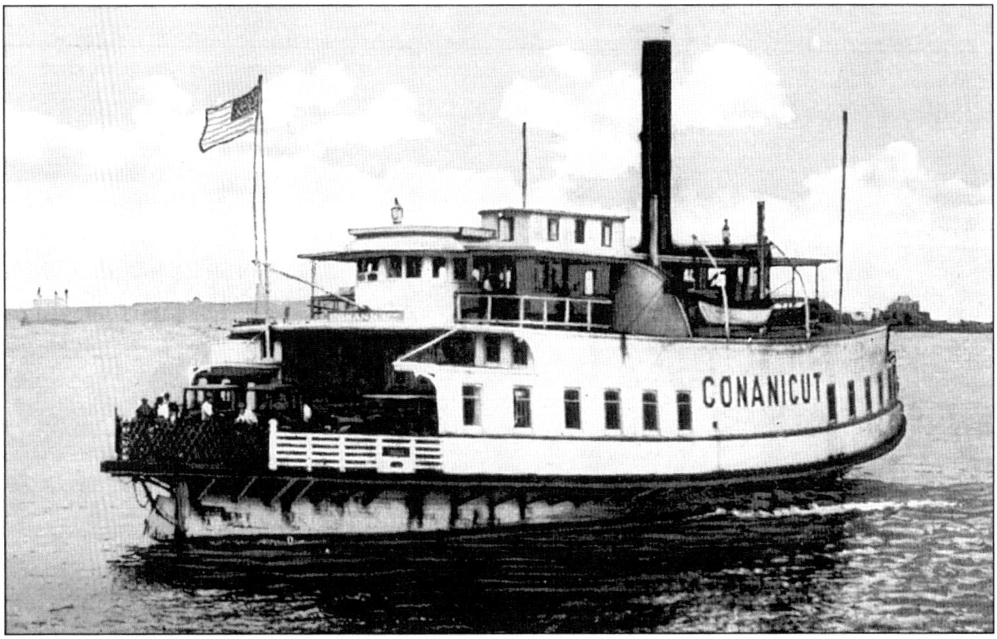

The Newport-Jamestown ferry *Conanicut* was put into service in 1886 to replace the *Jamestown*. The ship ferried passengers across Narragansett Bay until 1927, when it was replaced by the *Governor Carr*.

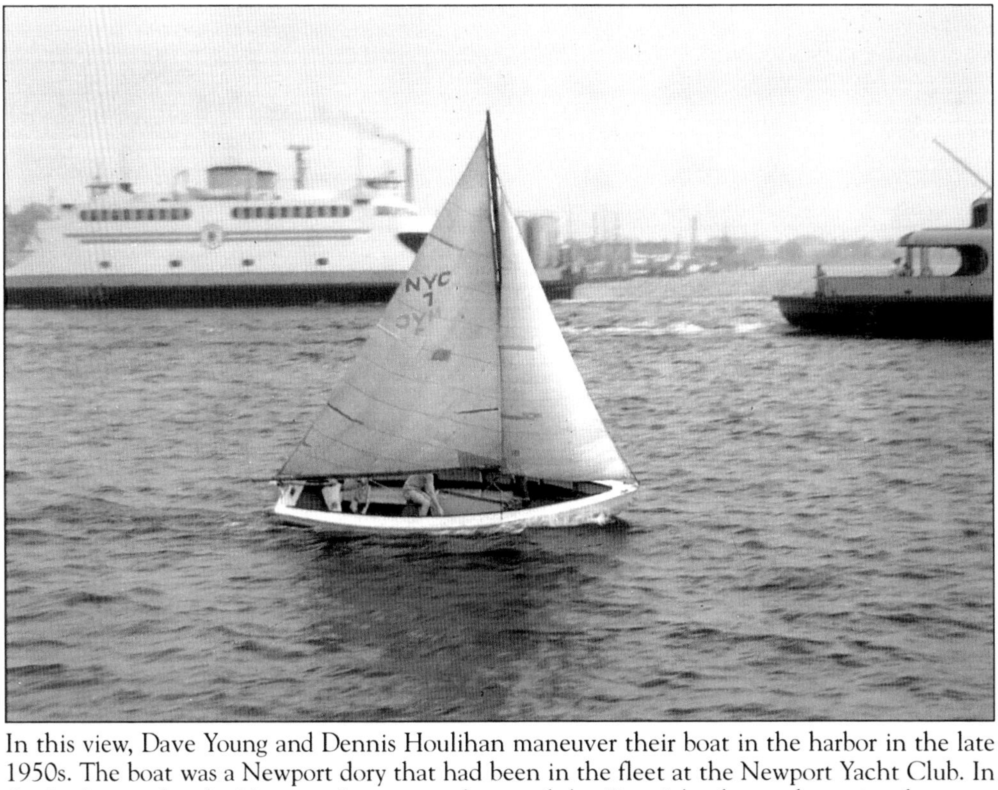

In this view, Dave Young and Dennis Houlihan maneuver their boat in the harbor in the late 1950s. The boat was a Newport dory that had been in the fleet at the Newport Yacht Club. In the background is the Newport-Jamestown ferry and the Goat Island torpedo station ferry.

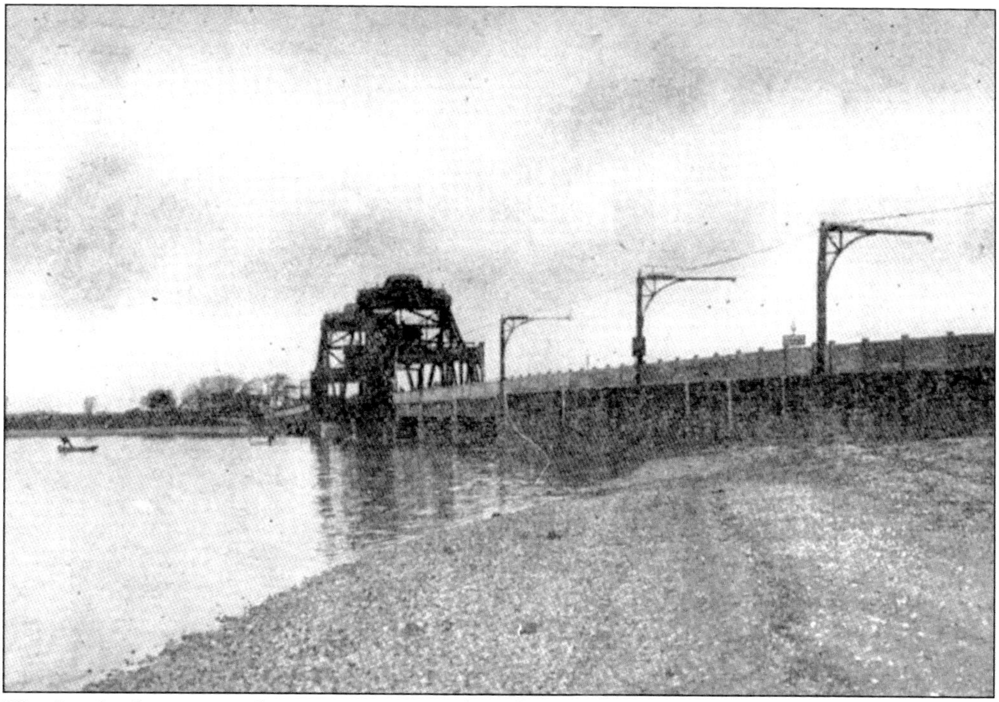

The first bridge to cross between Portsmouth and Tiverton was erected in 1795. It was washed out in January of the following year. The crossing was known as Howland's Ferry.

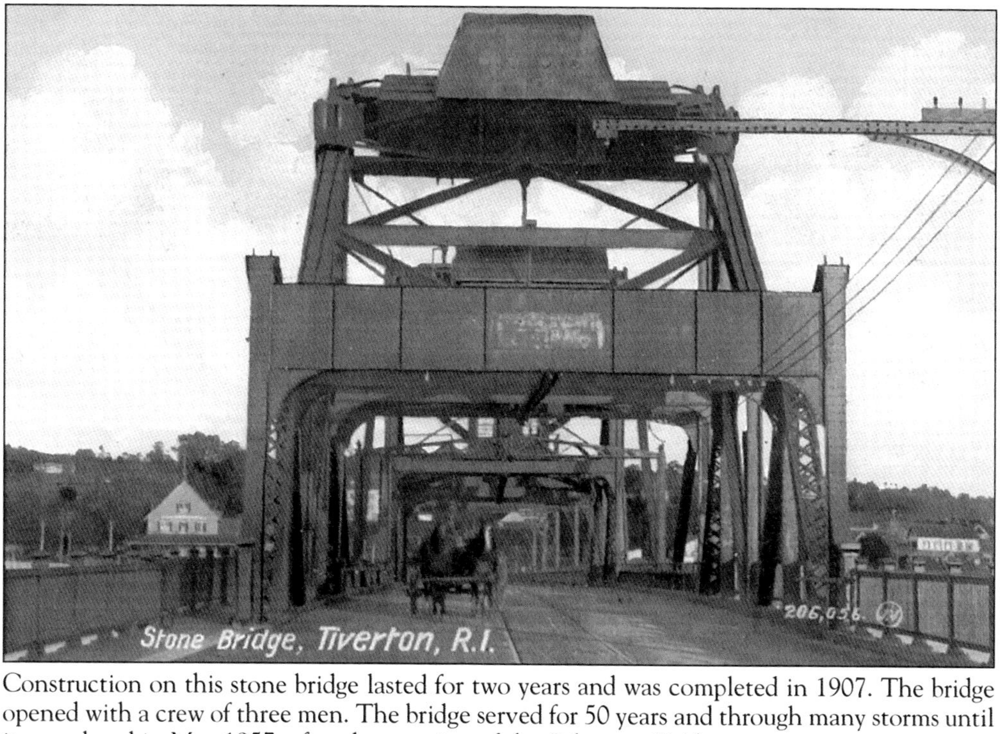

Construction on this stone bridge lasted for two years and was completed in 1907. The bridge opened with a crew of three men. The bridge served for 50 years and through many storms until it was closed in May 1957, after the opening of the Sakonnet Bridge.

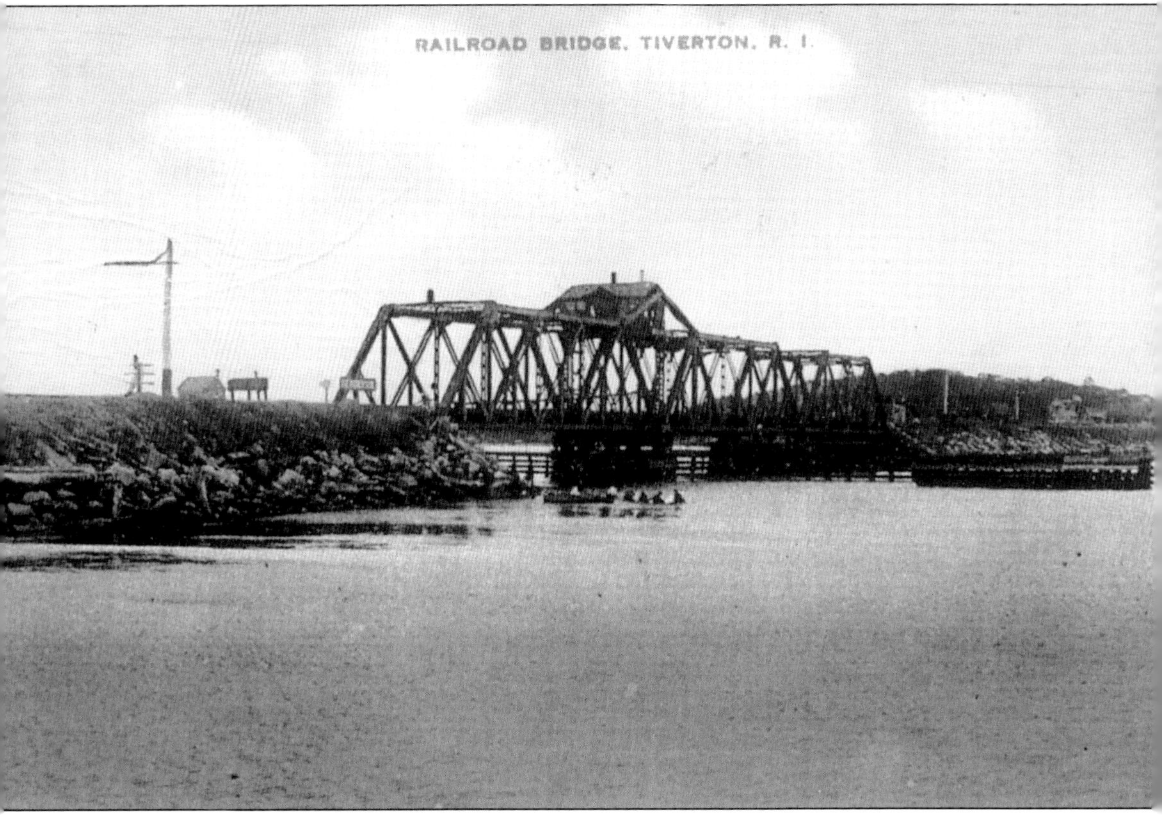

In 1861, lands were conveyed to the Old Colony and Fall River Railroad. This railroad bridge was built *c.* 1860 between Portsmouth and Tiverton. A steam railroad between Newport and Boston was a big turning point in the city's history.

The Mount Hope Bridge is shown with the towers built and the connecting cables strung. The bridge would eventually replace ferry service between Bristol and Aquidneck Island.

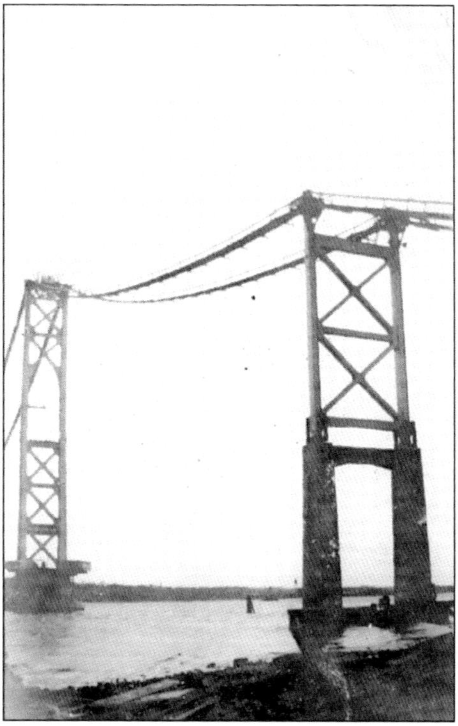

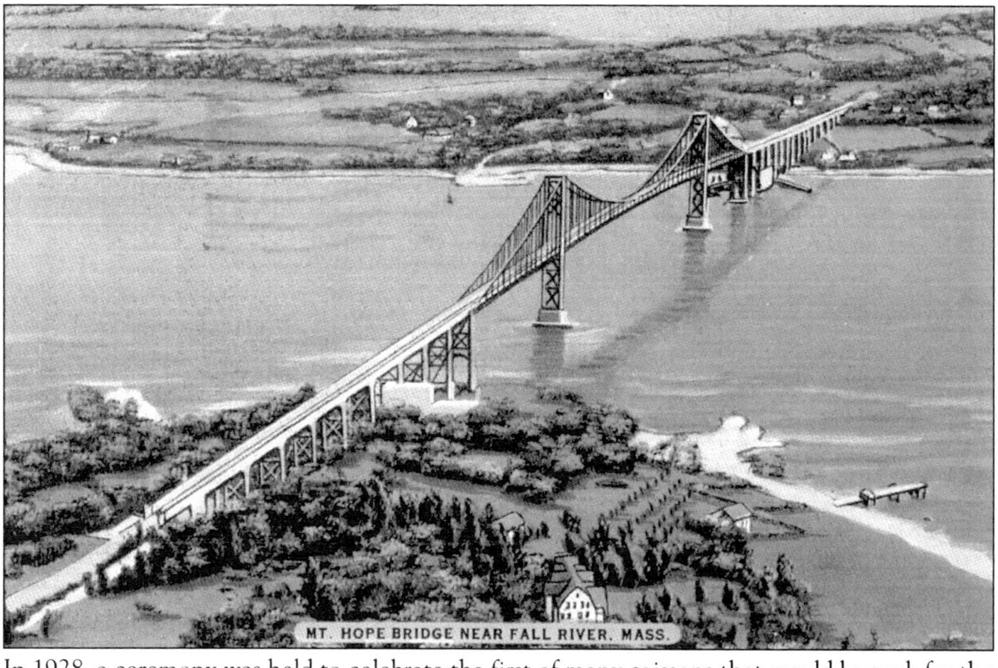

In 1928, a ceremony was held to celebrate the first of many caissons that would be sunk for the bridge. On October 24, 1929, the Mount Hope Bridge was dedicated.

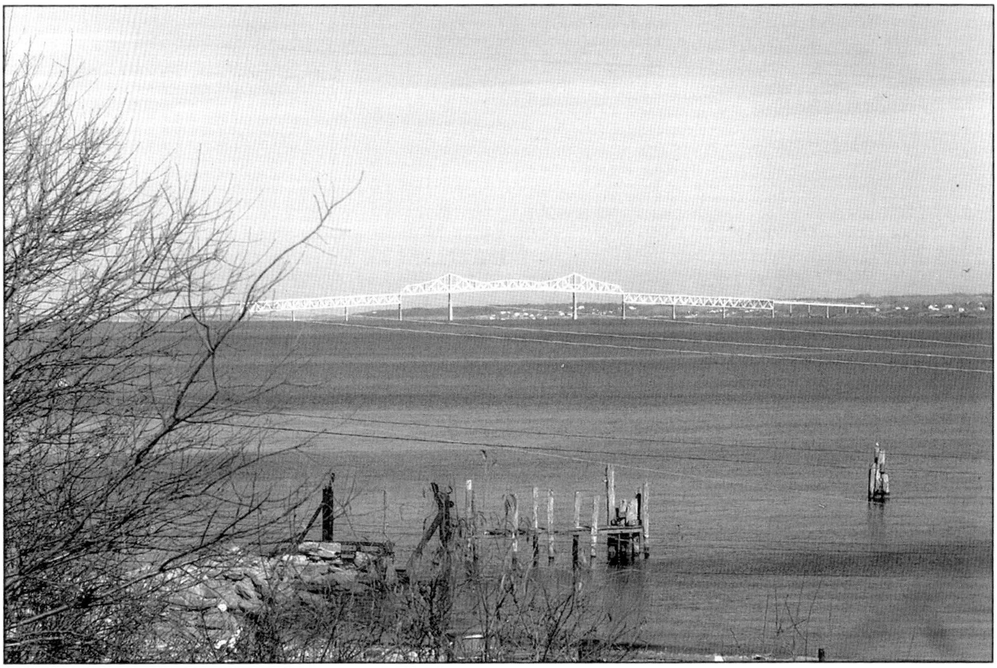

The Narragansett Bay Bridge was completed in under three years at a cost of $3 million.

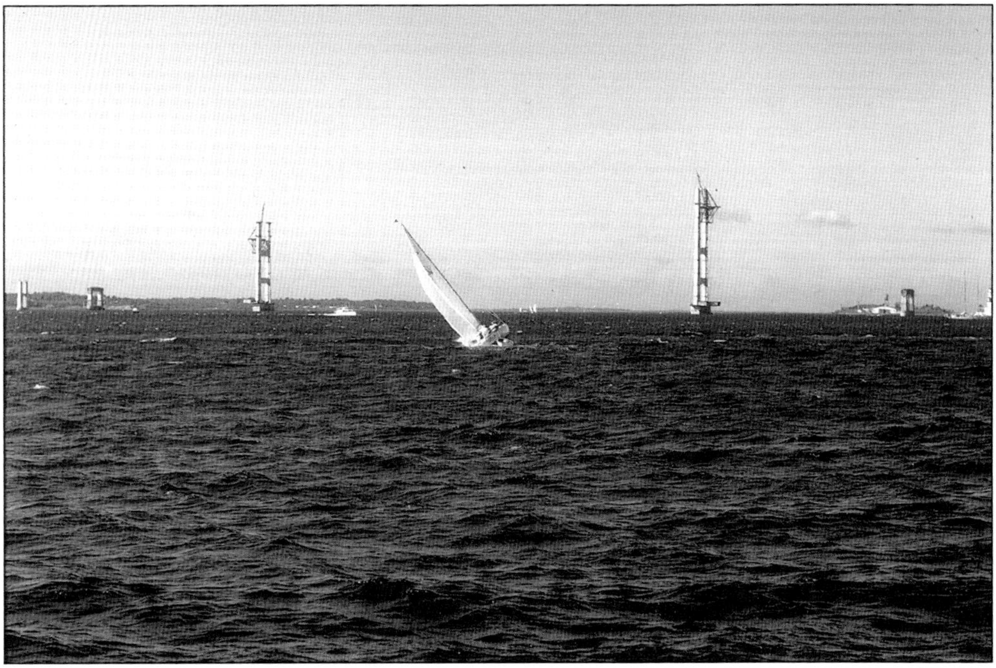

The towers for the Newport Bridge are shown here almost completed. In April 1965, the first pylon was driven into Narragansett Bay, marking the start of bridge construction, which would last for over three years.

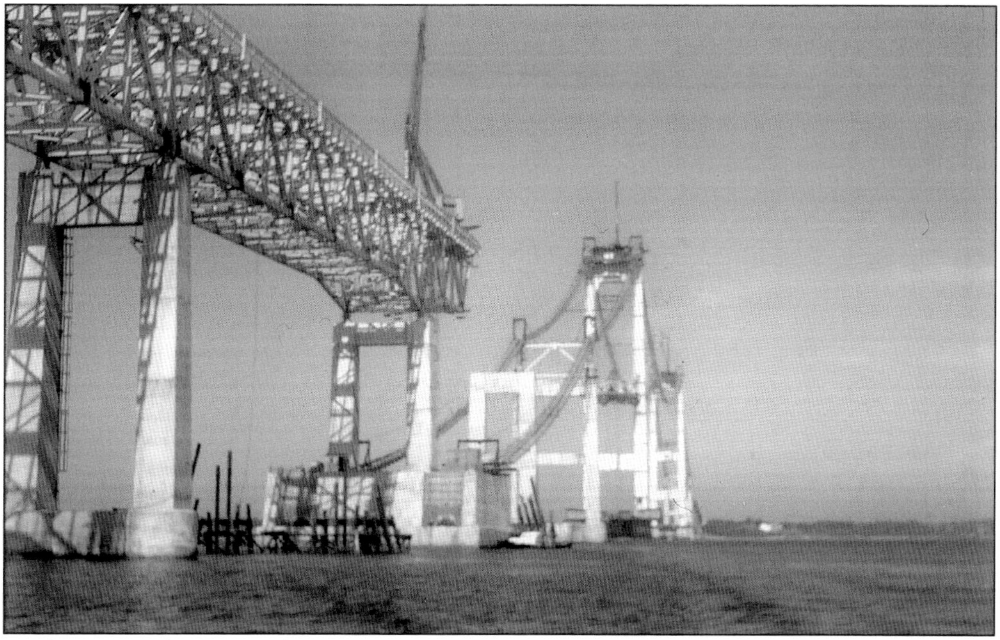

In this view, the towers have been completed, the cable has been strung, and the rigid framework for the roadbed is in place.

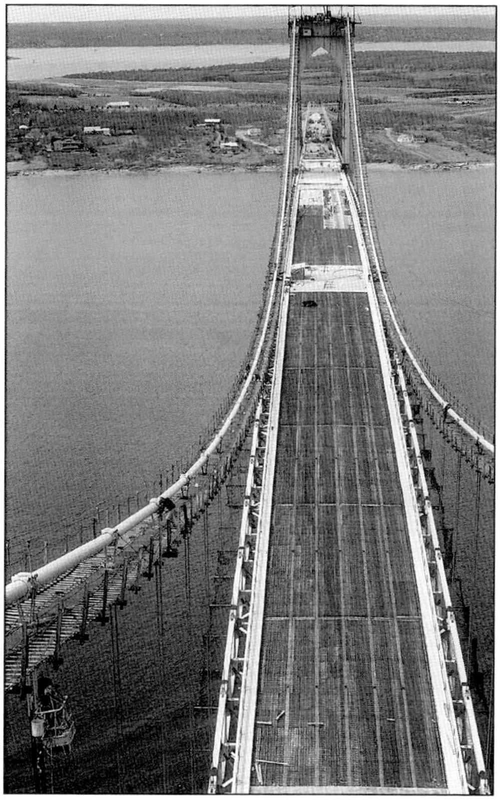

A view from the east tower shows the almost completed roadbed. Jamestown lies in the distance.

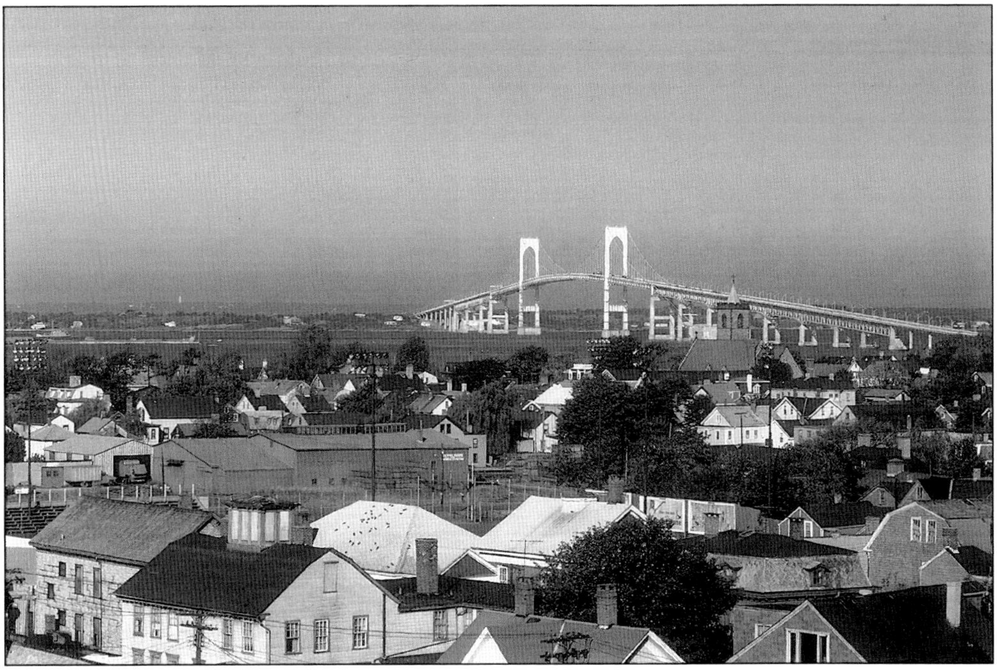

The completed bridge is shown c. 1970 from the YMCA building. The bridge was opened on June 28, 1969.

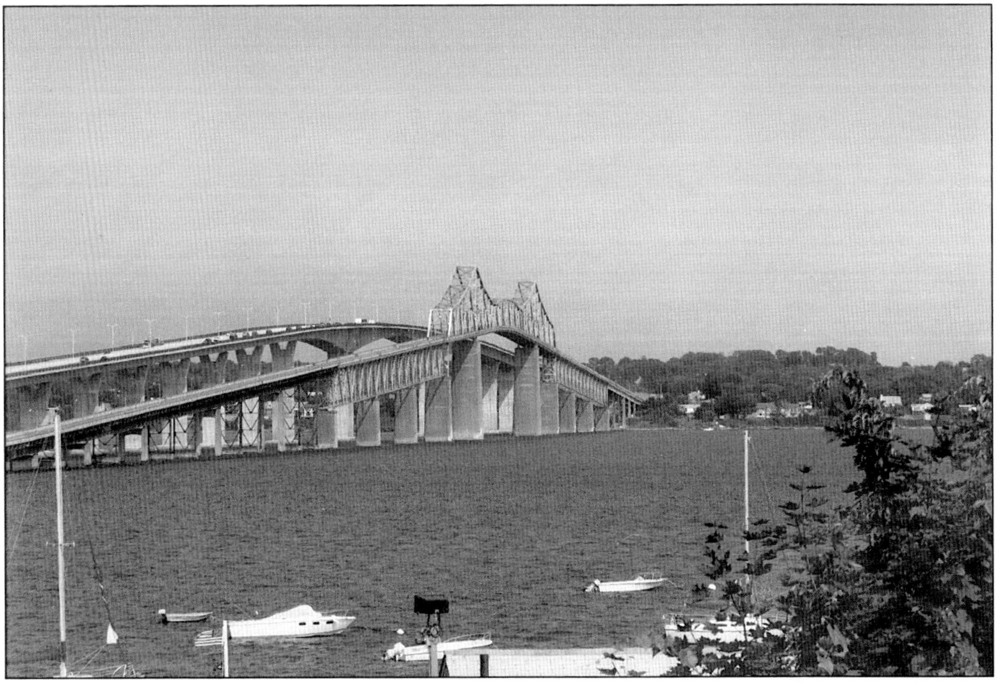

The new Jamestown-Verrazano Bridge opened in October 17, 1992. The bridge took eight years to build because of the many setbacks it experienced. Here, the two bridges echo one another. (Photograph by Dorothy Burnette.)

Four

Along the Water's Edge

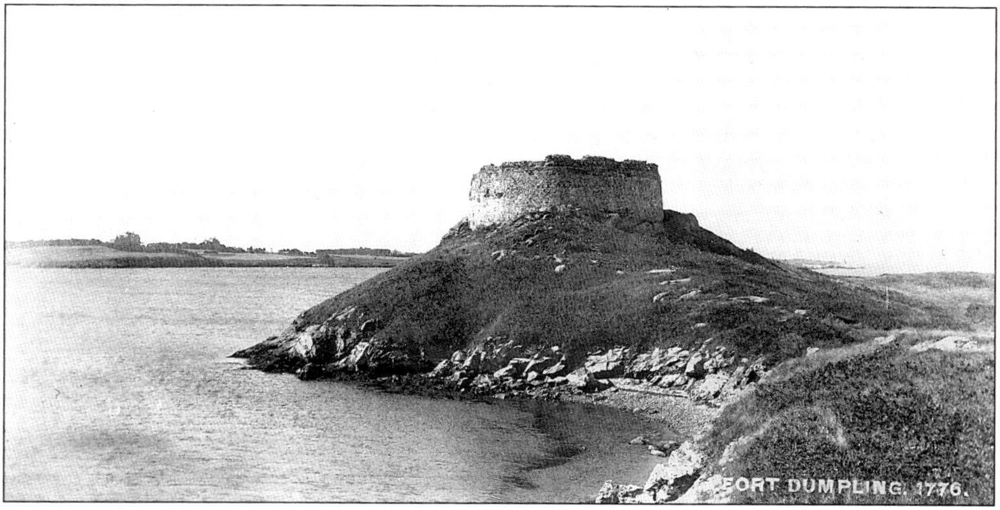

Fort Dumplings was built in the late 1790s at the mouth of the harbor. In the 1850s, it was badly damaged by target fire from Fort Adams. It was finally demolished in 1899.

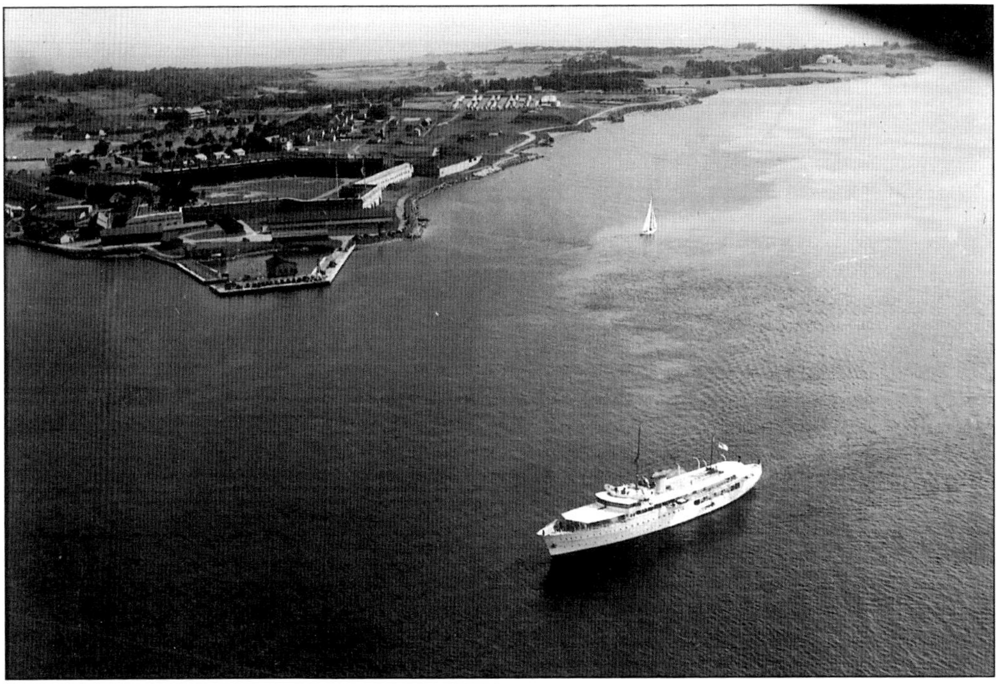

Construction of Fort Adams was begun in 1824 on land that was originally part of the Brenton Estate. The construction would last for years as the scale of the fort was increased. The fort was completed in 1841 with two companies of U.S. troops already stationed there.

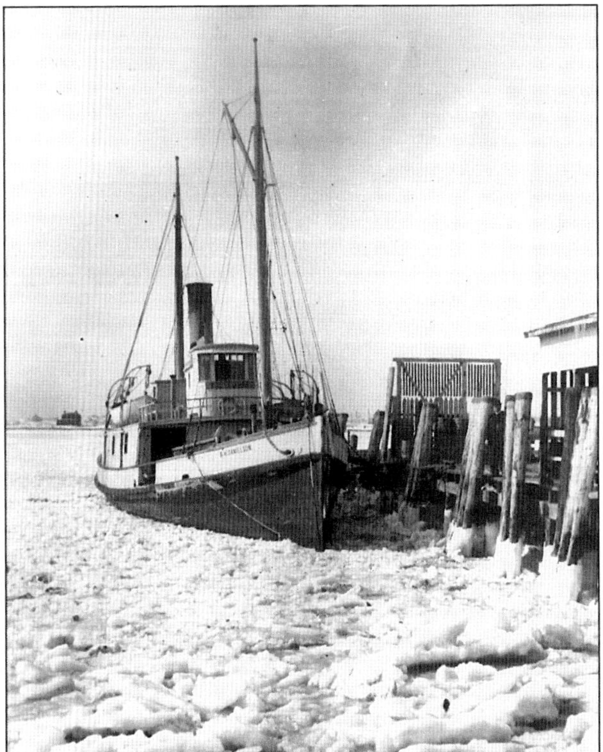

In 1875, Aquidneck Island experienced a very severe winter. For weeks the harbor was frozen solid and it was possible to walk to Fort Adams and Goat Island.

In the early 1700s, a fort was built on Goat Island and named in honor of King George. This 1938 aerial photograph shows the officers' quarters and torpedo station. (Courtesy of the William Bachus collection.)

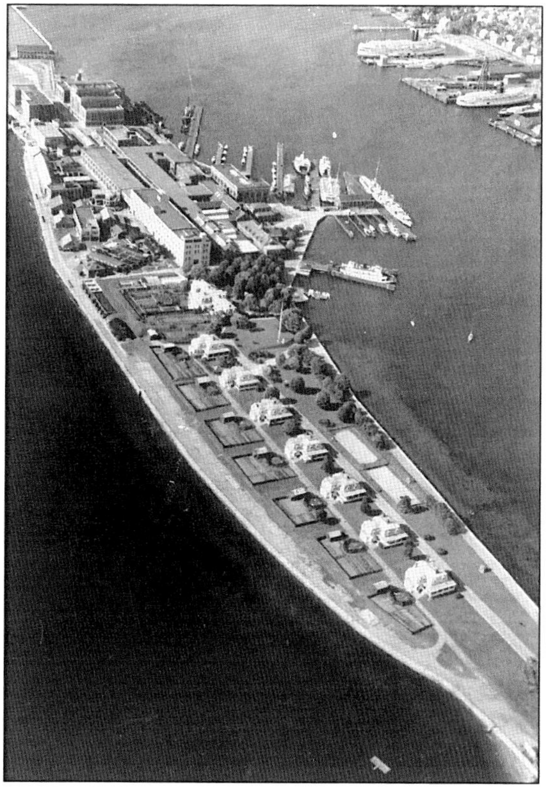

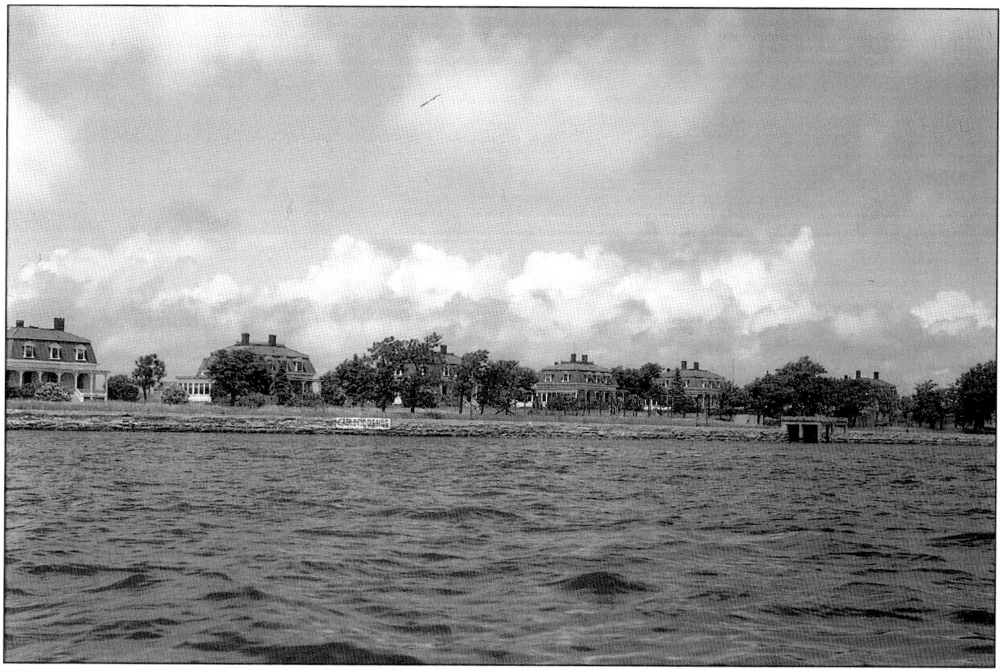

This photograph of Goat Island shows the officers' quarters lined up for inspection. In the mid-1960s, the navy offered Goat Island for private developments.

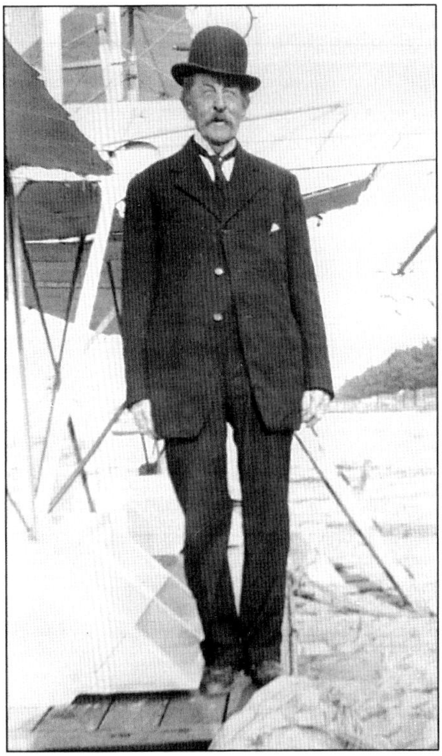

Shown here is Capt. Hugh L. Willoughby beside his plane on King's Beach. Willoughby resided in the Chateau on Halidon Hill. He lived in Newport for many years until his death in 1939 at the age of 84.

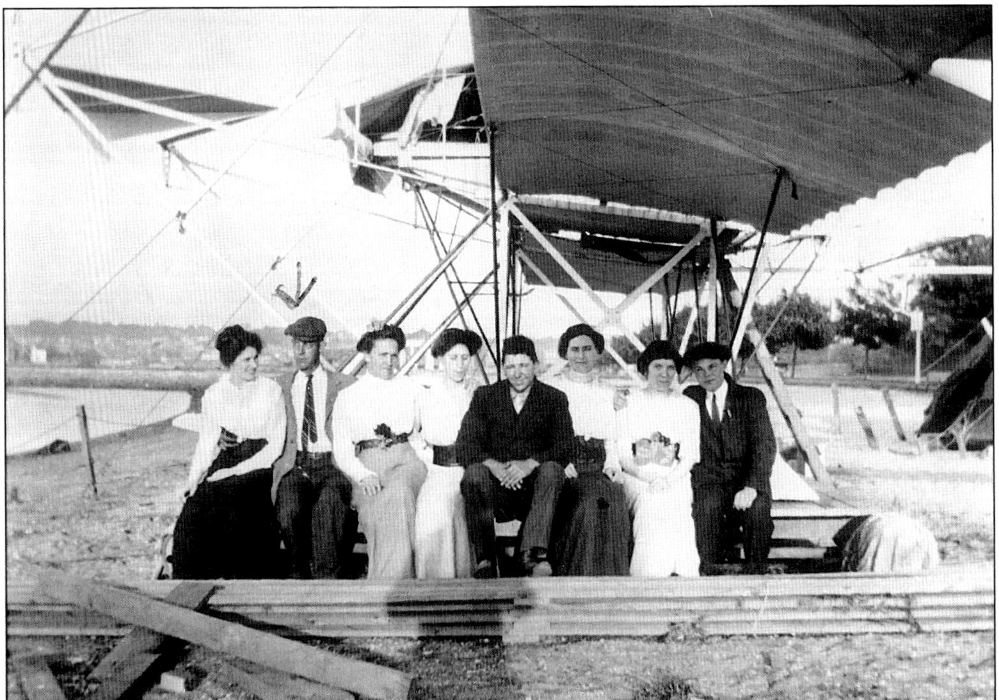

Friends of Capt. Hugh L. Willoughby pose in front of his plane, which was being assembled in King's Park at the base of Halidon Hill.

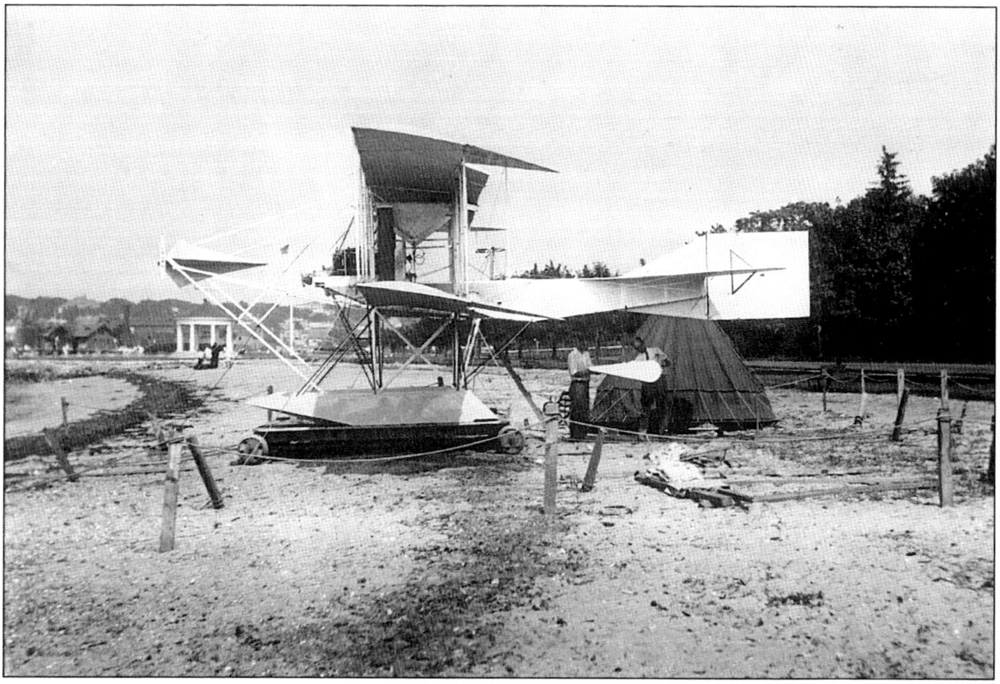

This is a view looking east on King's Park in 1915 with Capt. Hugh L. Willoughby's Model-F airplane almost ready for flight.

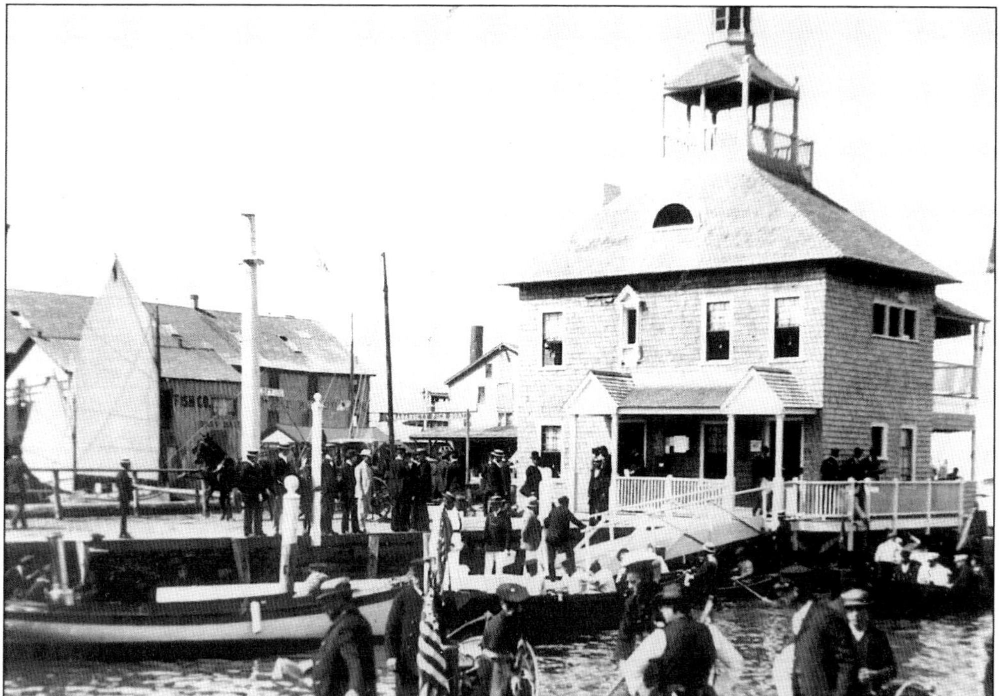

The New York Yacht Club, located at the end of Sayer's Wharf, is shown in the early 1900s. The club was organized in New York in 1844. The Newport chapter opened in 1897.

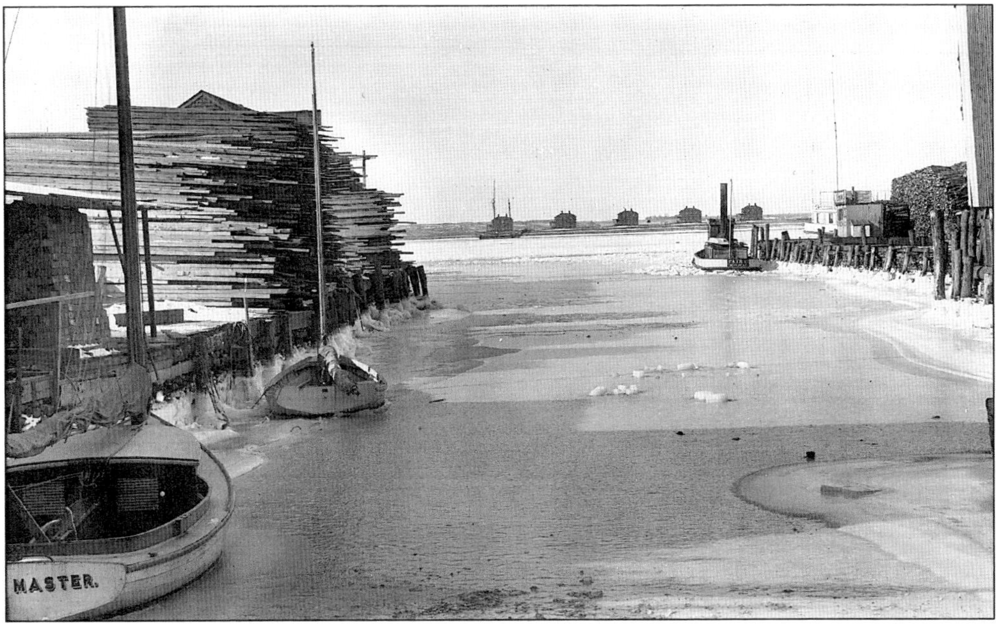

An icy view of Hammett's Wharf looking west toward Goat Island in the winter of 1910.

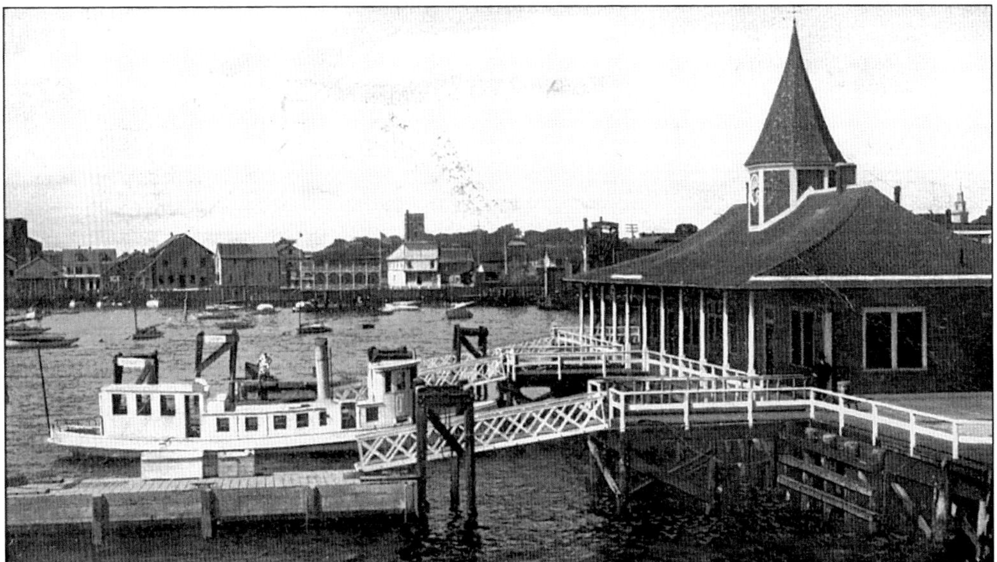
In 1903, the government purchased the Swinburne and Peckham Company with the intention of making an embarkation point for ferries between downtown Newport and its properties around the bay. This postcard shows an excursion boat docked at the landing.

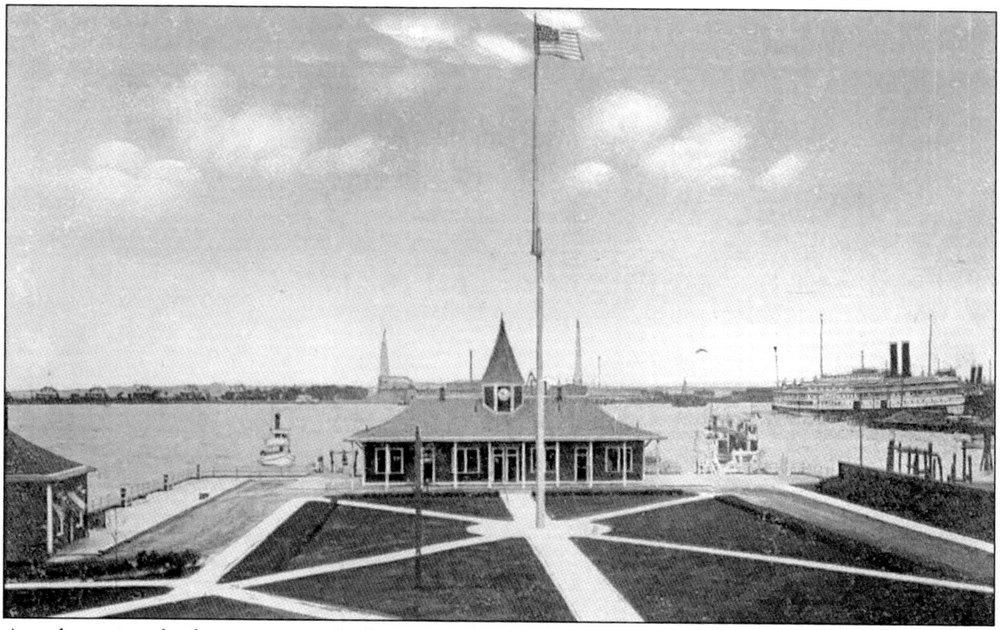

Another view looking west with the steamship *Puritan* to the right. The navy provided ferry service from Government Landing to its many properties around Narragansett Bay.

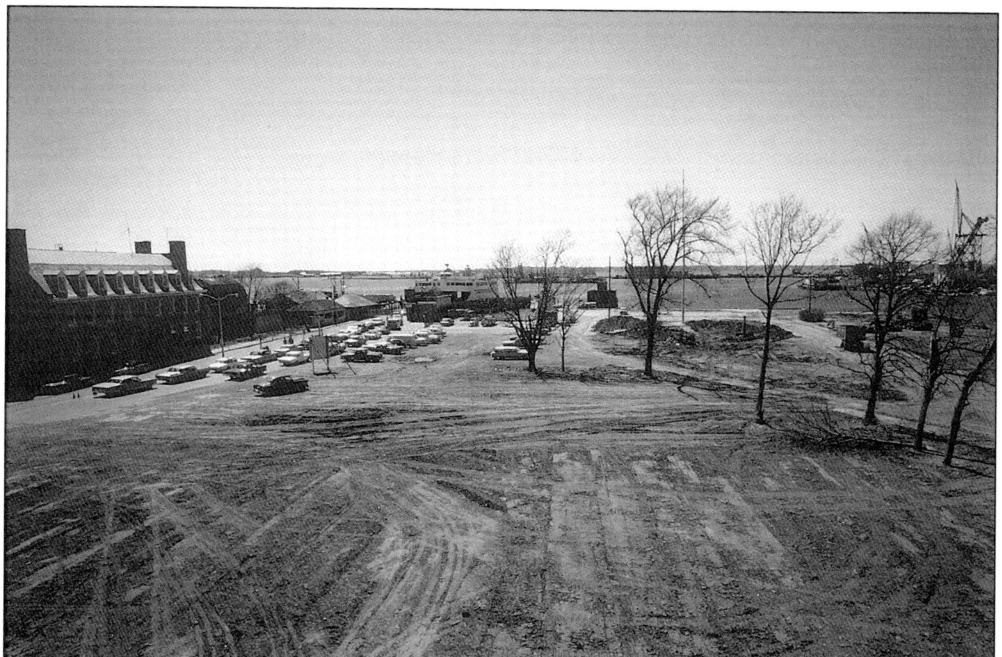

Government Landing is shown in this view in the late 1960s, just before ferry service between Newport and Jamestown was discontinued. The Newport Bridge was about to open.

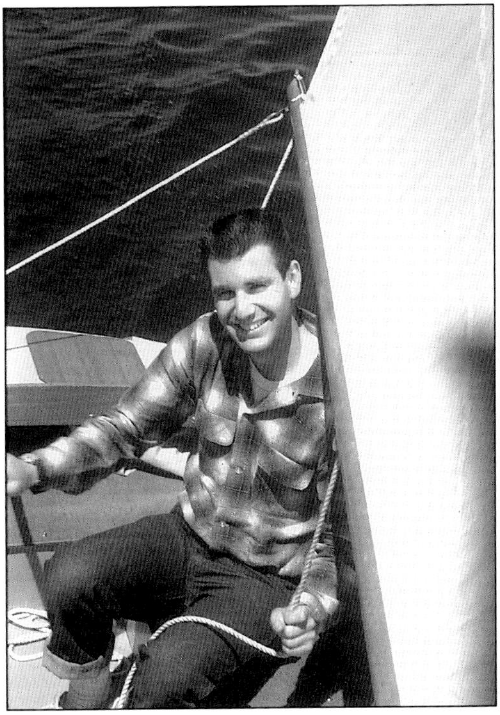

Dave Young poses c. 1962 in a 16-foot falcon sloop. Many times, Dave took the helm while his father, "Doc," took pictures around the bay.

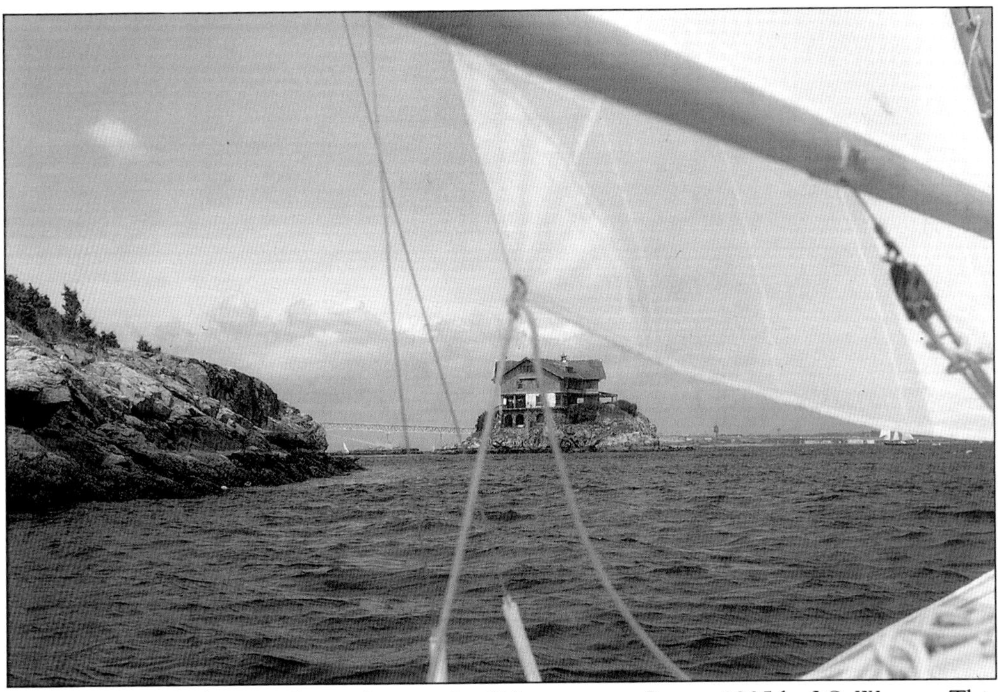

Clingstone was built on rocks, at the mouth of Narragansett Bay, c. 1905 by J.S. Warton. This late-1960s photograph shows the house after its 1962 restoration.

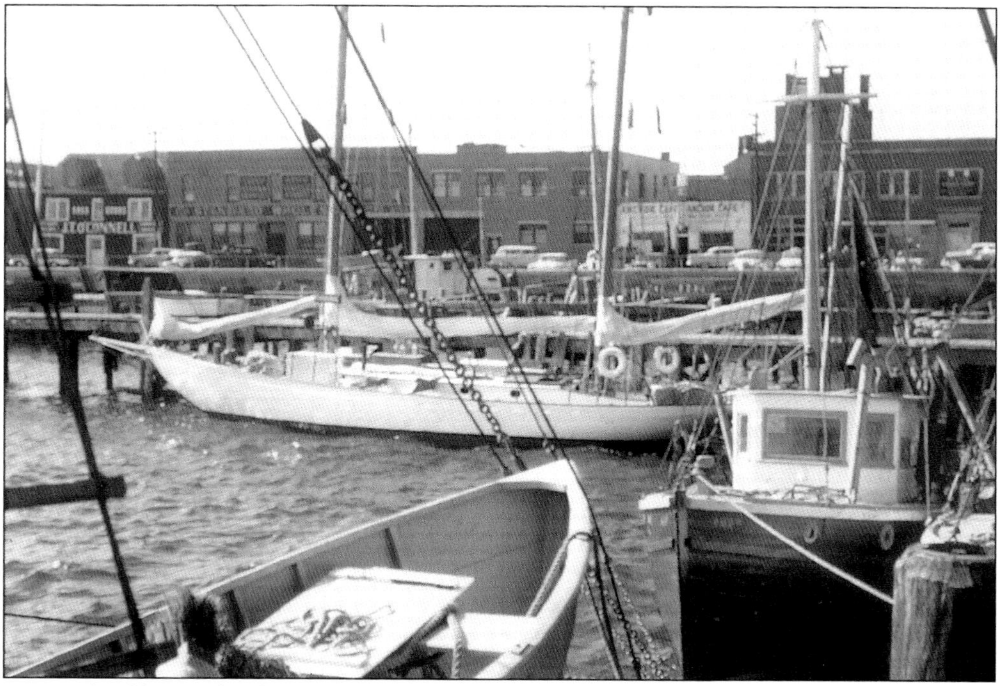

Long Wharf lies in the distance in this 1920 photograph. J.T. O'Connell's ship chandlery is to the left.

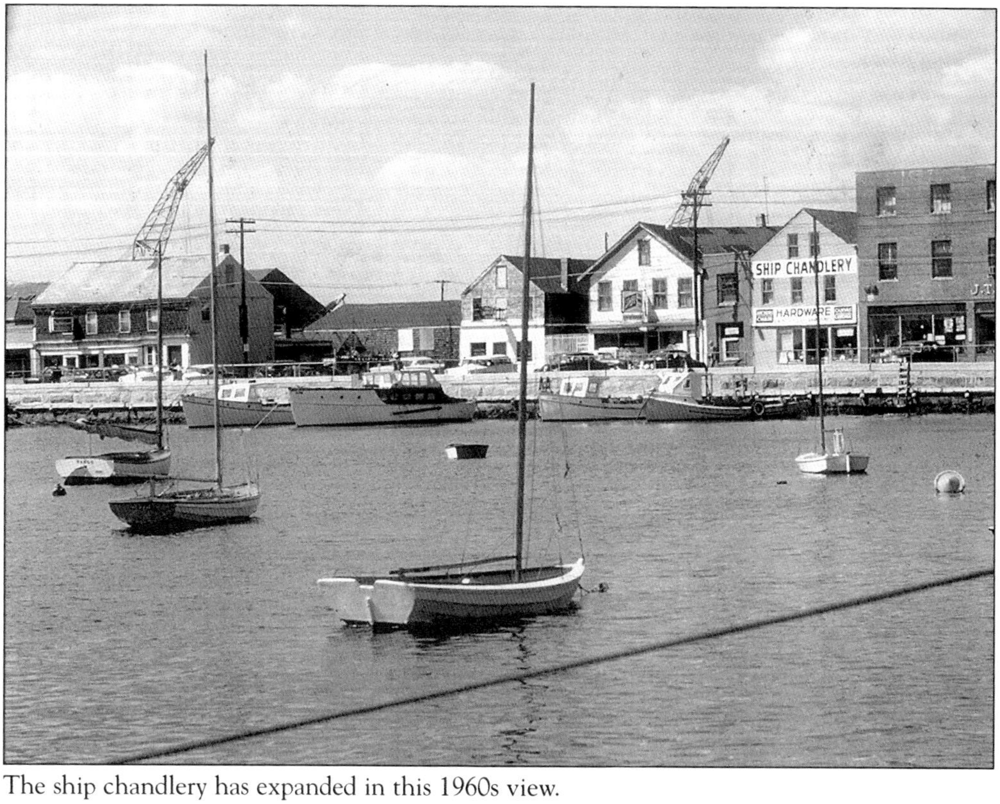

The ship chandlery has expanded in this 1960s view.

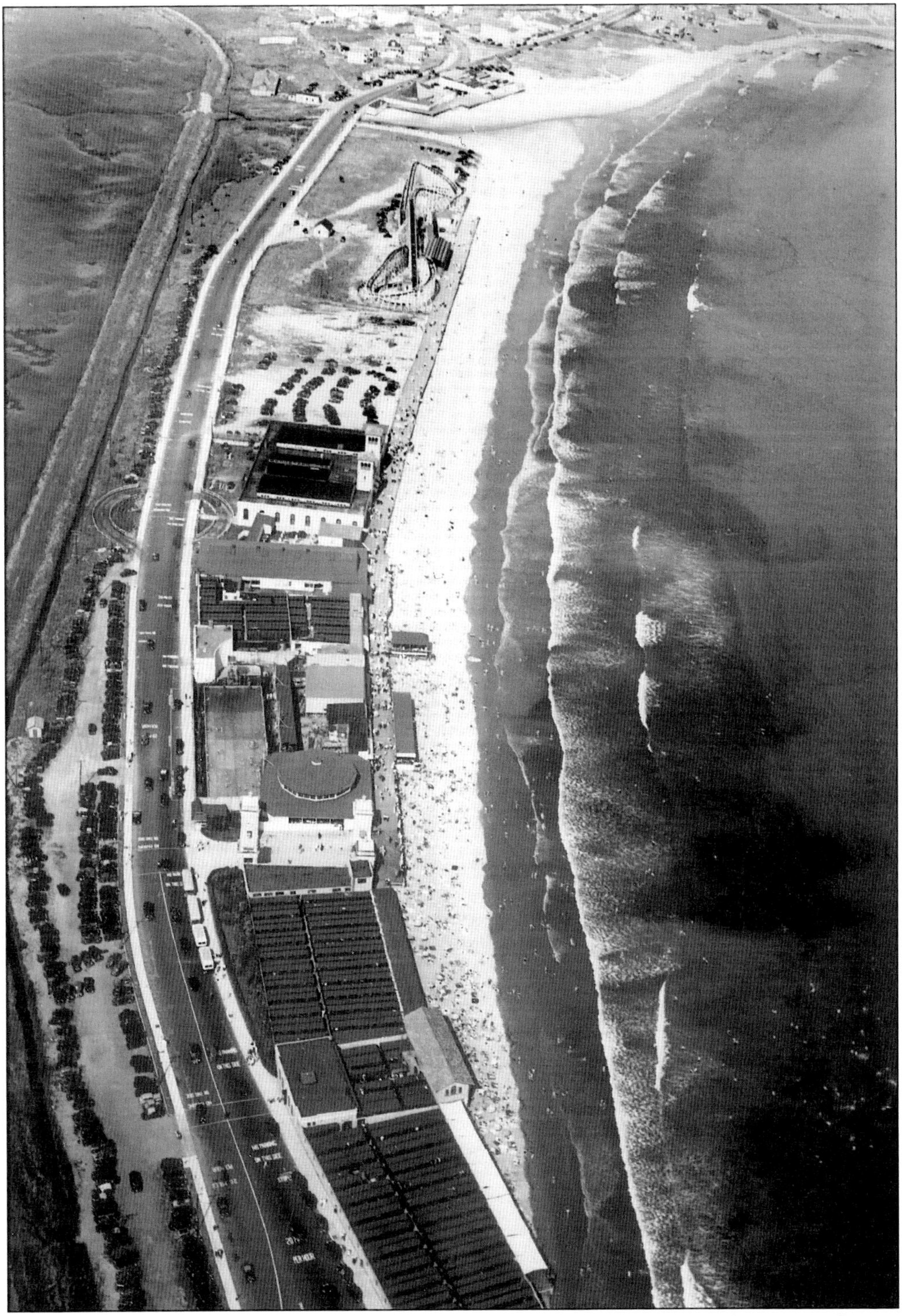

This aerial view shows Easton's Beach on July 4, 1938. The roller coaster can be seen in the top of the photograph. Less than two months later, the Hurricane of 1938 would destroy the beach. (See page 95.) (Courtesy of the William Bachus collection.)

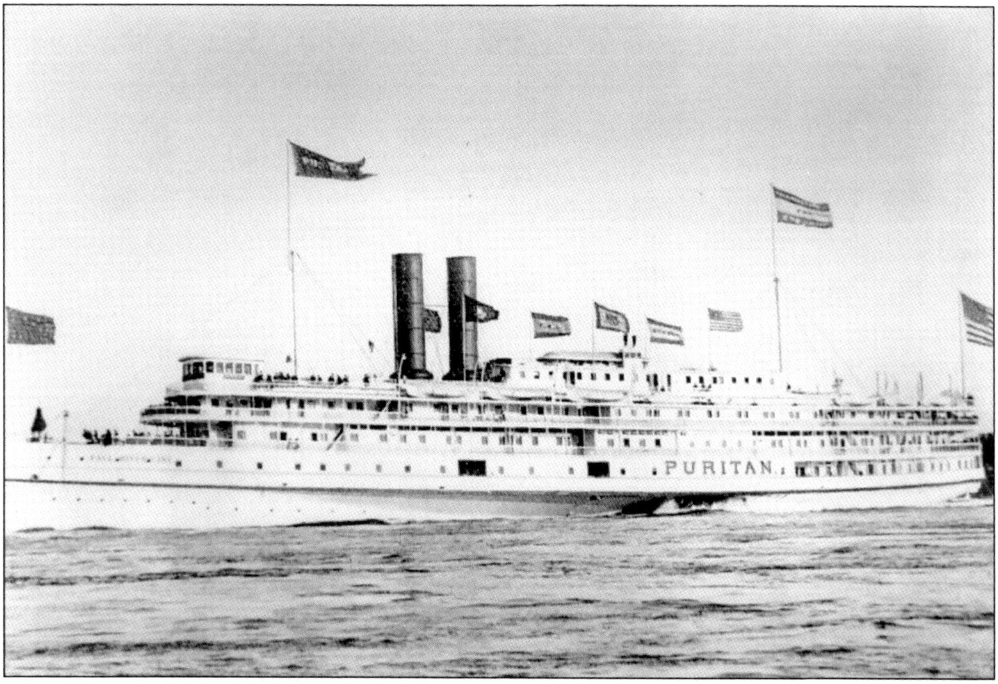

The *Puritan* was designed by George Pierce and went into service in June 1889. It was 420 feet long.

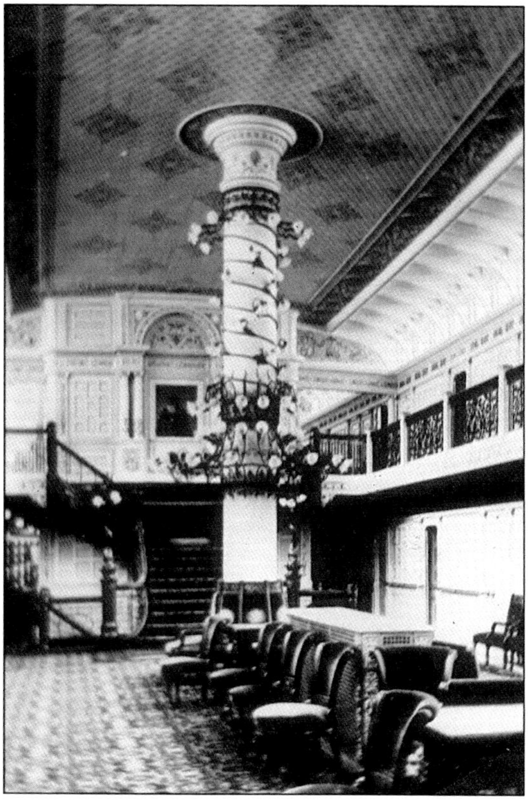

The *Puritan* was the second largest steamship built by George Pierce. This image shows the *Puritan*'s grand salon.

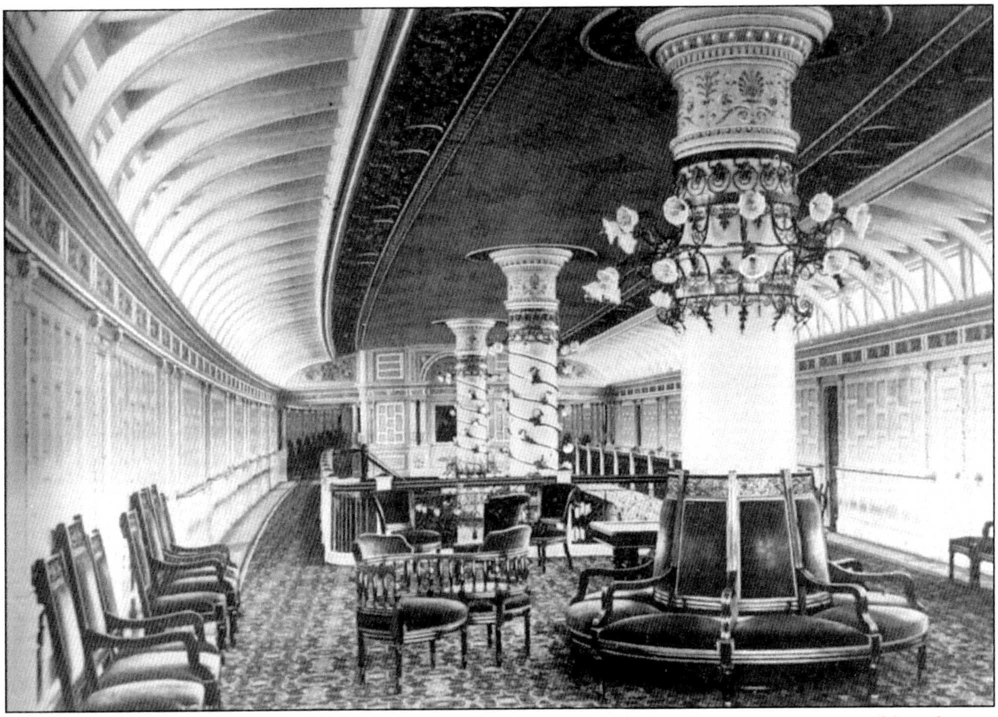

George Pierce designed many steamships in his career, and the *Puritan* was one of his finest. This is another view of the grand salon.

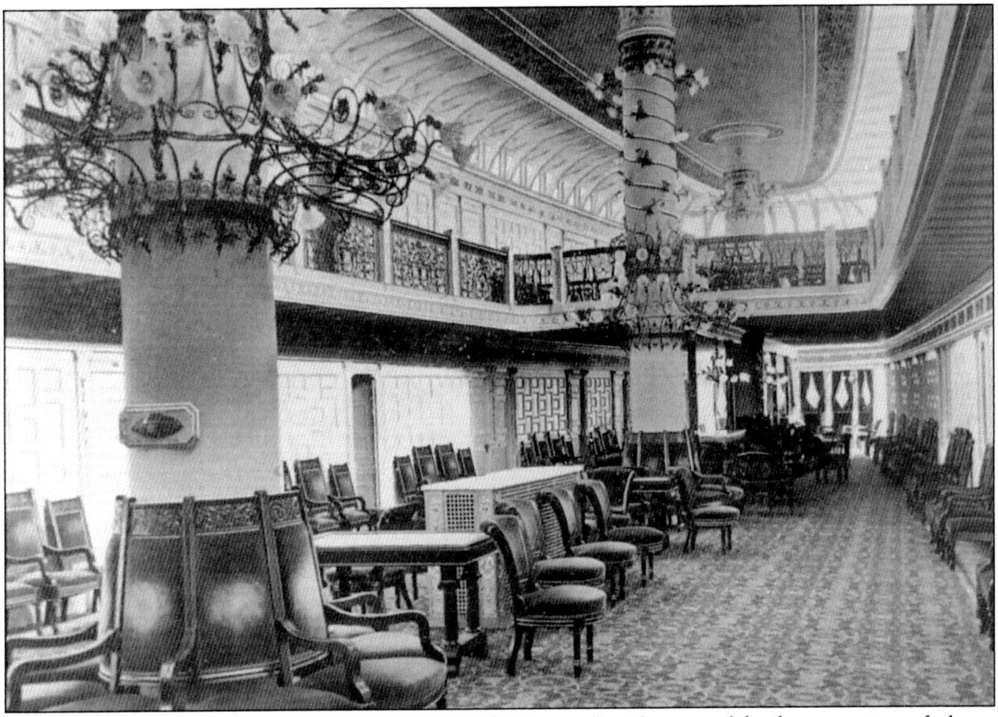

The *Puritan*'s grand salon is shown in a view looking aft. The vessel had a capacity of about 1,200 passengers.

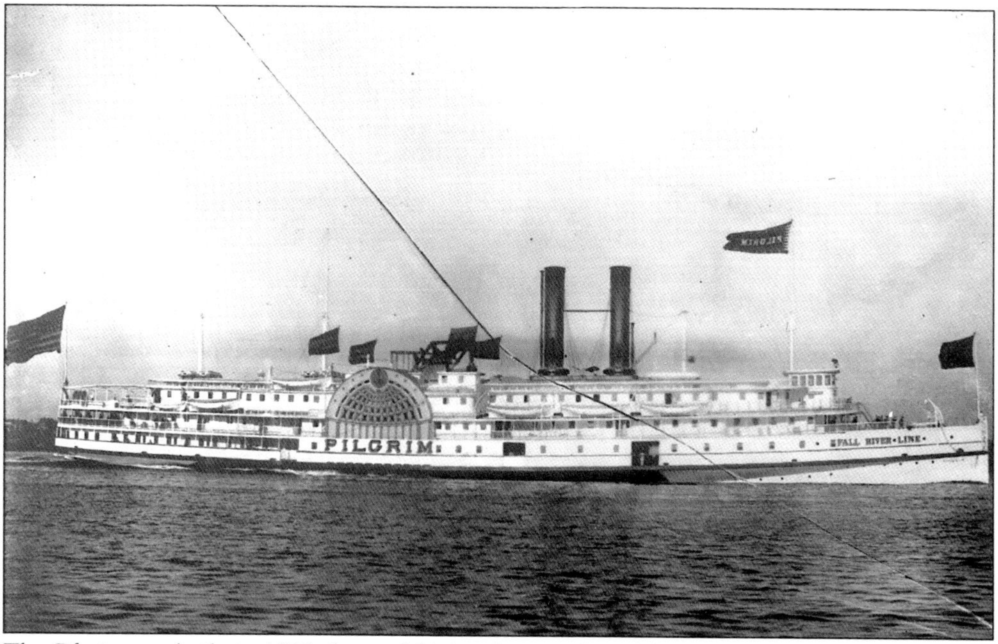

The *Pilgrim* was built in 1883. It was 390 feet long and could transport 1,200 passengers. The ship remained in service until 1913 and was scrapped in 1920.

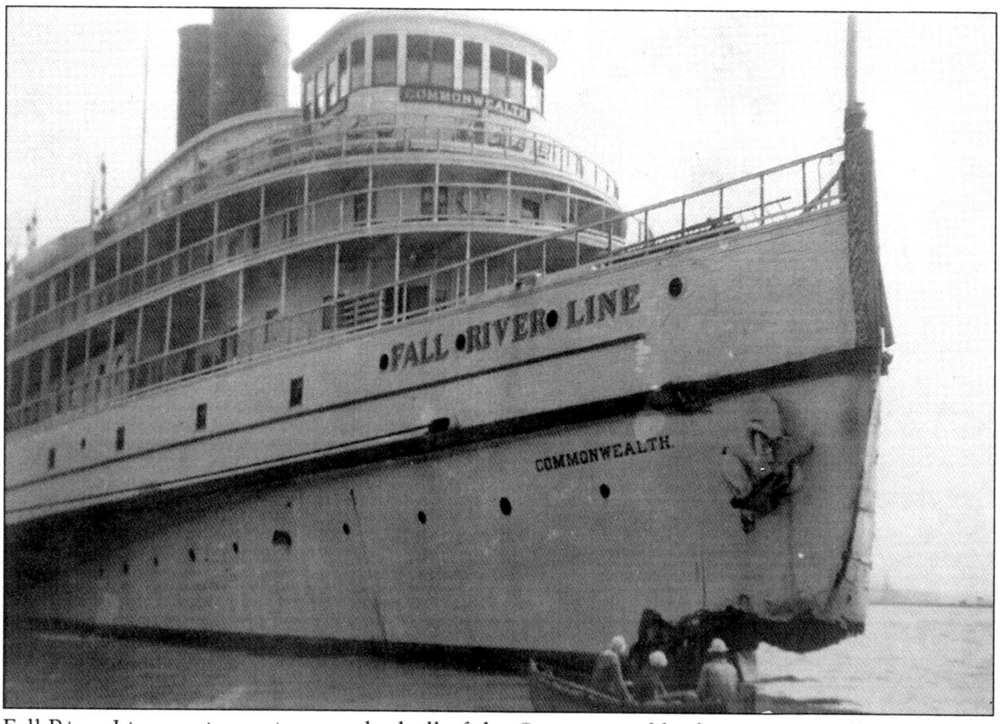

Fall River Line engineers inspect the hull of the *Commonwealth* after a minor collision.

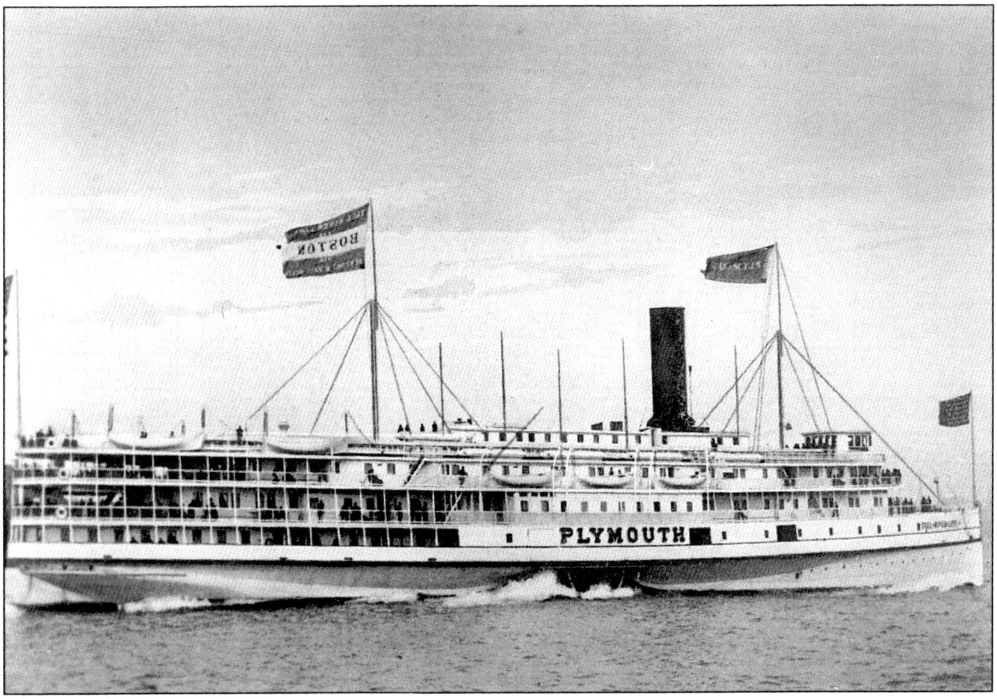

The *Plymouth* went into service in 1890 and plied the waters between Fall River and New York until 1937.

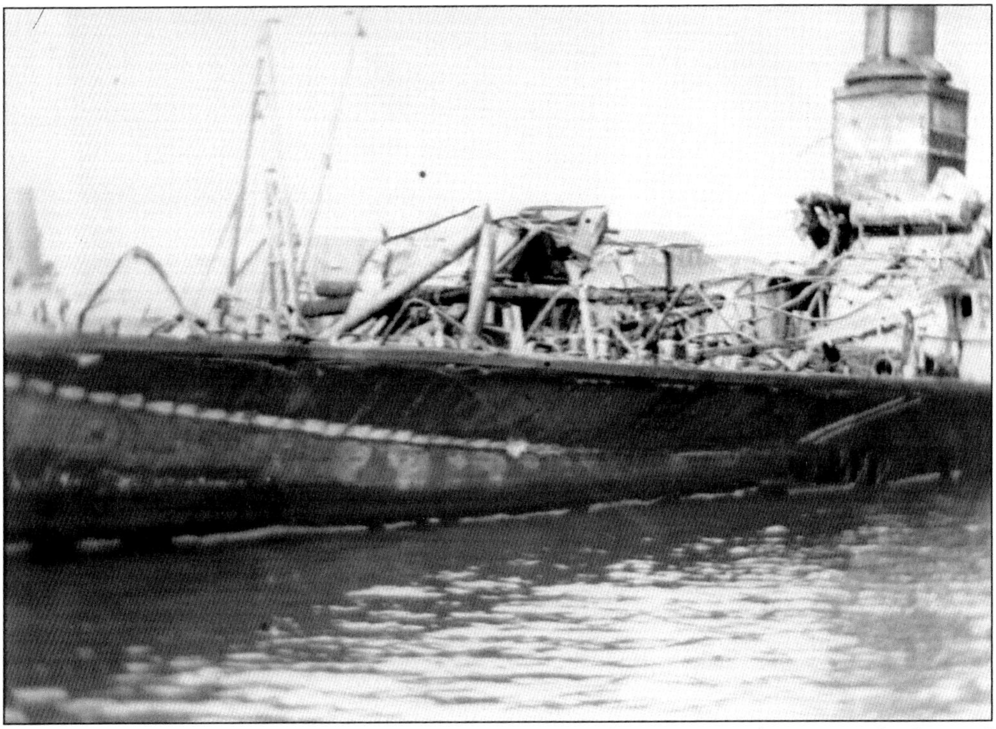

The *Plymouth* was docked in Newport the night of March 27, 1906, when it caught fire and burned to the waterline.

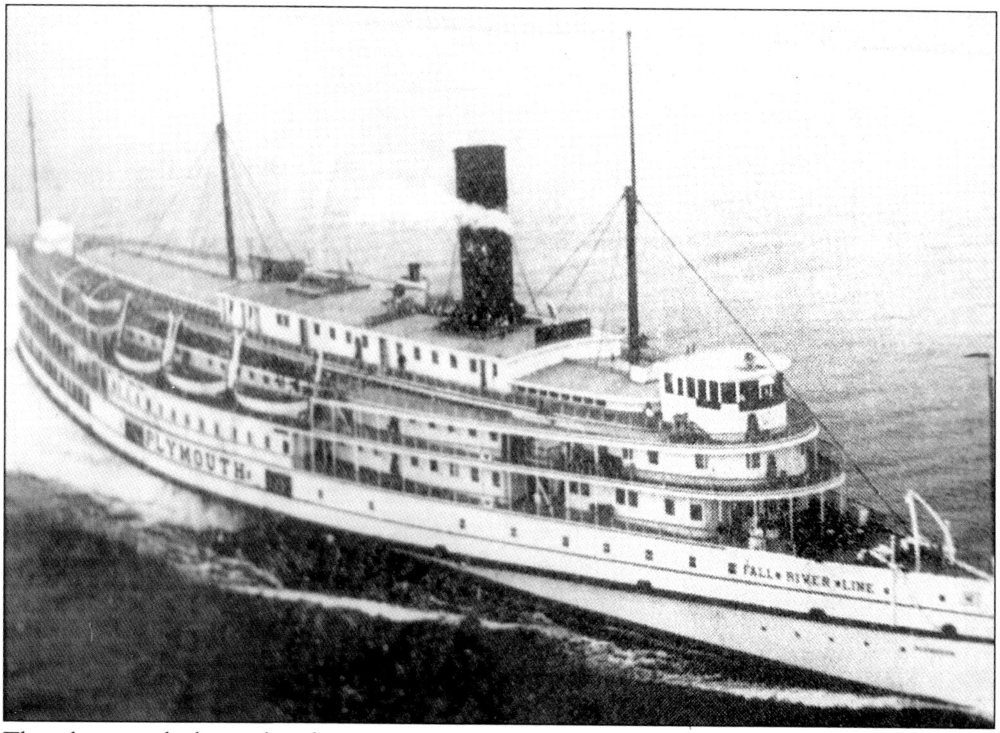

This photograph shows the *Plymouth* rebuilt after the 1906 fire.

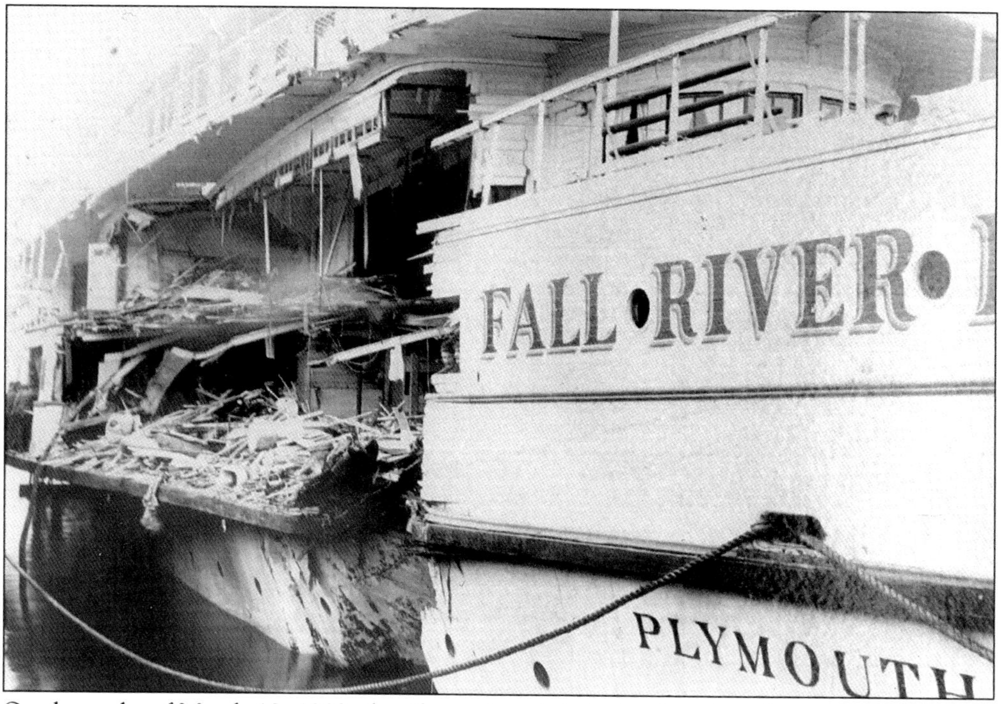

On the night of March 19, 1903, the *Plymouth* collided with the *City of Taunton* off the coast of Plum Island. During the mishap, a passenger and two crew members were killed and several others were seriously wounded.

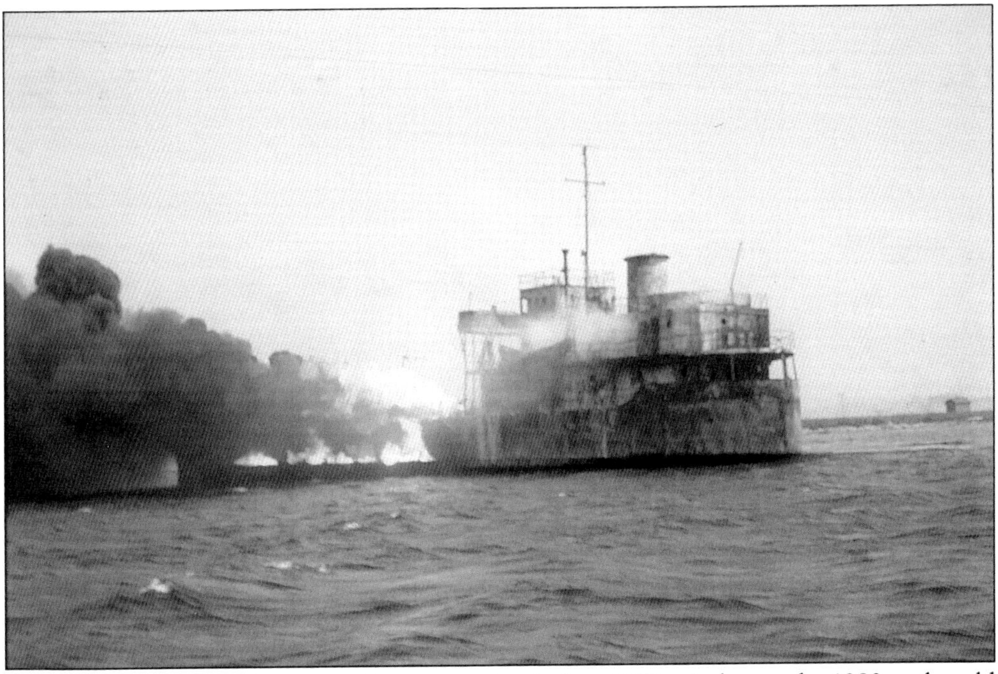

An oil tanker burns off the coast of Jamestown in the late 1950s. As late as the 1980s, oil could still be seen around the shore.

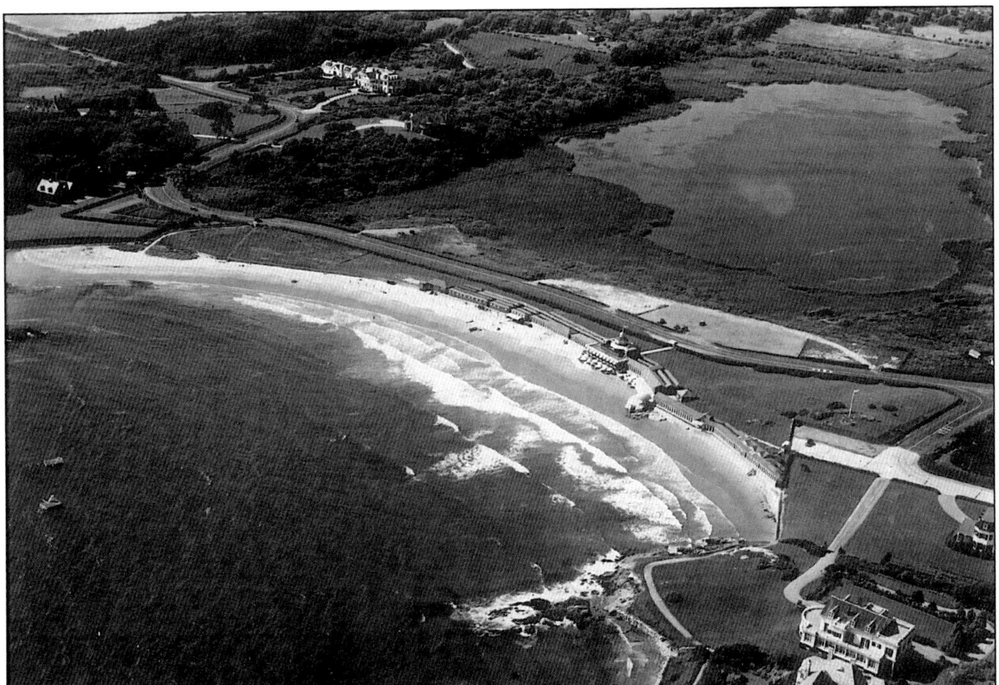

Bailey's Beach is shown in July 1938. A little over a month later, the beach would be destroyed by the Hurricane of 1938. (See page 92.) (Courtesy of the William Bachus collection.)

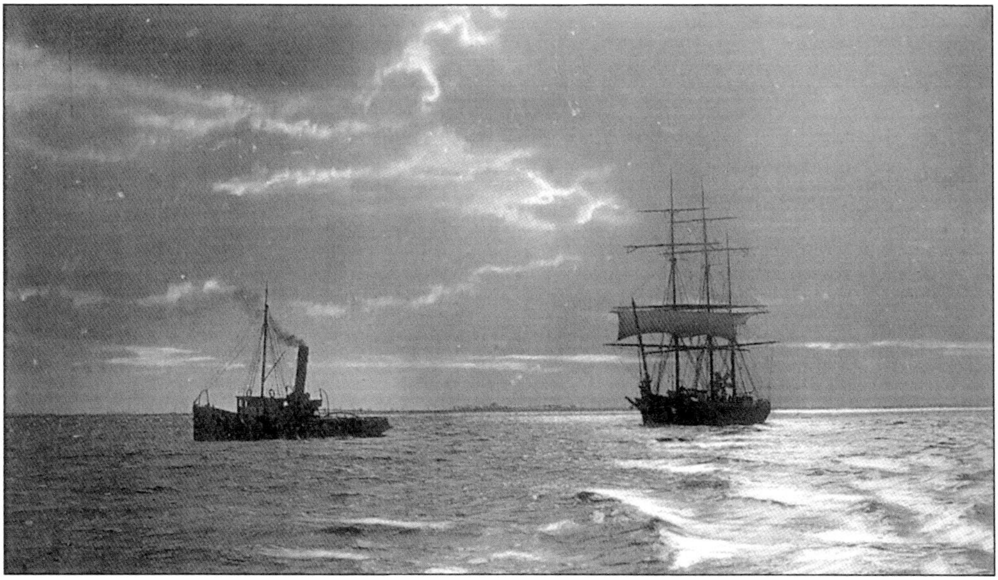

This 1905 postcard shows the outer harbor, near Brenton Point. From 1853 to 1962, a lightship was moored near this spot to provide a beacon for incoming vessels.

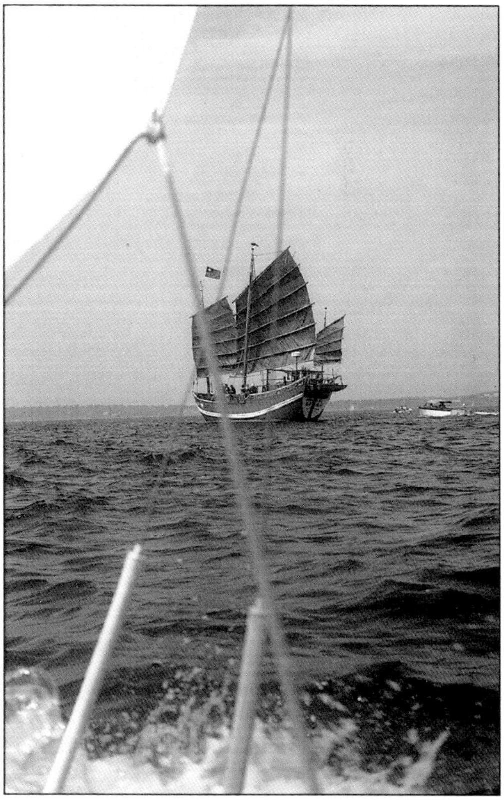

A junk sails around Newport Harbor during the 1976 Tall Ship Festival.

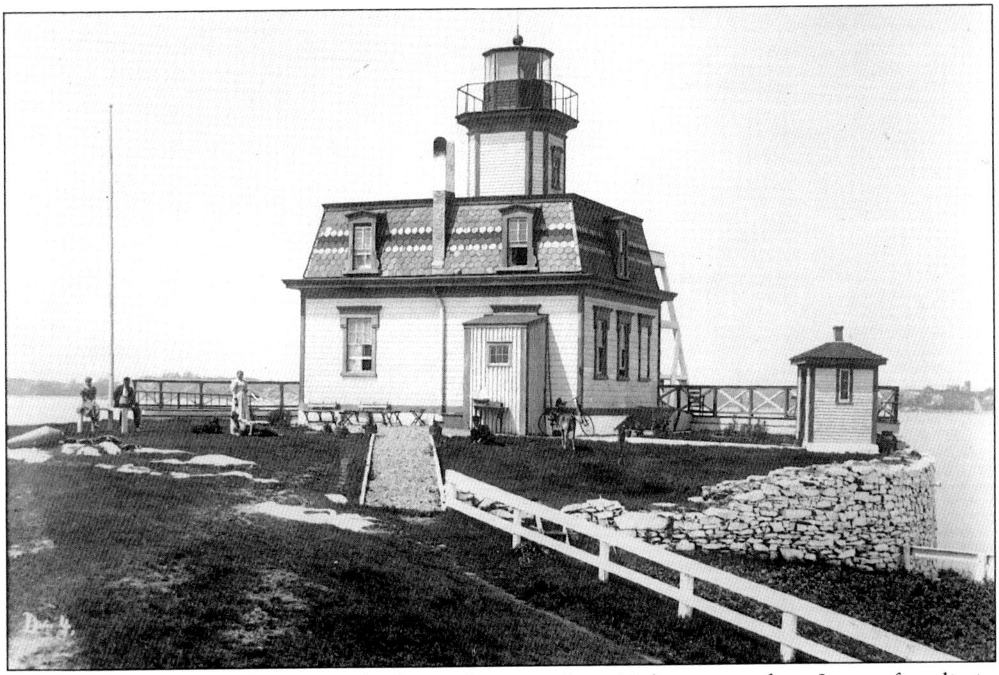

The Rose Island Lighthouse was built on the site of an 18th-century fort. It was first lit in 1870. The lighthouse stood abandoned for years until it was rescued by the Rose Island Lighthouse Foundation.

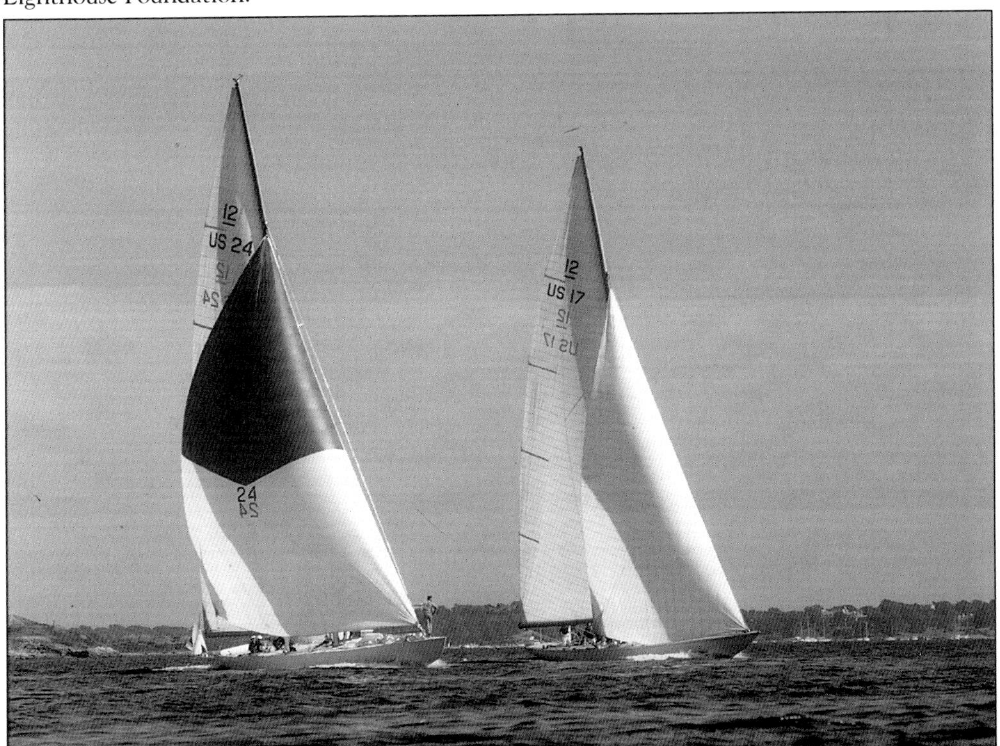

Twelve-meter ships sail in Newport Harbor in the early 1980s.

Five

Times to Remember

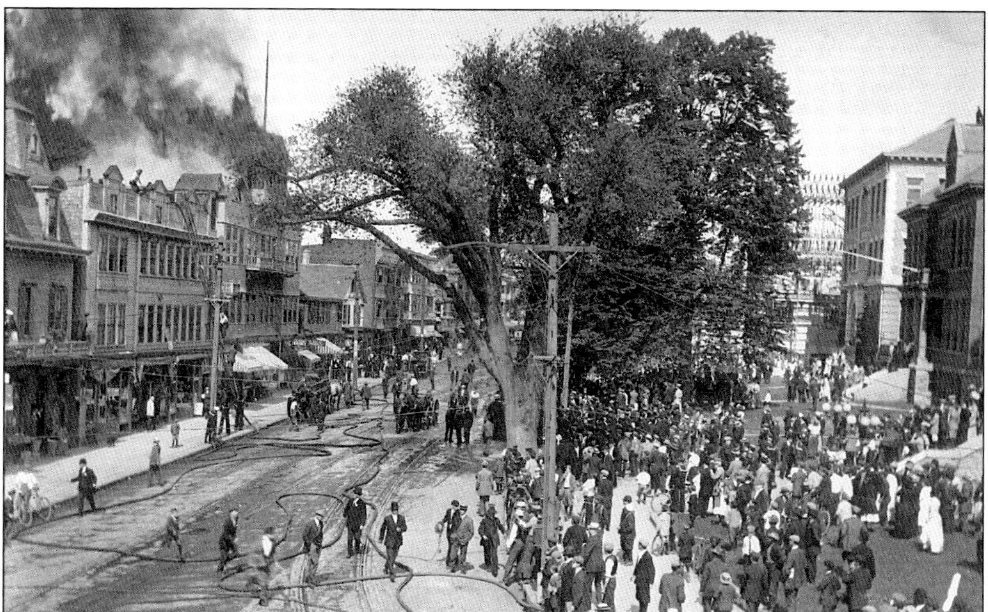

Smoke billows from the Consant J. Smith Block on Broadway. The Paramount Theater was built on the site not too long after this photograph was taken.

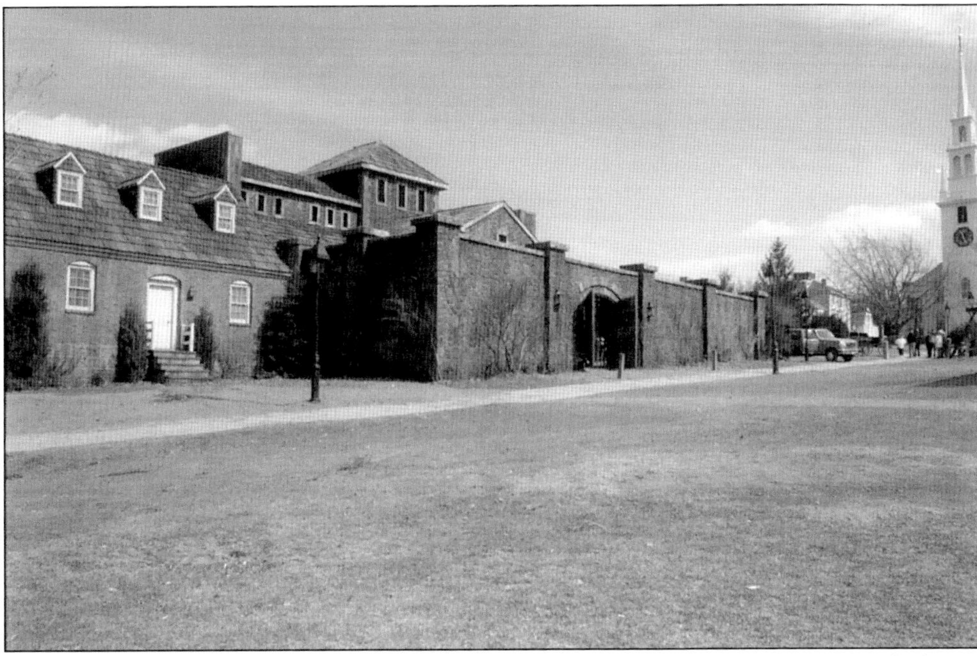

The jail set for the movie *Amistad* was built in Queen Anne Square at the corner of Thames and Church Streets. (Photograph by Dorothy Burnette.)

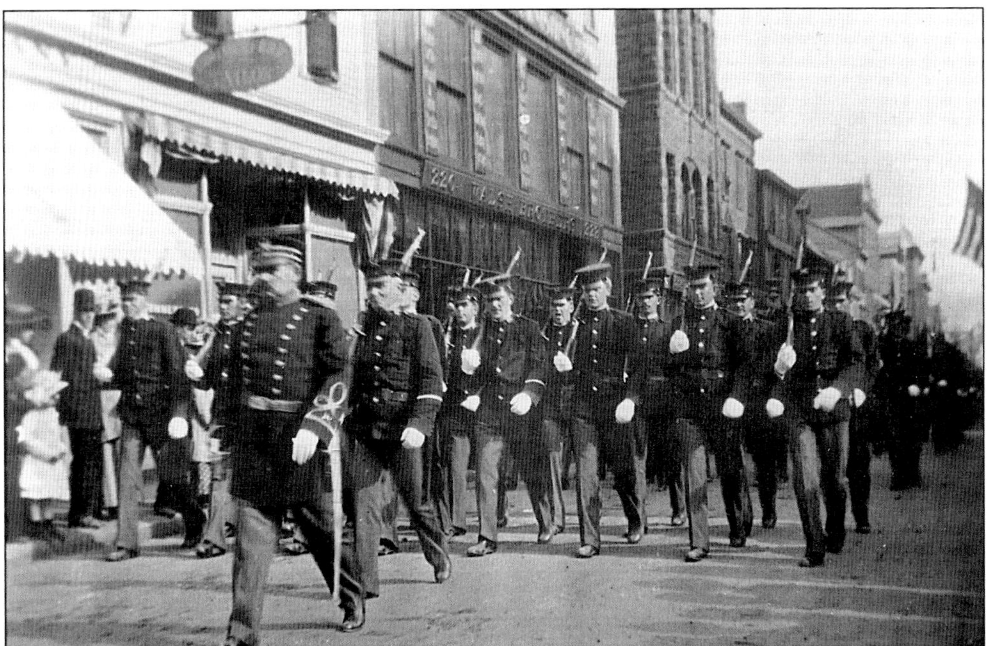

This parade was held on Thames Street in the 1920s. The Walsh Brothers store at 228 Thames Street can be seen in the center of the photograph.

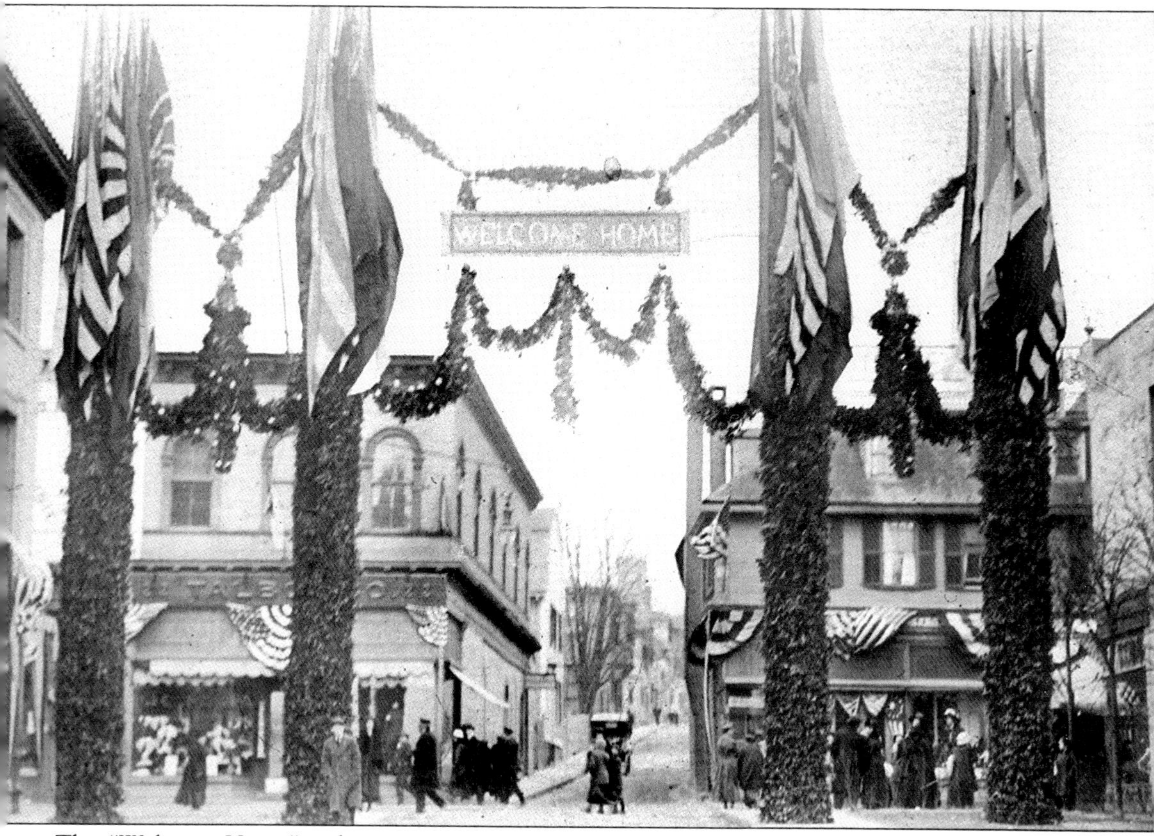

This "Welcome Home" arch was constructed at Government Landing at the corner of Thames and Church Streets. The triple arch was made of spun laurel and festooned with flowers. It was erected to honor Admiral Simms upon his return to Newport. The admiral took command of naval forces during World War I. He developed the convoy system in response to Germany's U-boats.

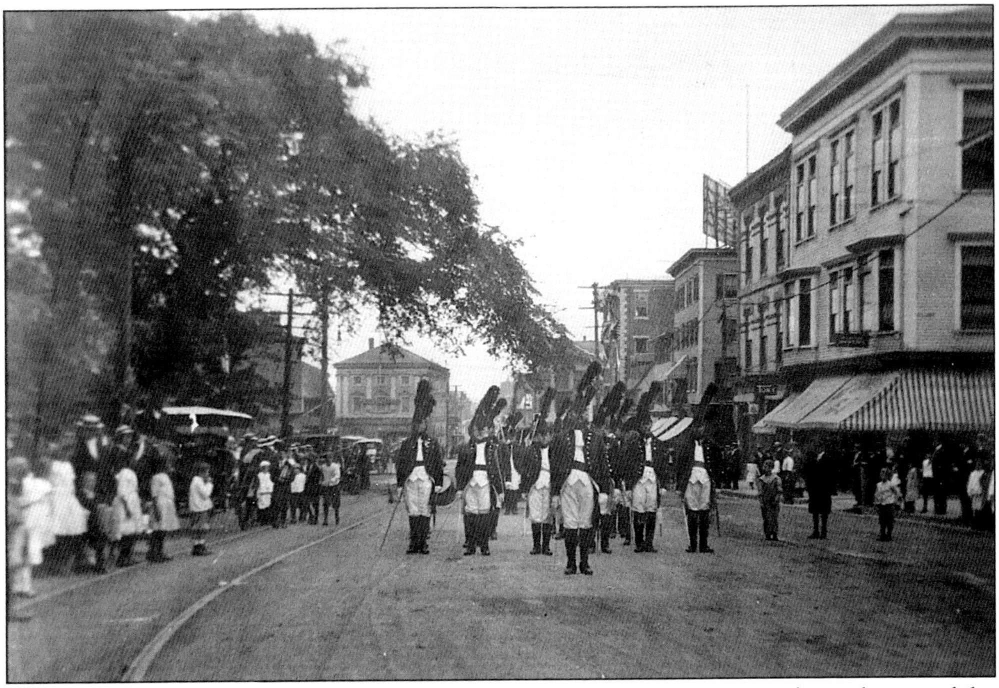

The Newport Artillery Company marches through Washington Square in the early part of the 20th century.

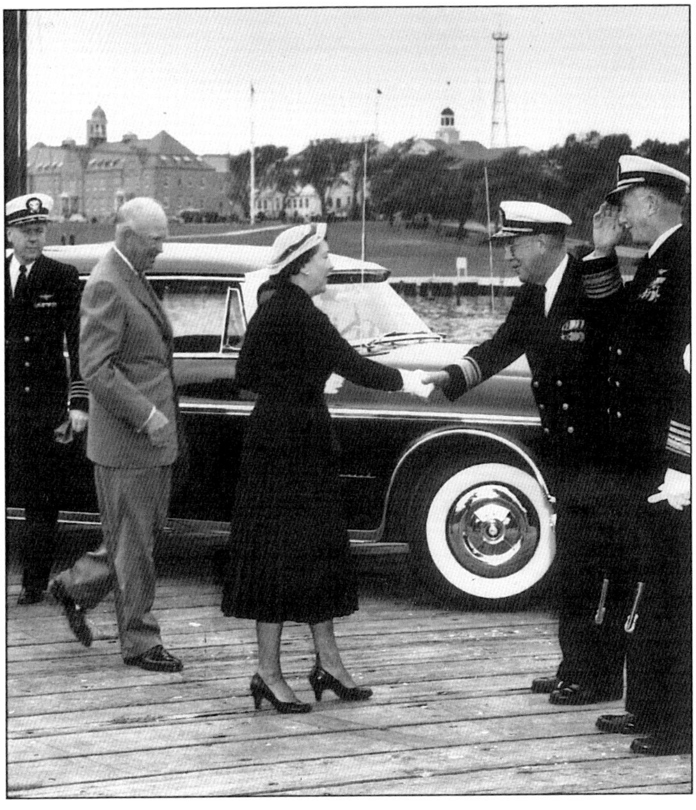

President and Mrs. Eisenhower are being greeted at the Naval War College in September 1957. The Eisenhowers were here to enjoy a three-week vacation.

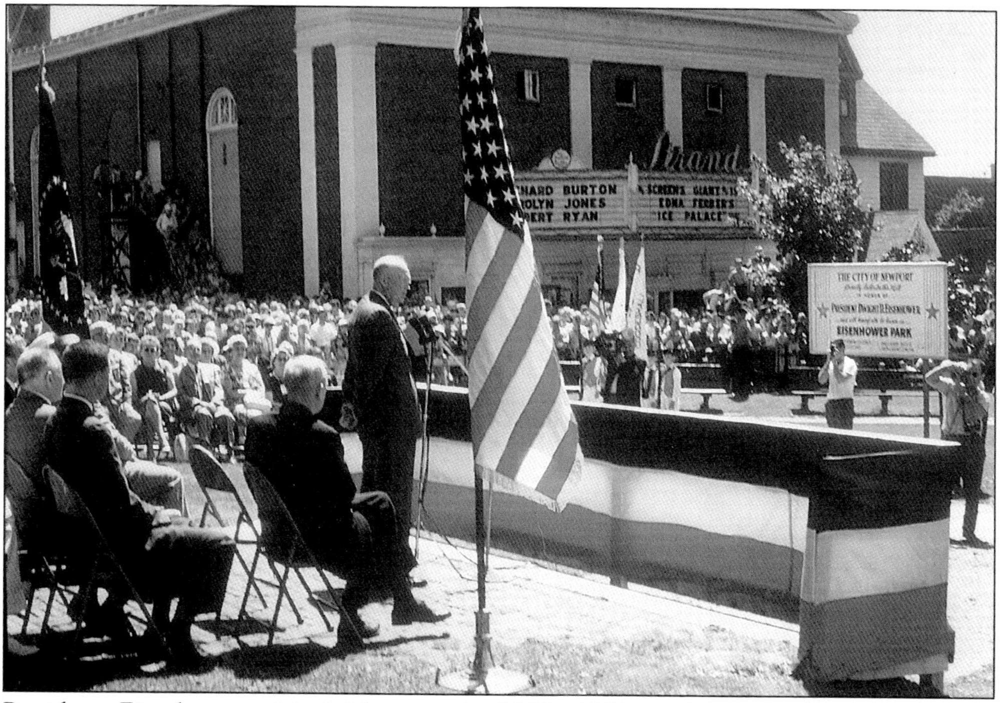

President Eisenhower visited Newport in 1957, 1958, and 1960. This visit was on September 26, 1960, for the dedication of a park named in his honor. The Strand Theater can be seen in the background.

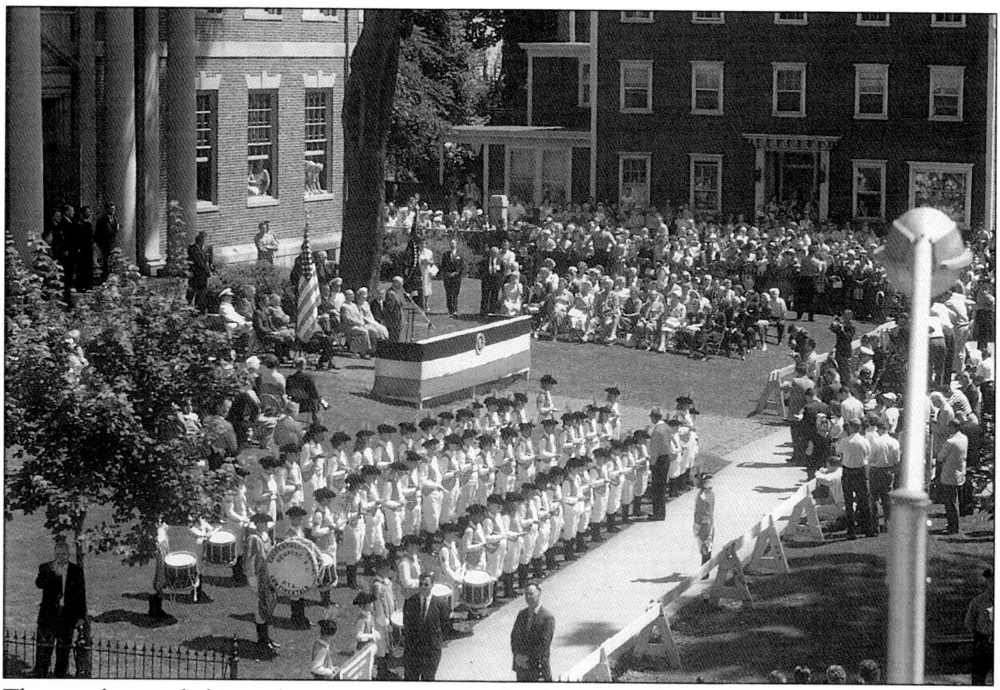

Thousands crowded into the square to witness the festivities.

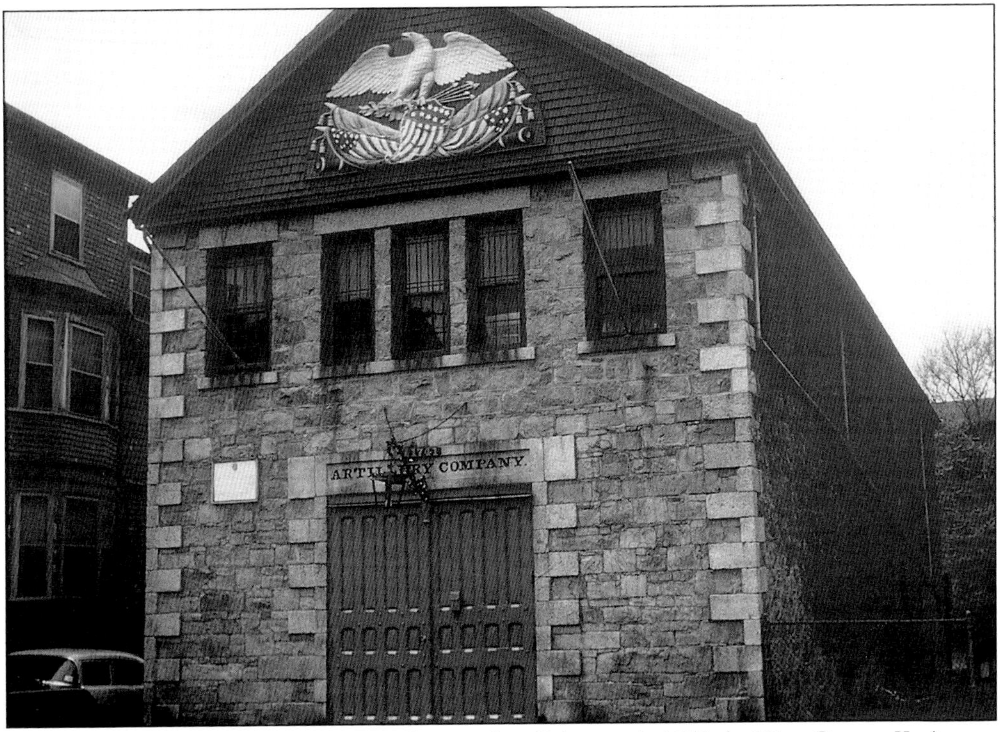

The Newport Artillery Company was chartered on February 1, 1741, by King George II. A one-story structure was built on Clarke Street in 1836. After a fire in 1907, the armory was rebuilt and a second floor was added.

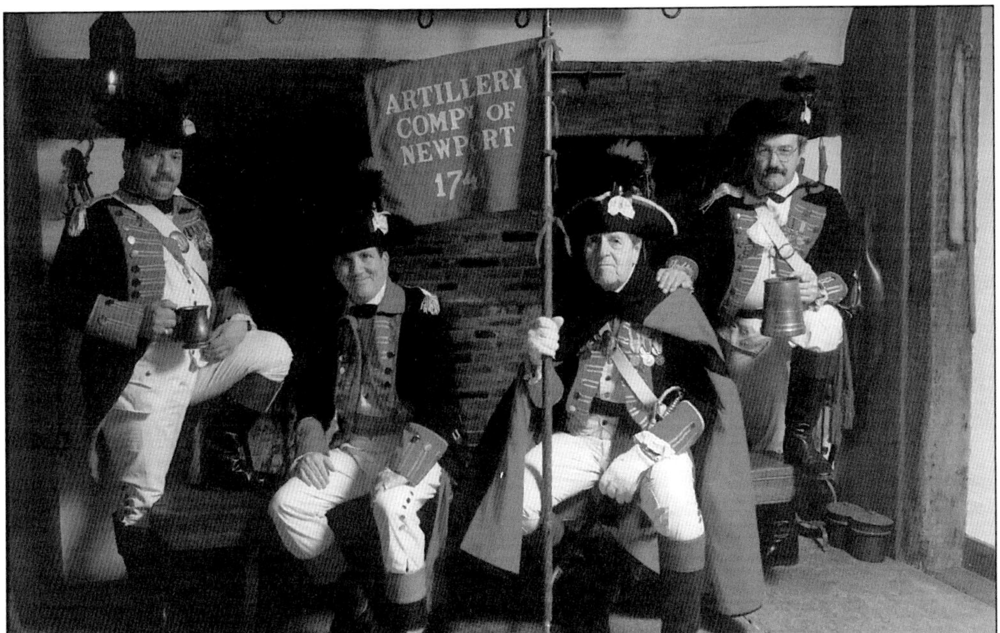

Members of the Newport Artillery Company pose in front of the hearth of the Rhodes-Peace-King House. (Photograph by Rob Lewis.)

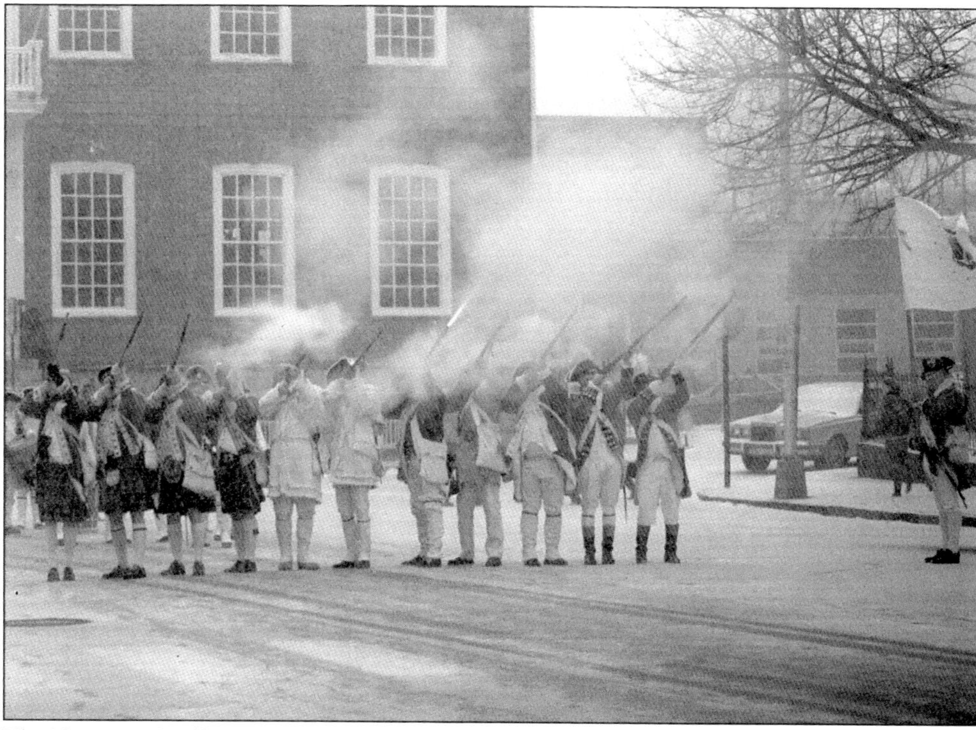

The Newport Artillery Company discharges its muskets in Washington Square during the 1993 St. Patrick's Day parade. A light dusting of snow during the parade added to the excitement of the day.

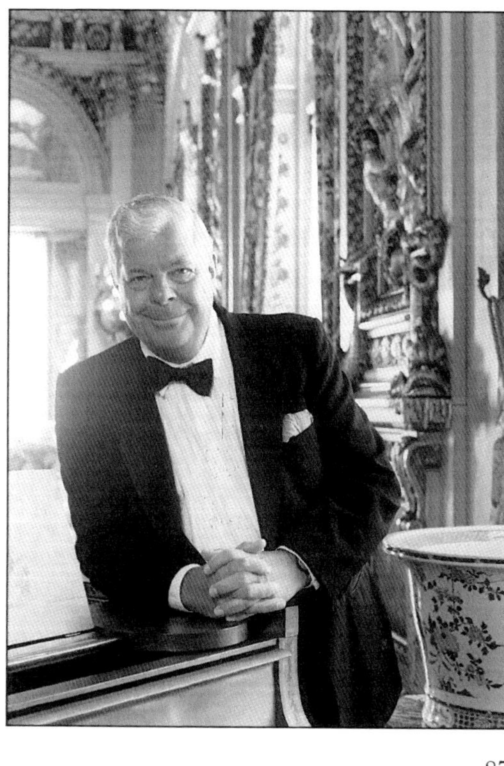

The Newport Music Festival was founded in 1969 to promote a summer venue for the Metropolitan Opera. Dr. Mark P. Malkovich III has been the driving force behind the festival for 27 years. (Photograph by Rob Lewis.)

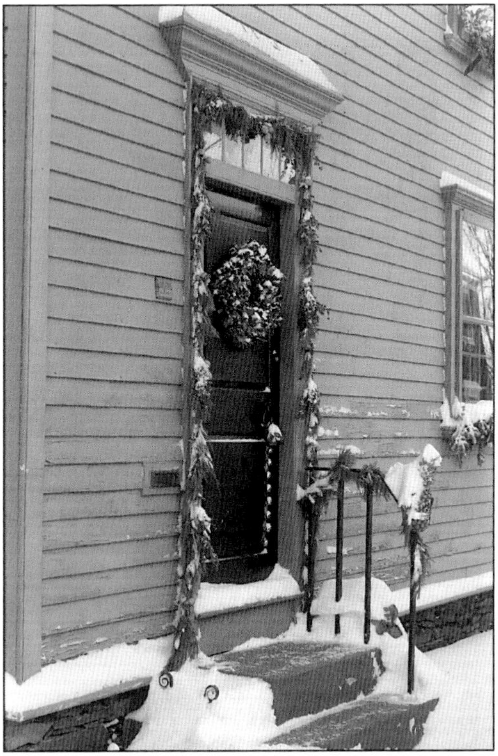

The Rhodes-Pease-King House (c. 1700) on Clarke Street is shown decorated for a Christmas-in-Newport event. (Photograph by Rob Lewis.)

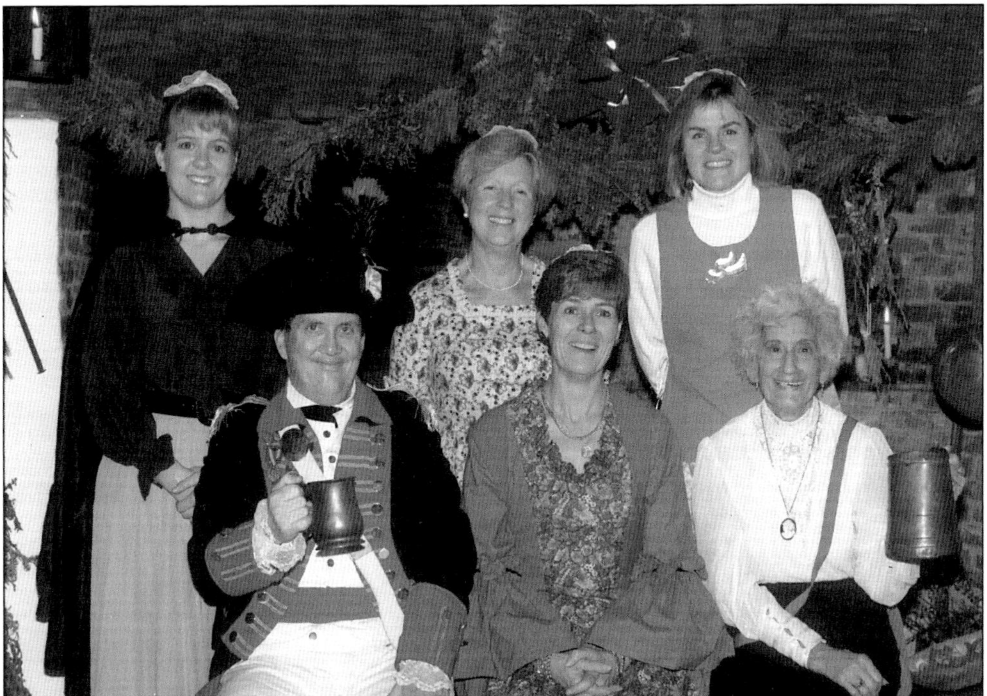

Matthew Dick and friends are dressed for the period as they serve as docents for a Christmas-in-Newport event.

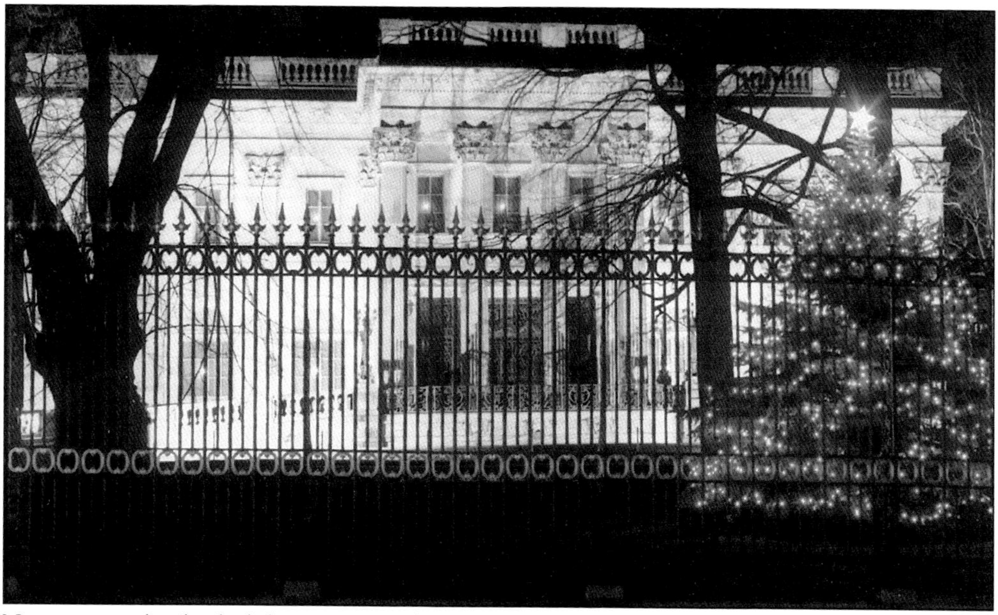

Newport marks the holiday season with a month-long celebration of Christmas in Newport. Here the Marble House is decked out for the holidays.

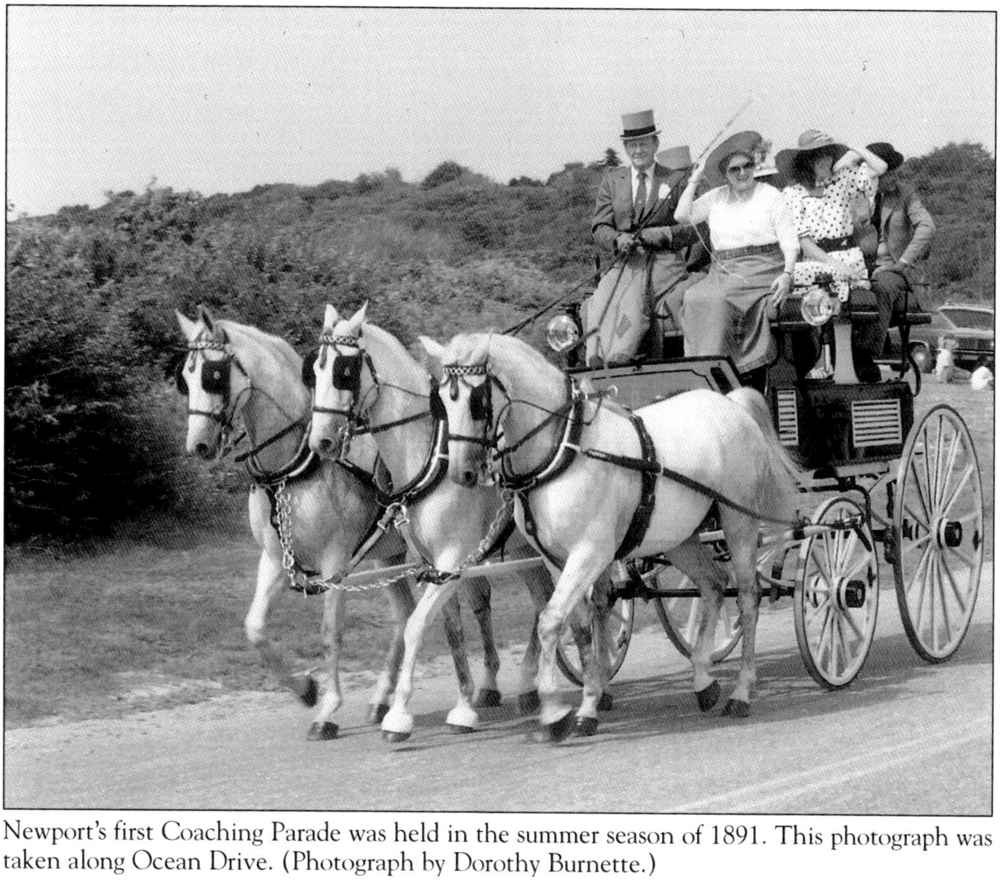

Newport's first Coaching Parade was held in the summer season of 1891. This photograph was taken along Ocean Drive. (Photograph by Dorothy Burnette.)

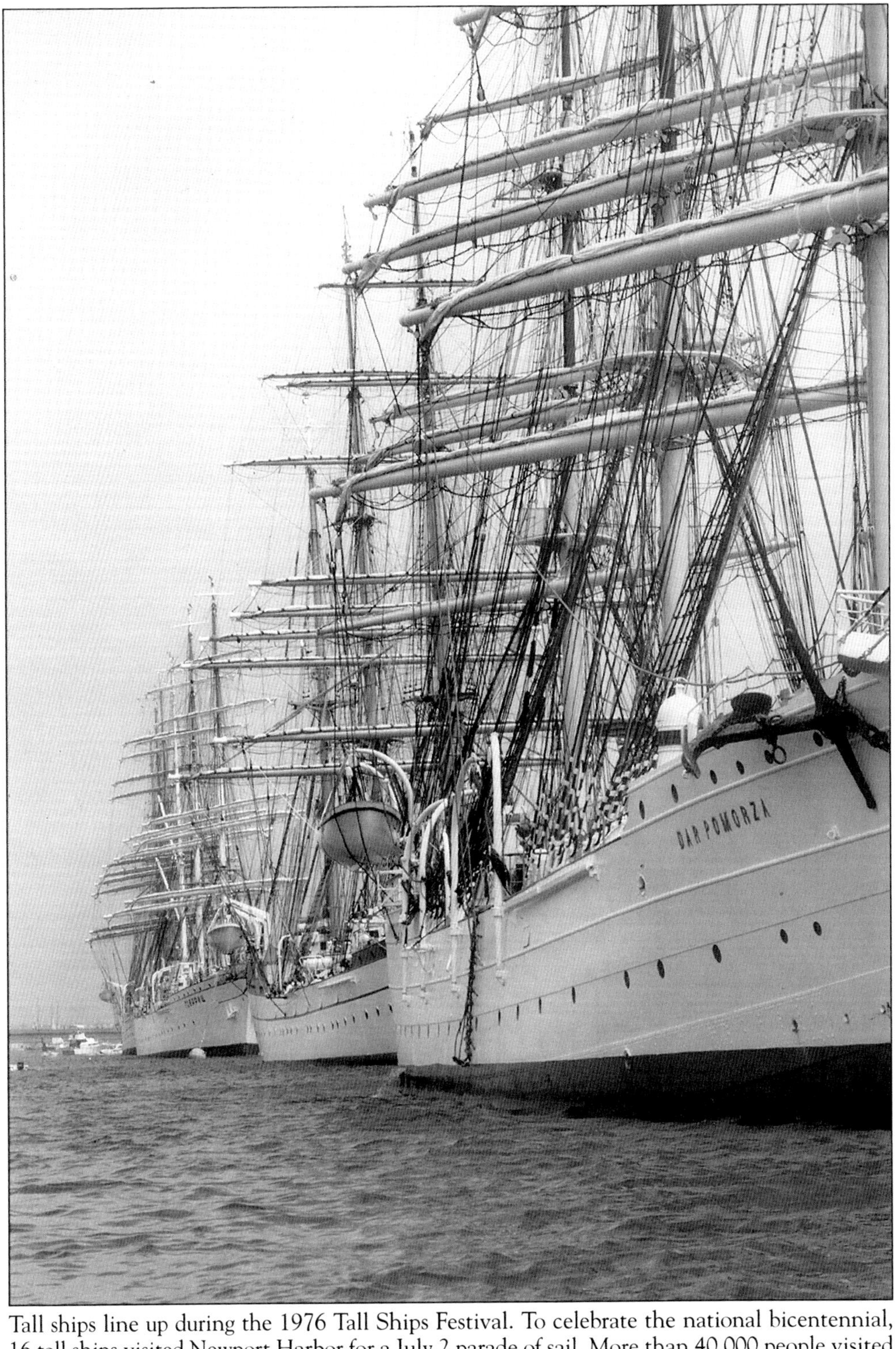

Tall ships line up during the 1976 Tall Ships Festival. To celebrate the national bicentennial, 16 tall ships visited Newport Harbor for a July 2 parade of sail. More than 40,000 people visited Newport during the four days that the ships were here.

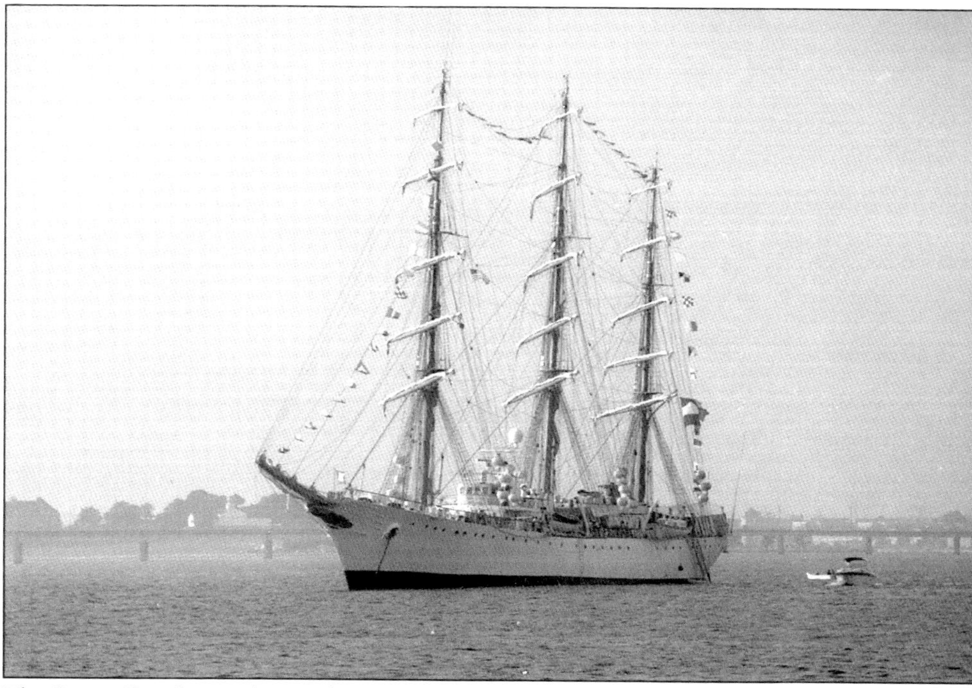

The *Sagres II* is shown during the 1983 visit of the tall ships. The vessel was built in 1937 and is 293 feet long. Its home port is Lisbon, Portugal.

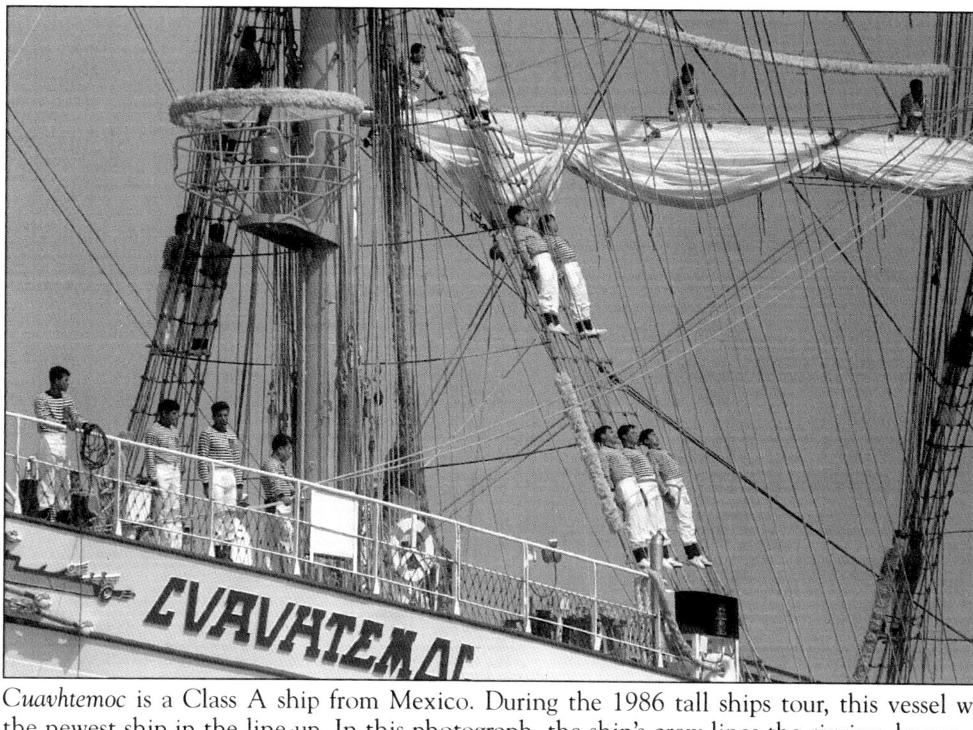

Cuavhtemoc is a Class A ship from Mexico. During the 1986 tall ships tour, this vessel was the newest ship in the line-up. In this photograph, the ship's crew lines the rigging, known as "dressing the ship."

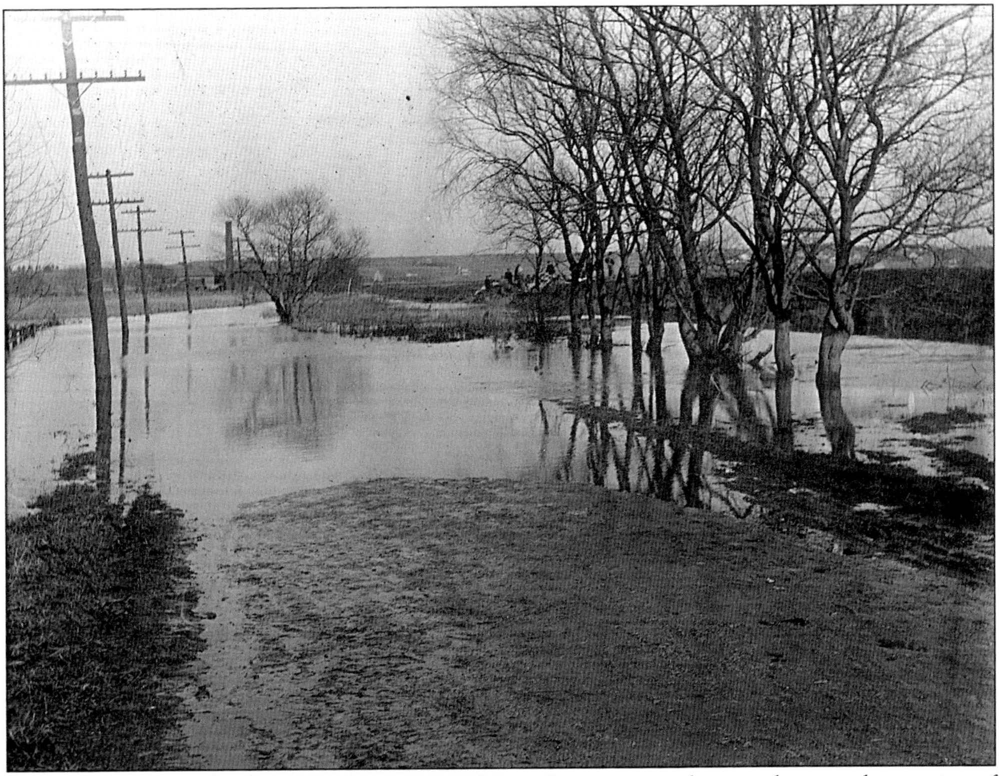

An 1873 storm floods the area surrounding the waterworks at the northern tip of Easton's Pond.

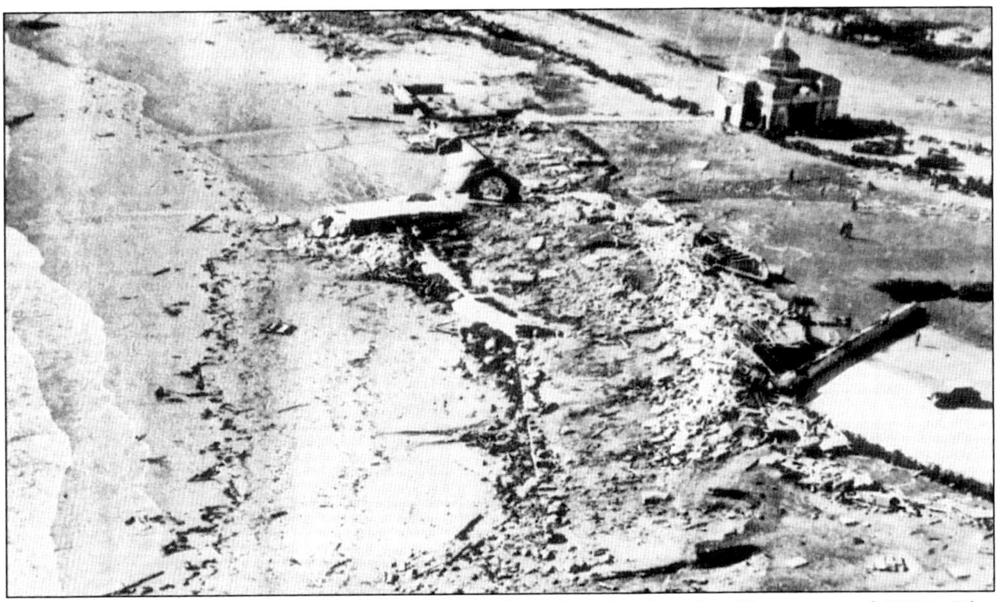

This aerial view shows the devastation at Bailey's Beach after the Hurricane of 1938. The beach's rotunda was lifted from its foundations by the tidal surge and was amazingly set down on Brenton Drive in one piece.

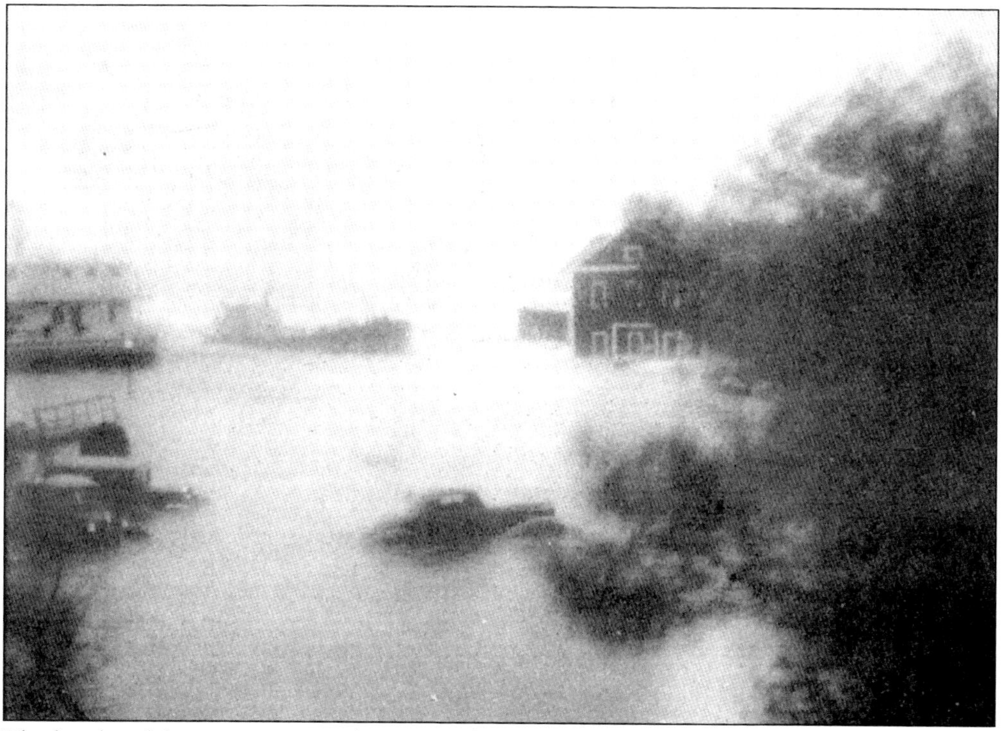

The height of the storm surge is documented in this U.S. Navy photograph in 1938.

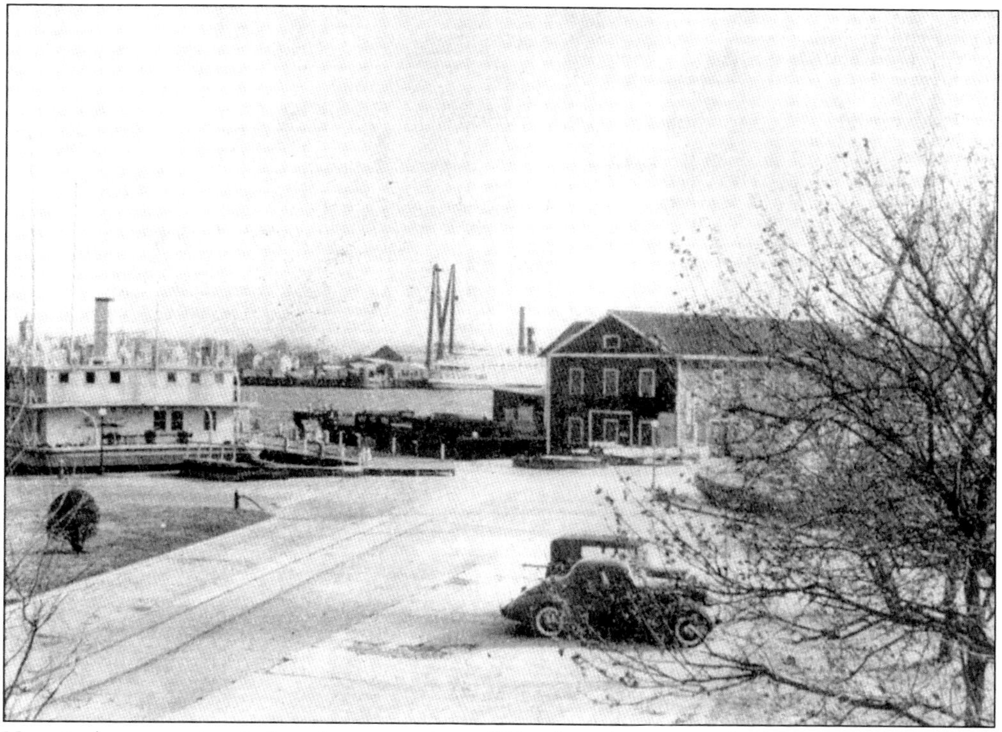

Here is the same view before the storm. Long Wharf can be seen in the distance.

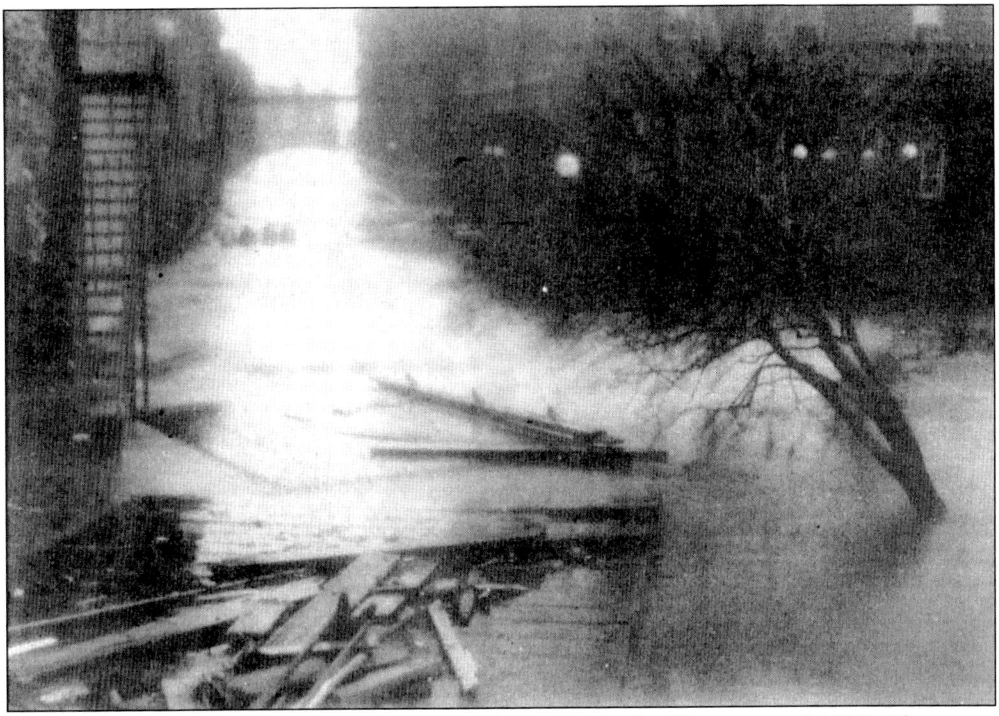

This is another photograph taken on Goat Island during the Hurricane of 1938. The storm struck in the late afternoon on the high tide, bringing a huge wall of water up the bay.

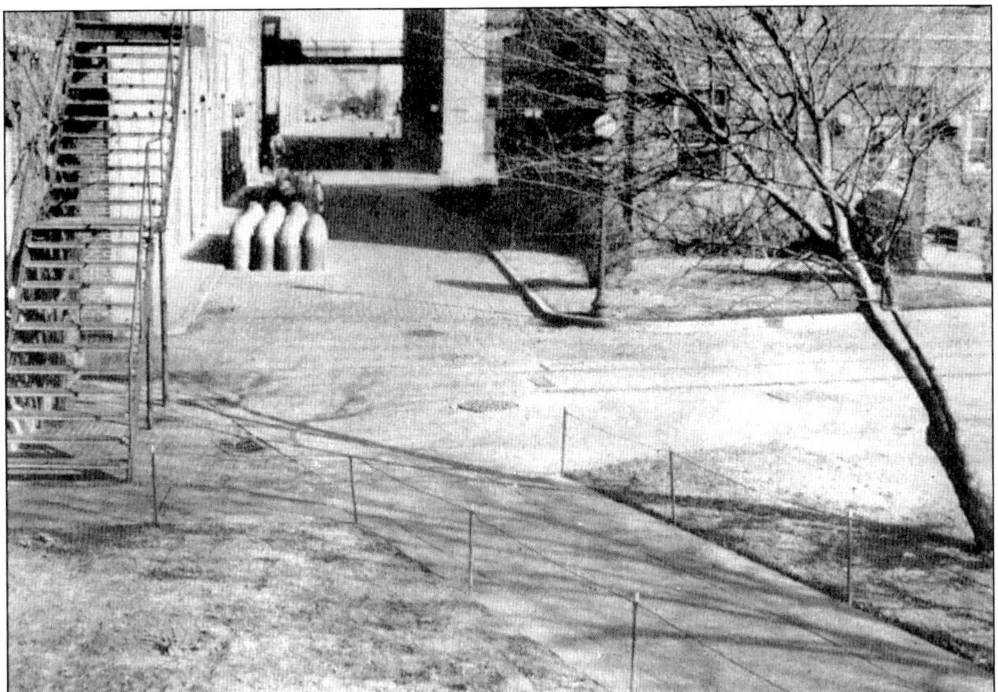

The same area is shown before the storm. In 1966, demolition of the torpedo station was begun. Debris from the buildings was used to build a breakwater at the north end of Goat Island.

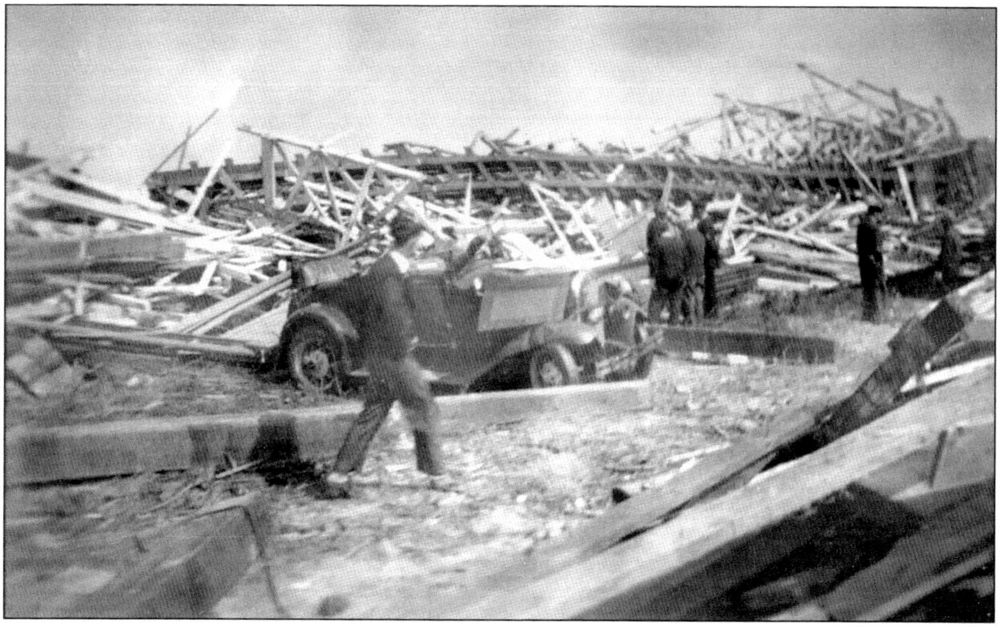

The roller coaster on Easton's Beach was reduced to kindling in the Hurricane of 1938. (Courtesy of John Caruthers.)

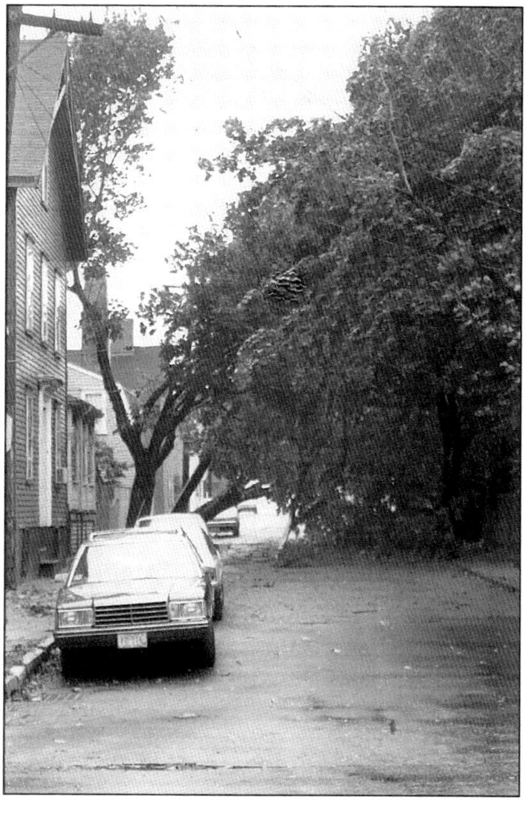

Hundreds of trees were downed or severely damaged throughout the city. It took days for some streets to be made passable, and thousands of electric customers were without power for extended periods. (Photograph by Rob Lewis.)

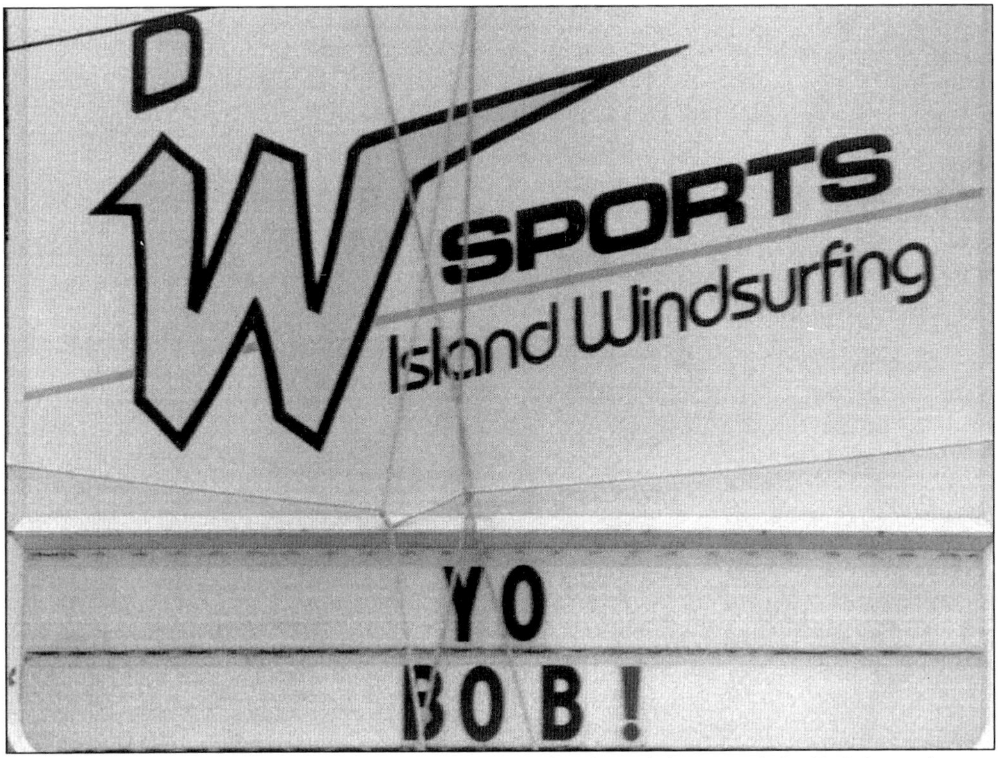

Hurricane Bob is taunted by the staff at Island Windsurfing. (Photograph by Rob Lewis.)

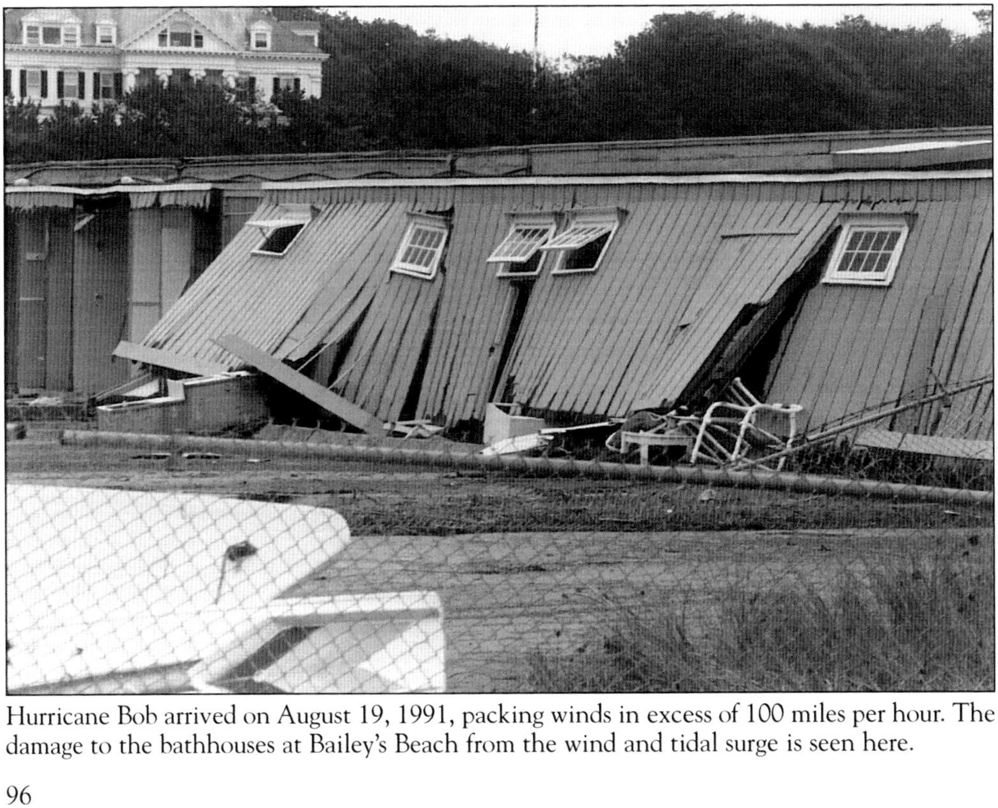
Hurricane Bob arrived on August 19, 1991, packing winds in excess of 100 miles per hour. The damage to the bathhouses at Bailey's Beach from the wind and tidal surge is seen here.

Six

CASTLES BY THE SEA

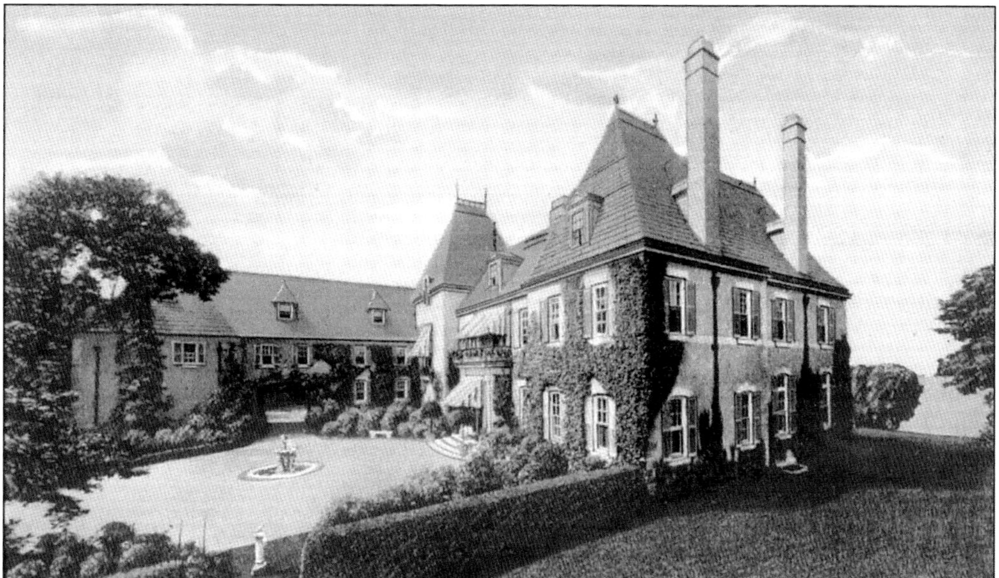

Harbour Court was designed by Cram, Ferguson, and Goodhue and erected in 1904–1906. After building the magnificent house, John Nicholas Brown had the landscaping done by the Olmsteds.

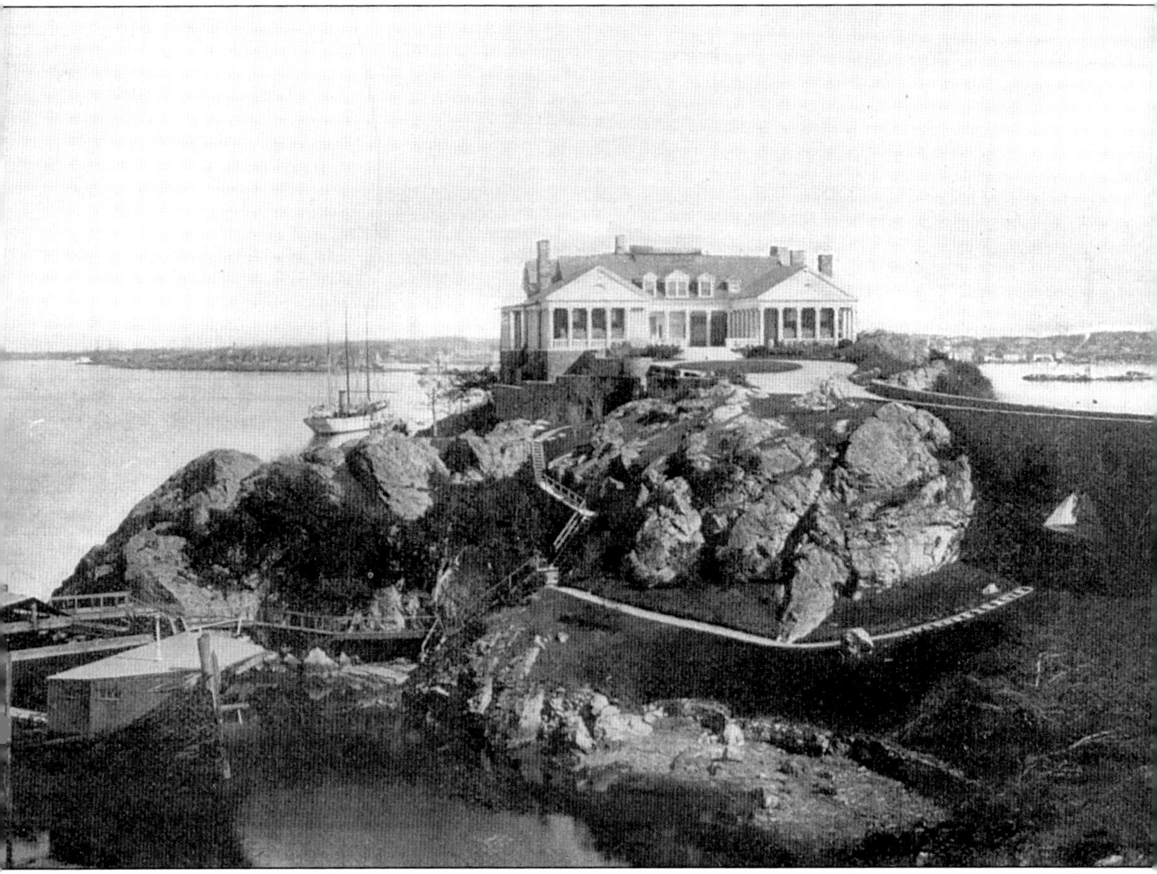

Beacon Rock was designed by McKim, Mead, and White and was built in 1890–1891 for Edwin D. Morgan.

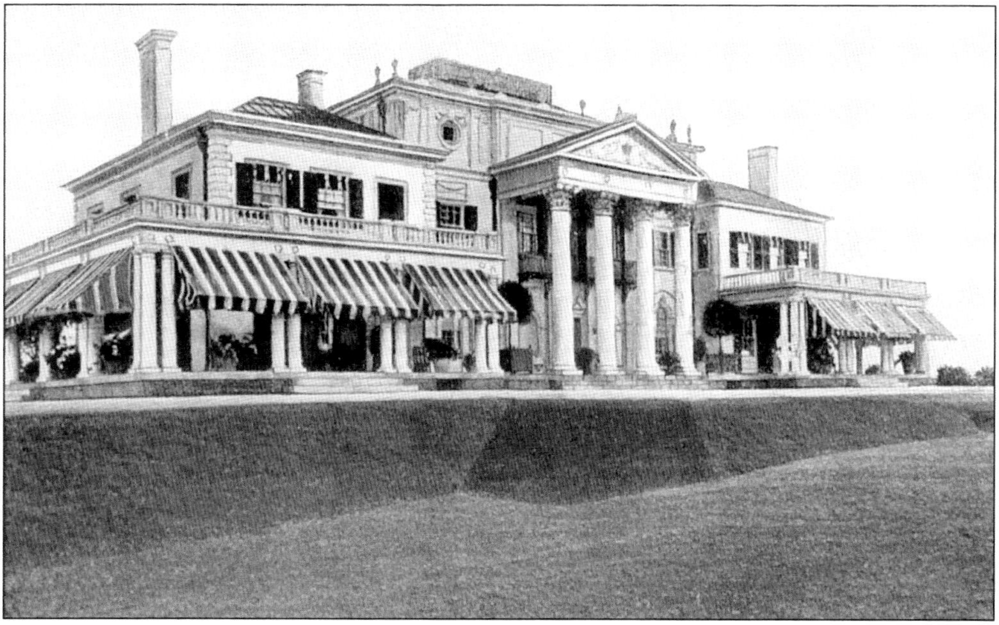

Armsea Hall was built on Ridge Road near Harrison Avenue. It was the home of Charles F. Hoffman.

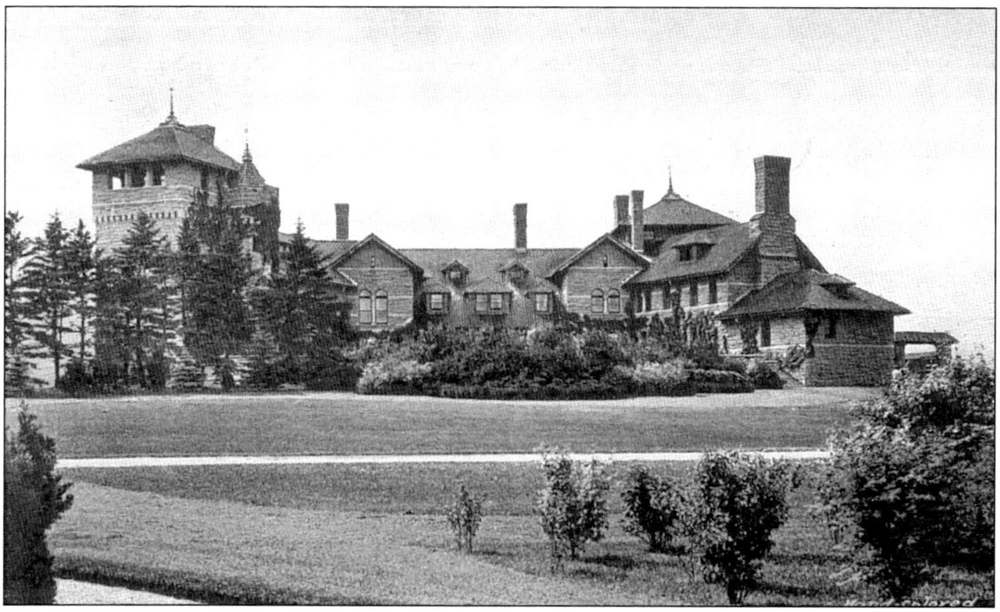

Shamrock Cliff was built in 1894–1896 by the Boston firm of Peabody and Stearns. The mansion sits on the cliffs off Ridge Road and was originally built for G.M. Hutton.

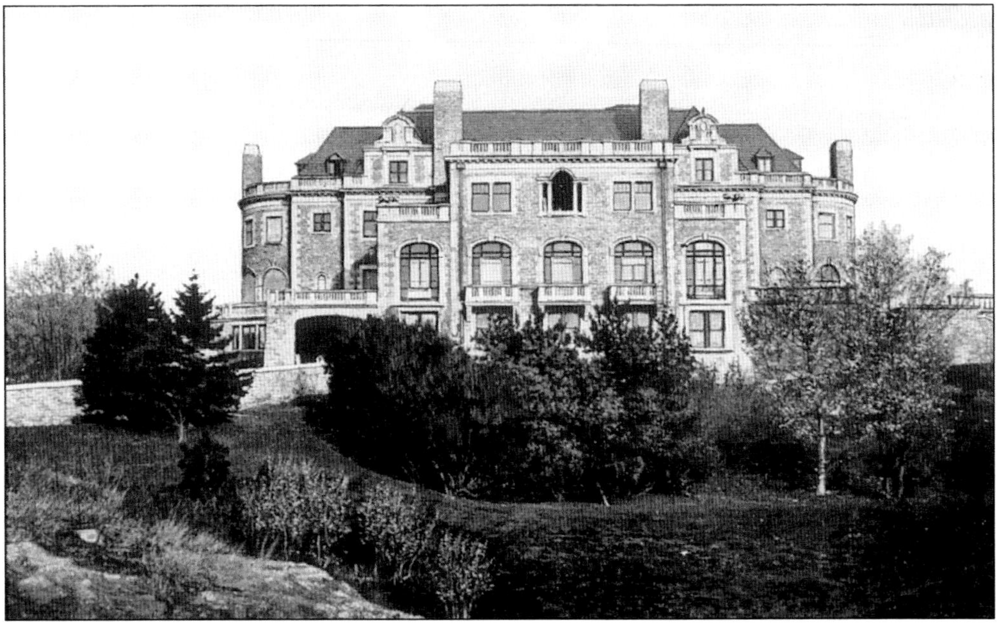

Beacon Hill House was built in 1910 by Arthur Curtis James. The house was surrounded by formal sunken gardens. The gardens were planted in sunken beds to protect them from the sea breezes.

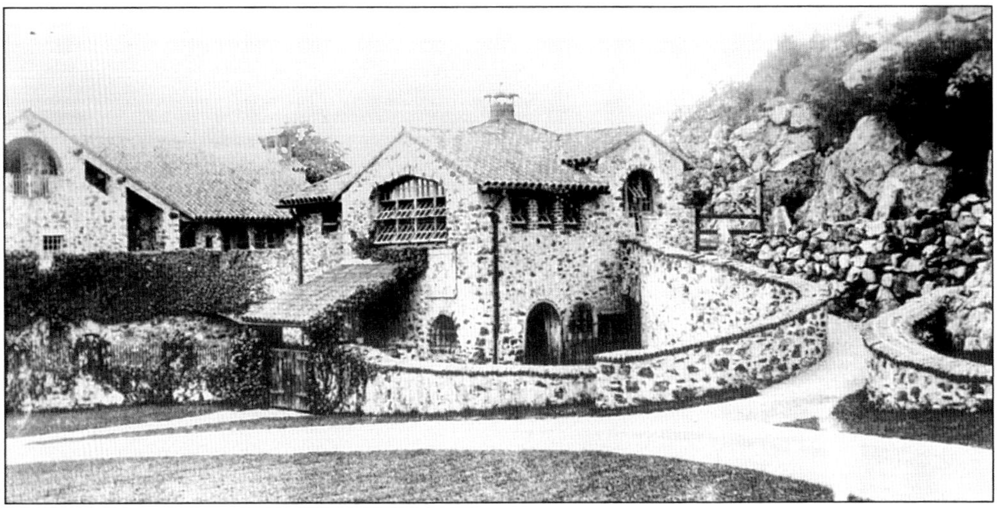

The Swiss Farm was part of the James residence. This photograph is from the early 1930s.

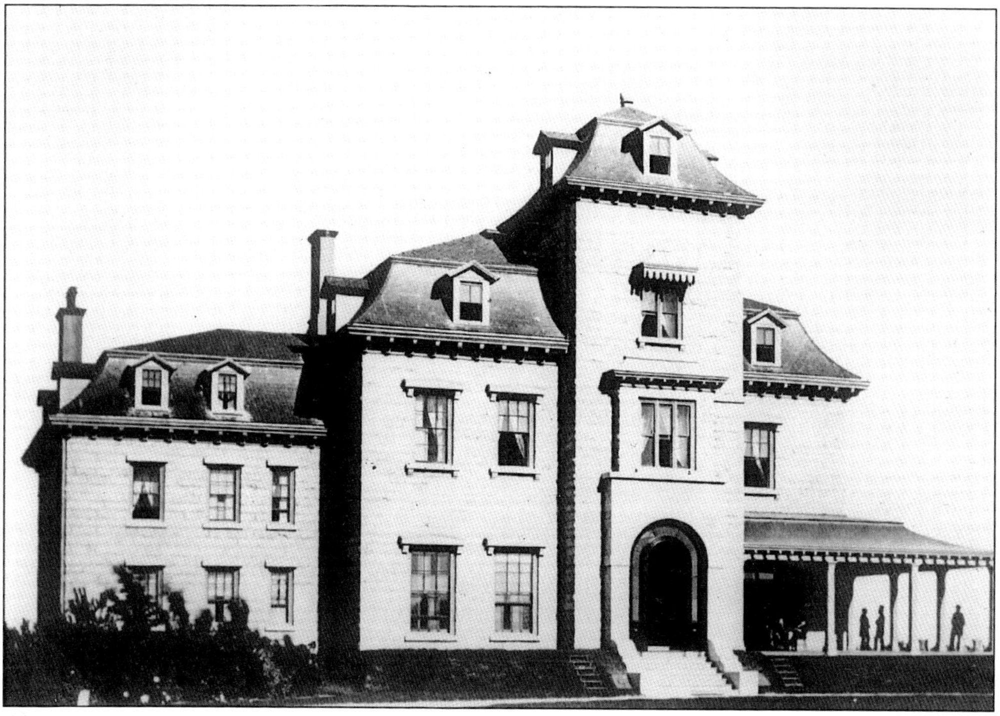

Chateau Sur Mer was built on Bellevue Avenue for William Wetmore in 1851. In 1872, Richard Morris Hunt was commissioned to enlarge the mansion.

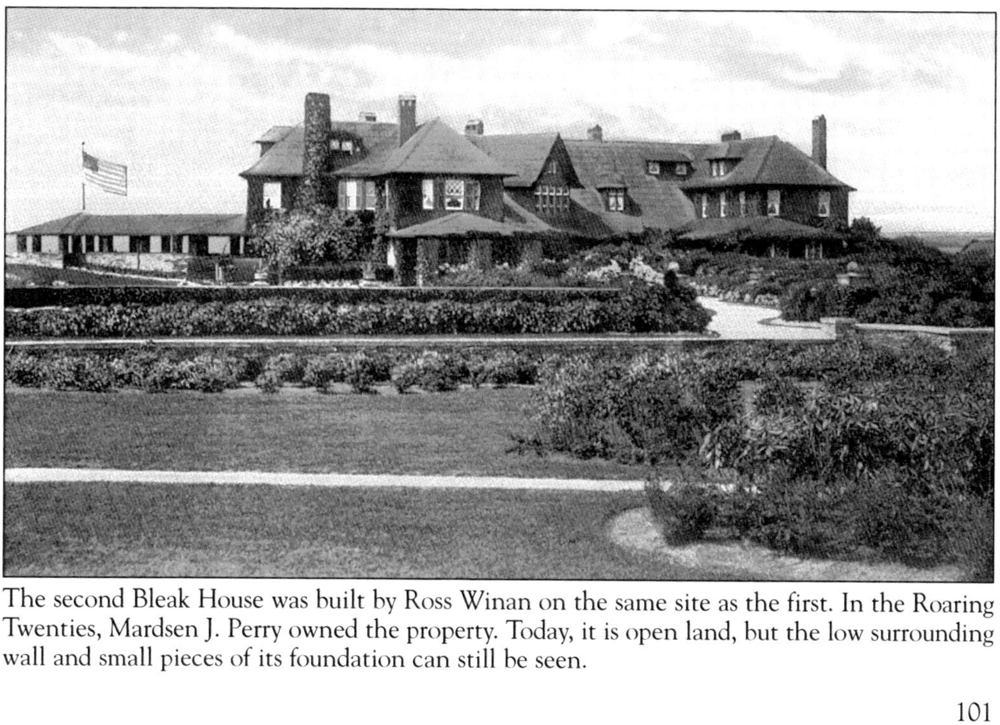

The second Bleak House was built by Ross Winan on the same site as the first. In the Roaring Twenties, Mardsen J. Perry owned the property. Today, it is open land, but the low surrounding wall and small pieces of its foundation can still be seen.

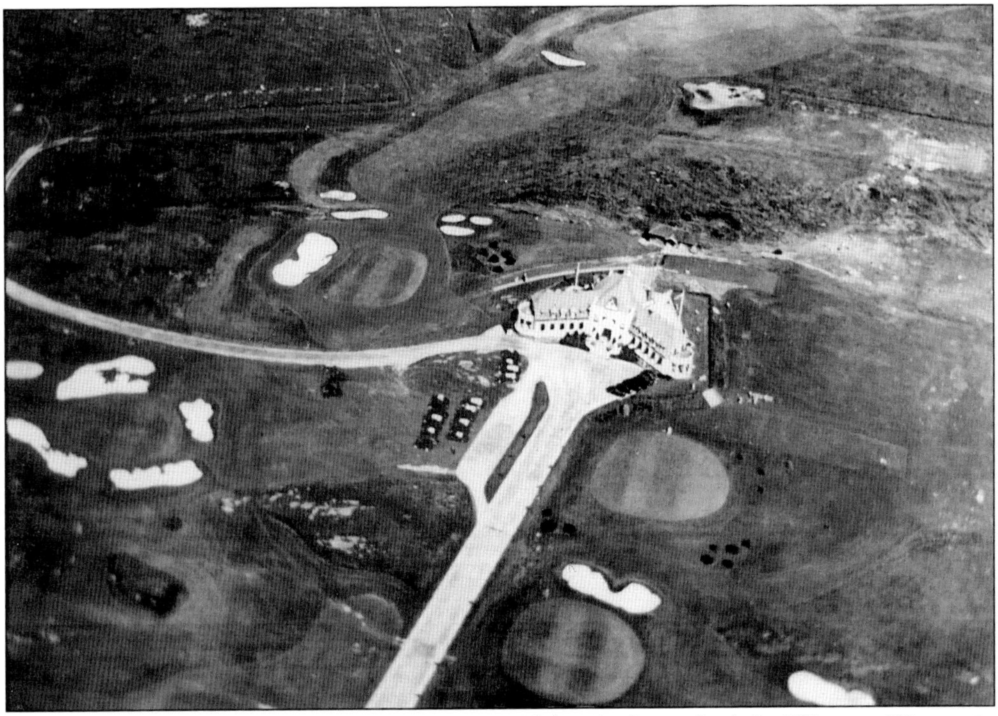

This aerial photograph of the Newport Country Club, which was built by Whitney Warren in 1894, was taken in July 1938 by H.H. Harris. As he was photographing the area, he was also flying the plane.

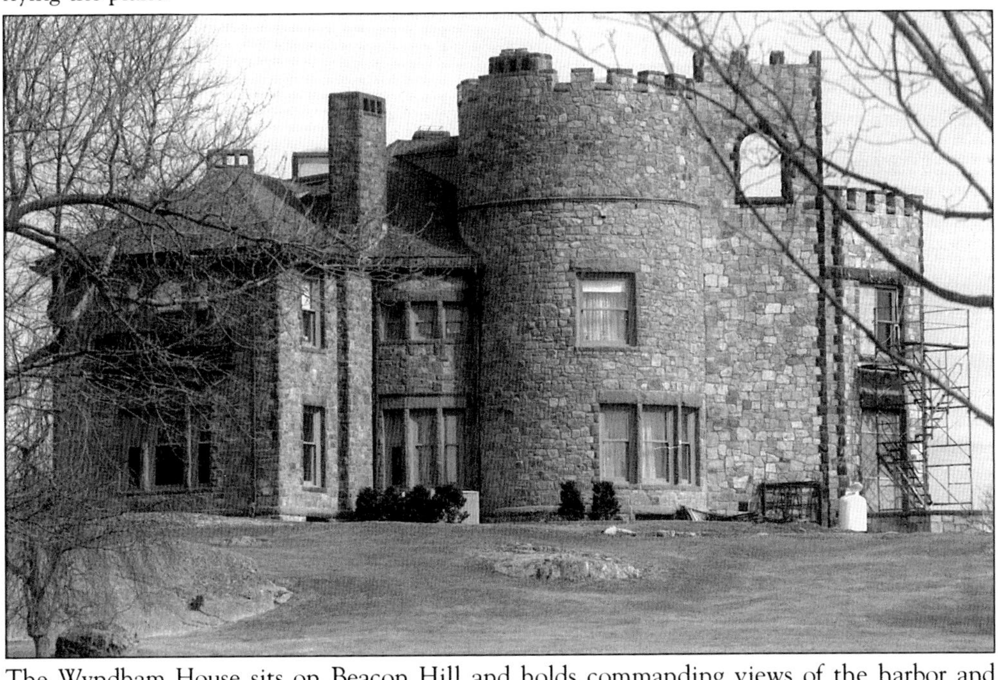

The Wyndham House sits on Beacon Hill and holds commanding views of the harbor and Ocean Drive. It dates to the beginning of the 1900s. Beacon Hill got its name from the beacon that was lit during Revolutionary times.

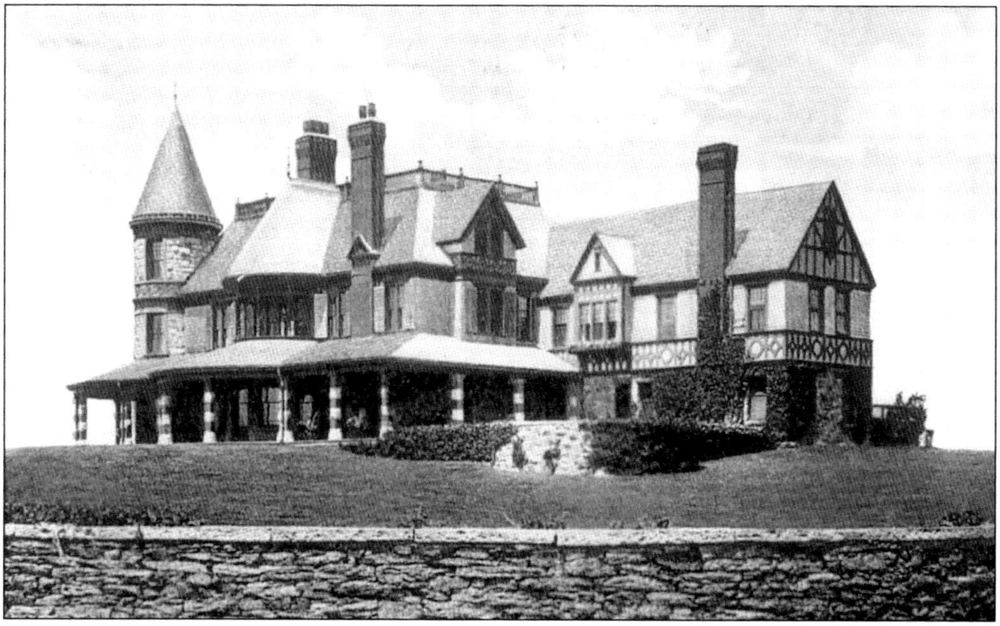

The Reef was built for Theodore M. Davis in 1882 on Brenton Point. The house was later owned by Milton Budlong and his family until it was deserted in the early 1940s. It fell into disrepair for over a decade until it was ravaged by a fire in the late 1950s. It was demolished in the early 1960s. Today, it is the site of Brenton Point State Park.

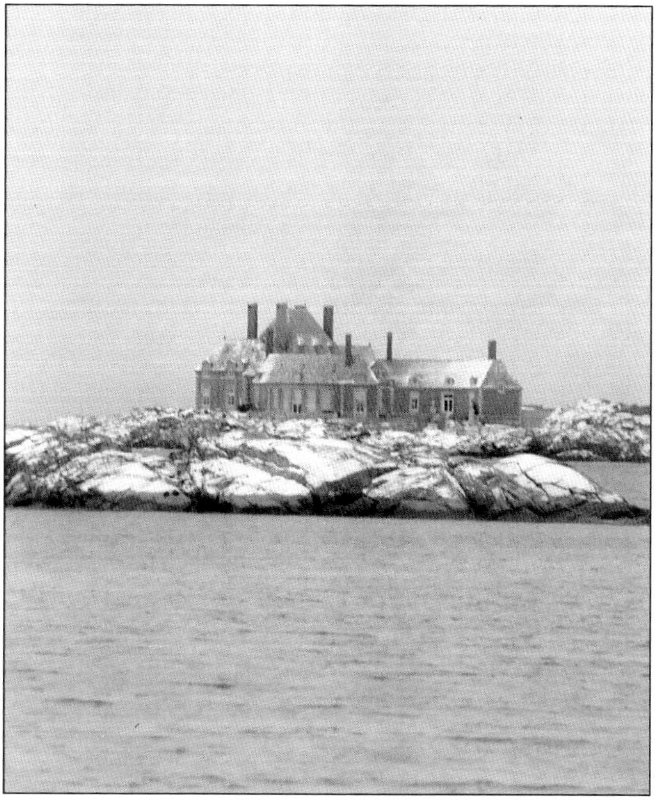

The mansion known as SeaFair is located at the tip of Cherry Neck, just past Green Ridge. It was built in the classic style of a French chateau in 1936. Sometime in the 1980s, the structure was converted into condominiums. William MacKenzie was the architect.

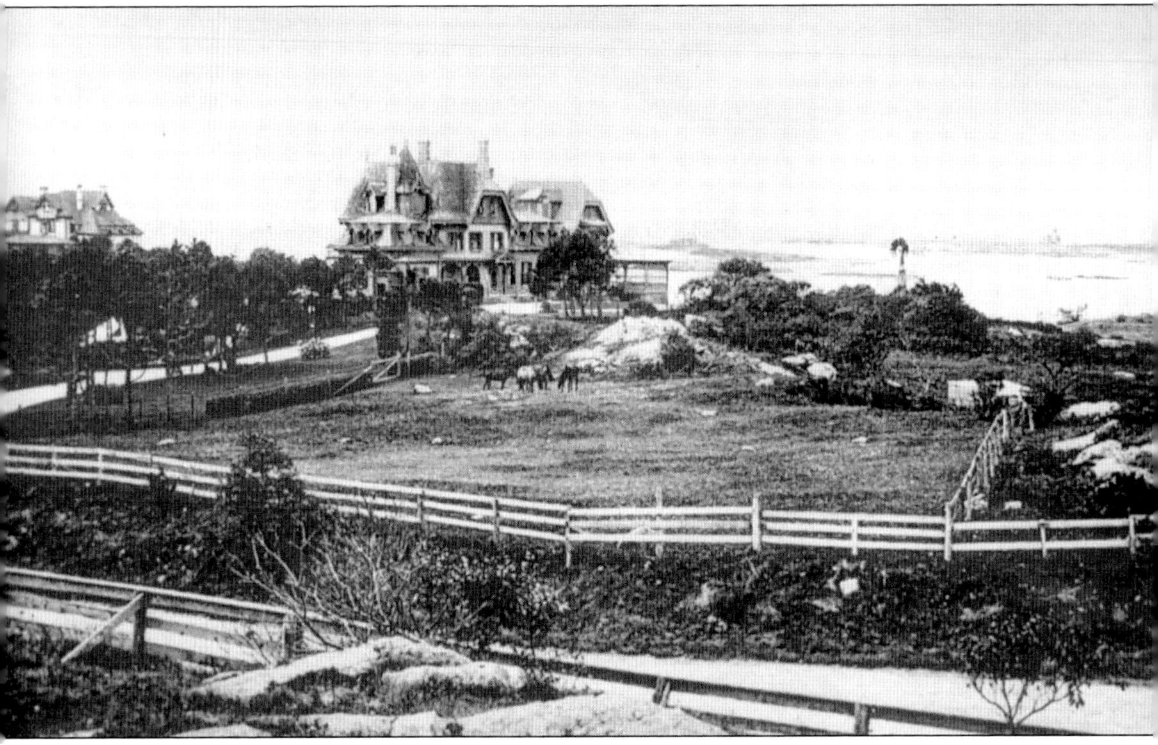

Rocky Farm was the ancestral home to John Alfred Hazard. The farm stretched from Bailey's Beach west along the ocean to what is today Hazard's Beach. It also bordered on Almy's Pond and Lily Pond. Upon his death in May 1880, Hazard willed all his property to Newport Hospital. In 1882, the land was valued at $123,000. Early on, the trustees of Newport Hospital realized the value of the land as Newport was becoming a playground for the wealthy. They joined with other landowners in cutting adjoining roads between Ocean Avenue and the harbor, creating many desirable building sites. As these were sold off, huge funds were generated to support the hospital's ever increasing expansion.

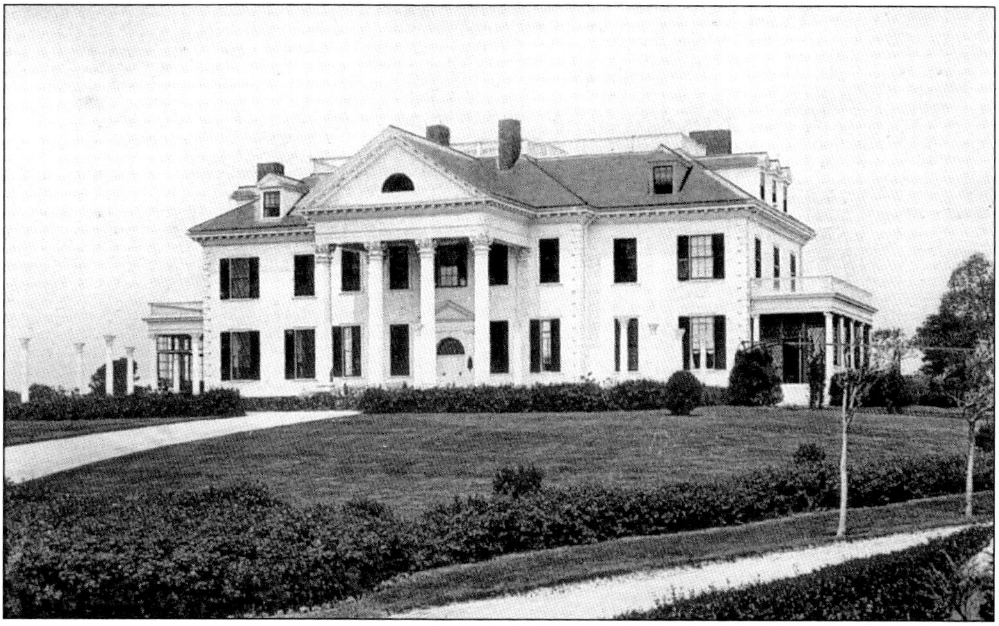

The Crossways was designed by McKim, Mead, and White and was built in 1898 as a Colonial Revival mansion for Stuyvesant Fish. It stands on Ocean Avenue at the corner of Jeffery Road.

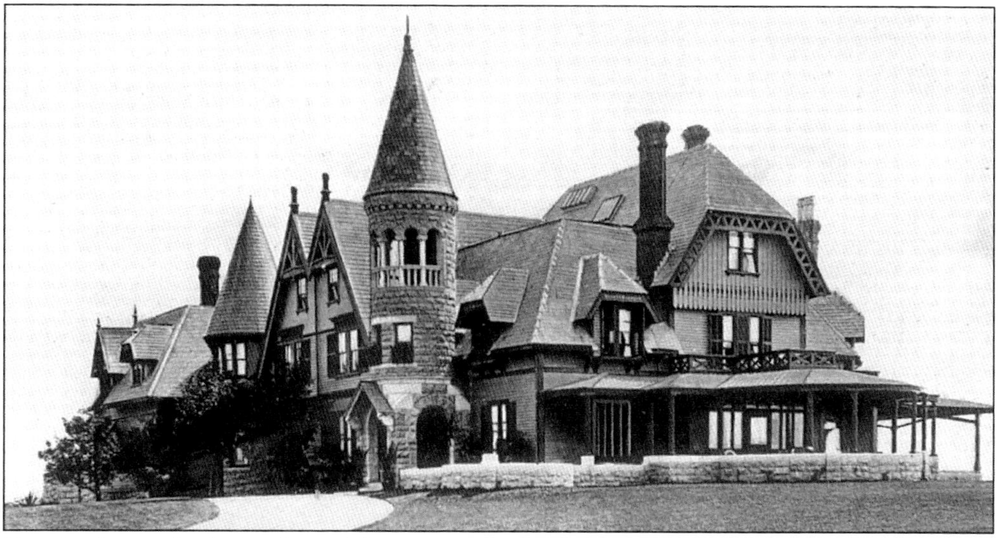

The Rocks was built by Henry Clews, west of Bailey's Beach. Directly below the house was Spouting Rock. Clews held a prominent position as a broker and banker on Wall Street. In 1862, Clews was elected as a member to the New York Stock Exchange.

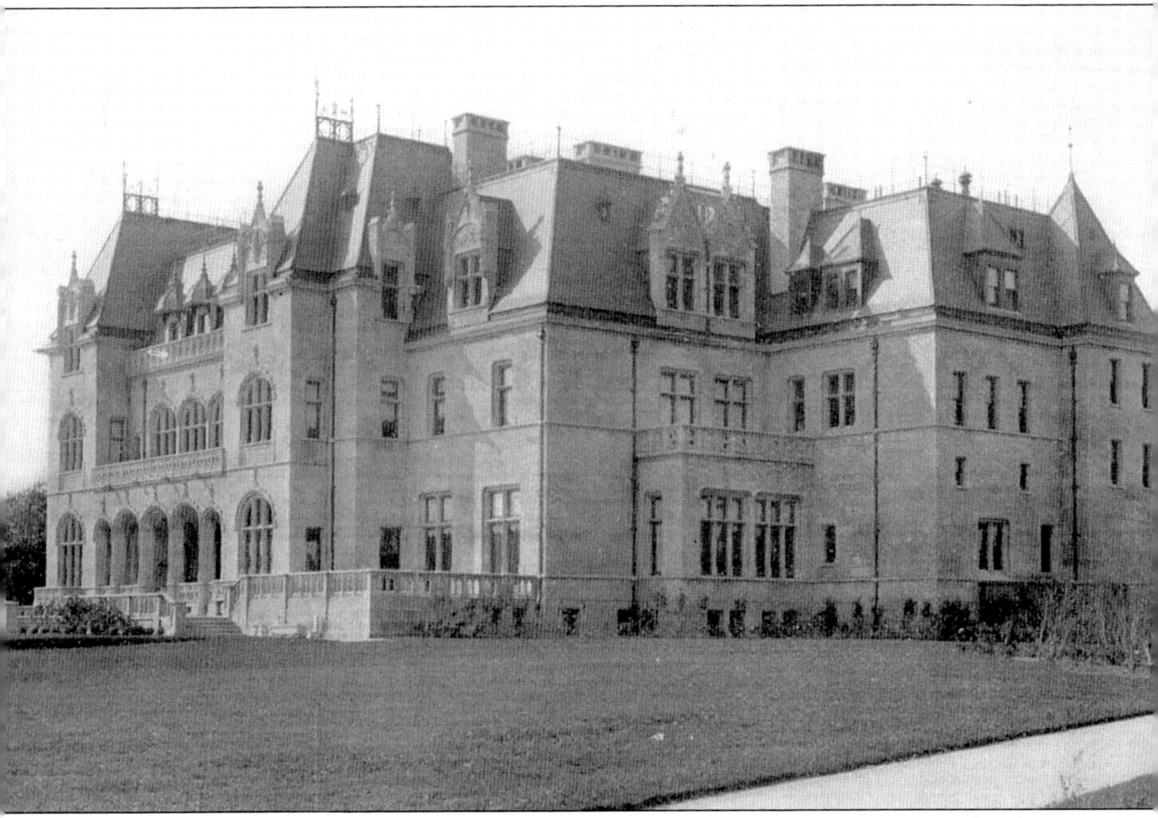

Ochre Court was designed by Richard Morris Hunt for Ogden Goelet in 1888. This 50-room Gothic French chateau was built to provide Mrs. Goelet, an important hostess in her time, with a grand house to entertain in. The house was surrounded by formal gardens and offered spectacular views of the Atlantic Ocean. In 1947, the house was given to the Sisters of Mercy, who shortly after opened Salve Regina College. Today, Salve Regina University encompasses more than 60 acres and has acquired several of Newport's mansions, which they maintain and preserve while serving the university in a variety of ways.

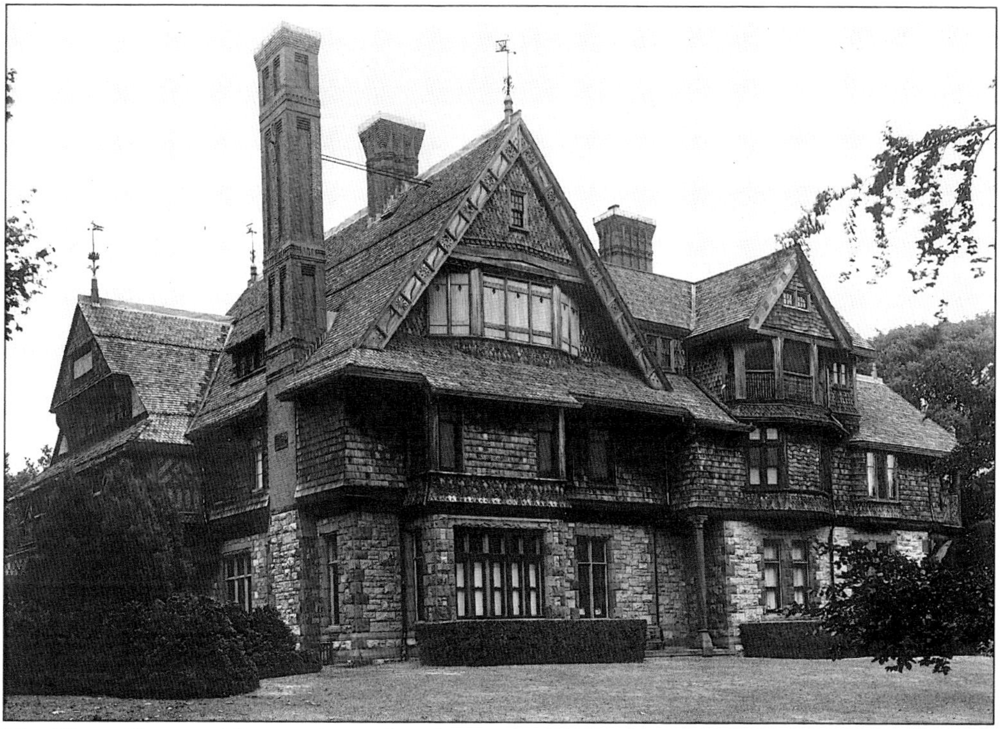

The Watts Sherman House is located at the corner of Lawrence and Shepard Avenues and was built in 1874 for William Watts Sherman and his wife, Anne Wetmore. The house was designed by Henry Hobson Richardson and stands today as one of Newport's greatest examples of Queen Anne architecture.

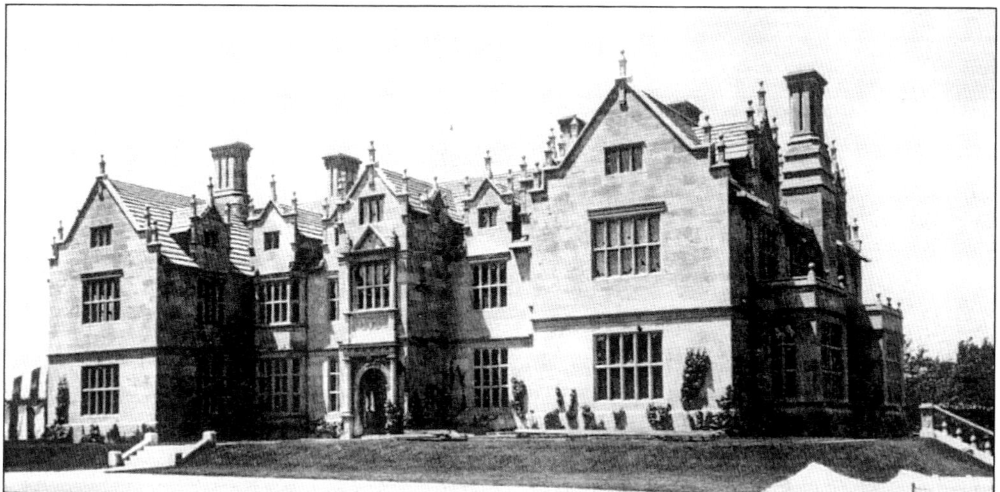

In 1888, James J. Van Allen built Wakehurst on Ochre Point Avenue. It was modeled after a castle in Sussex, England, that dated to 1590. Salve Regina University purchased the property in 1972 and, today, it is used as a student center.

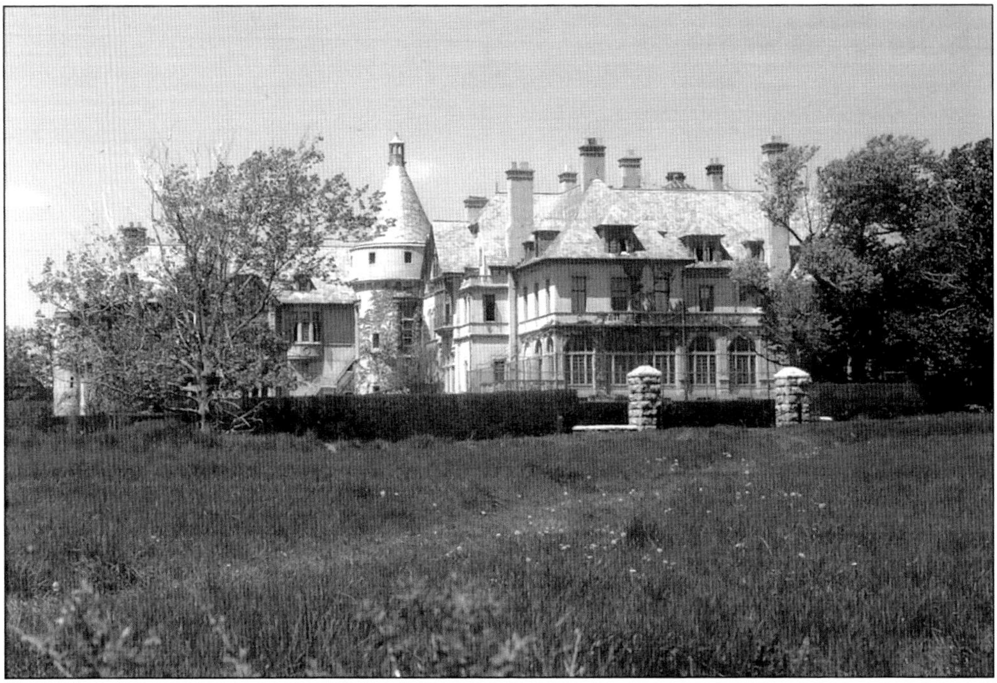

Seaview Terrace was designed by Howard Greenley in 1924 and built between 1927 and 1929. Edson Bradley was the mansion's first occupant. The 65-room house is now owned by Salve Regina University and serves as a student residence.

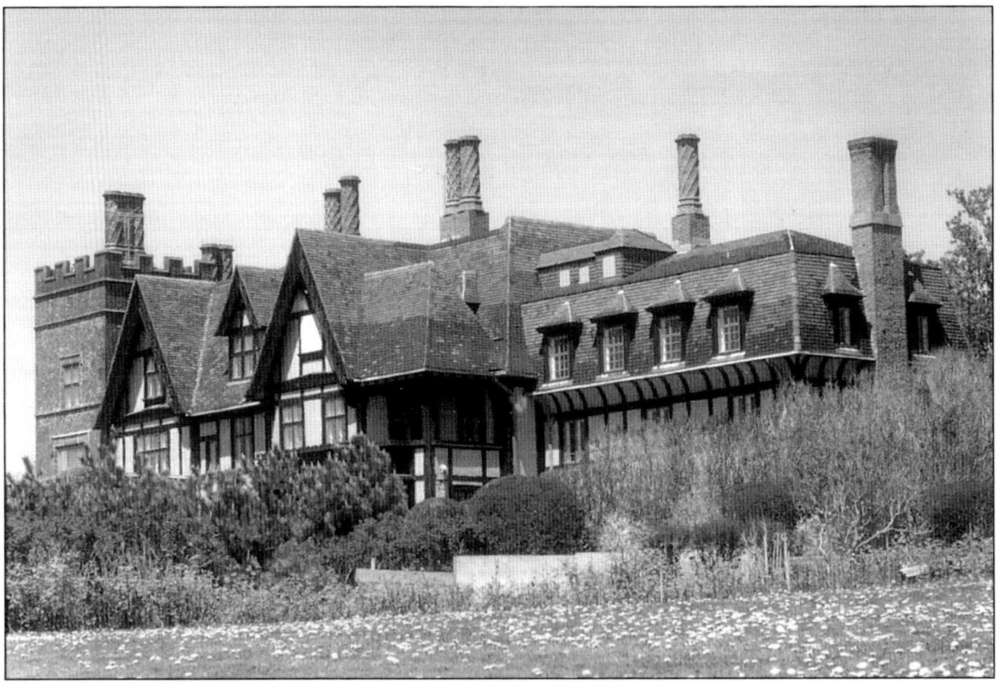

Fairholme was built in 1870 for John R. Drexel in the classic Tudor style. It was enlarged c. 1930.

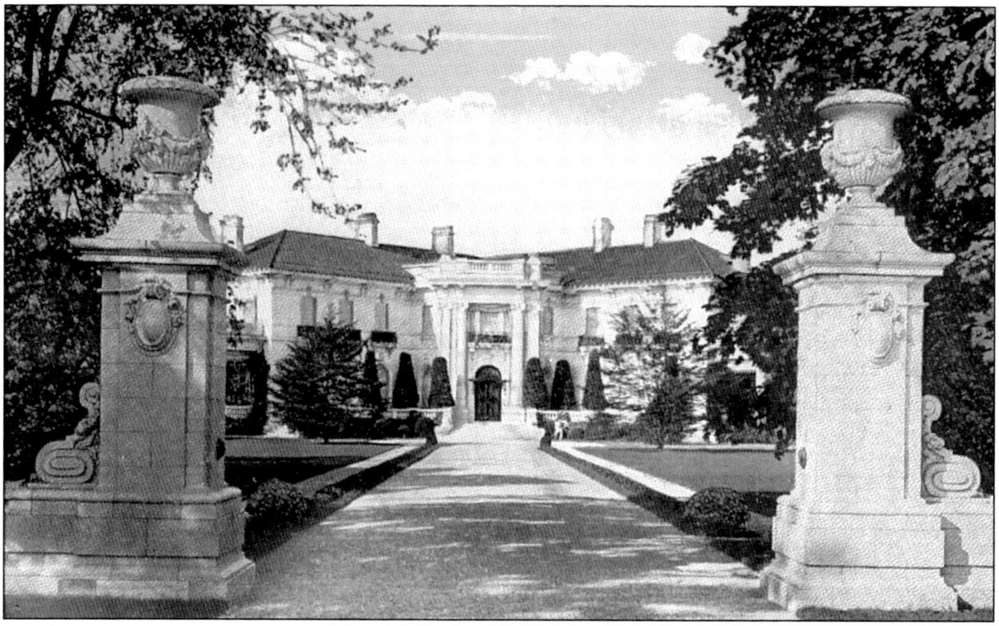

Dr. Henry Barton Jacobs of Baltimore built Whiteholme *c.* 1905 on Narragansett Avenue at the corner of Ochre Point Avenue. It was later replaced by Miley Hall.

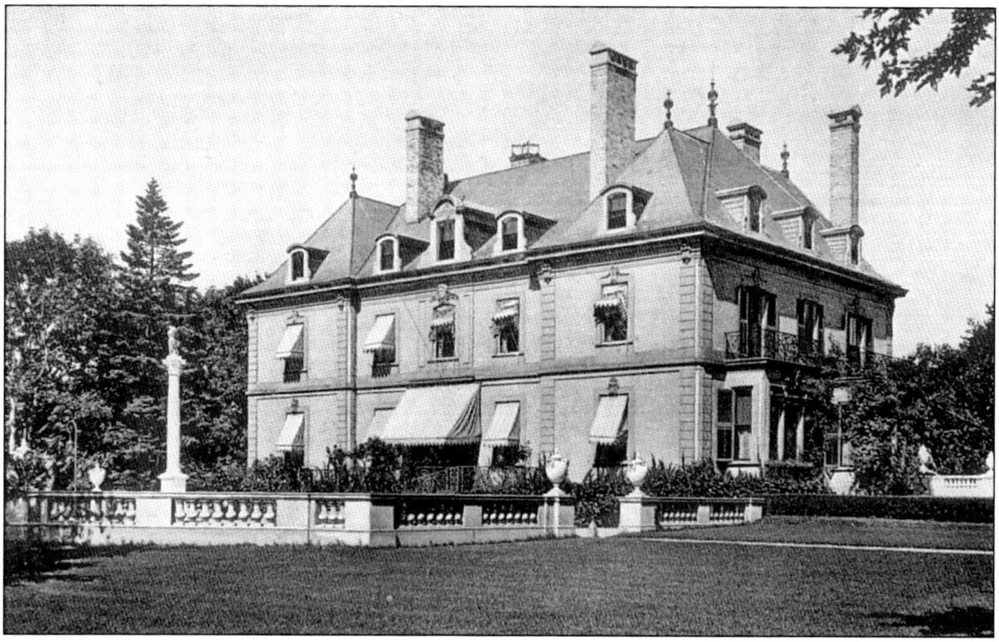

The George Richmond Fearing House, known as the Orchard, is located on Narragansett Avenue and was built in 1871. In more recent times, it was known as the Firestone Estate.

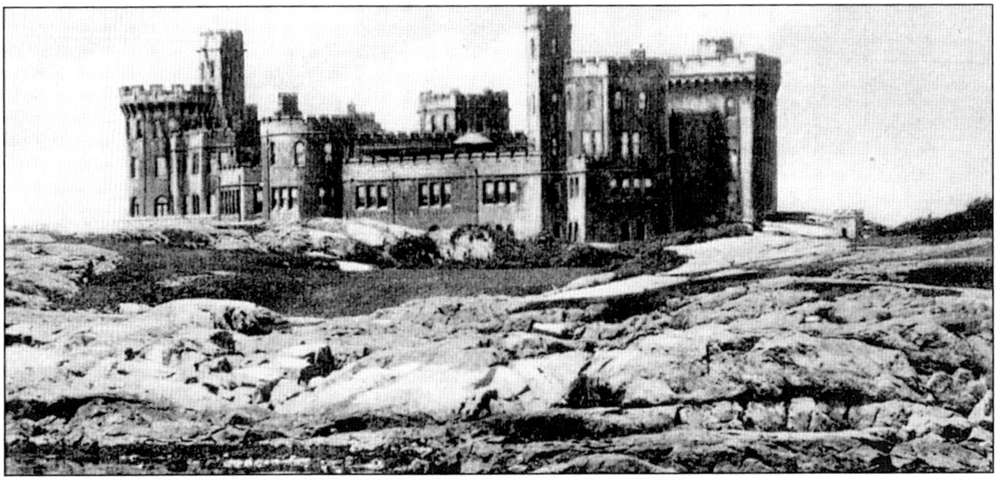

The Breakwater was built in 1899 by Charles Warren Lippitt at the end of Ledge Road. The structure was known locally as Lippitt's Castle and was razed *c*. 1925.

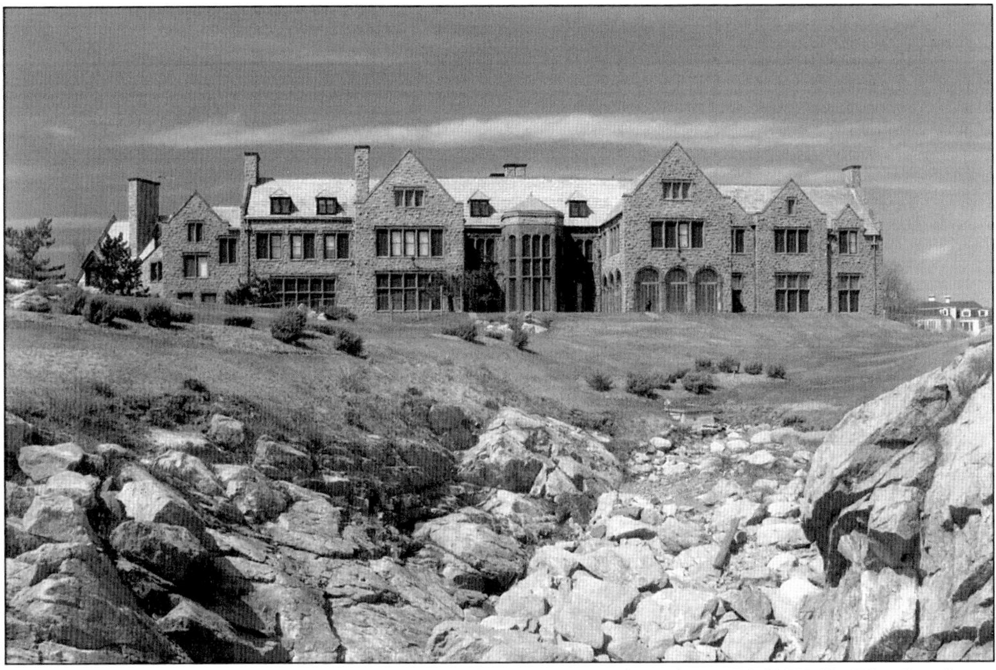

This photograph of the Duke Estate on Rough Point was taken from Cliff Walk. The land was originally owned by Frederick Vanderbilt and was purchased by James B. Duke, who made his fortune in tobacco. The house stayed in the hands of Doris Duke until her demise in the early 1990s. Today, the house is a museum curated by the Newport Restoration Society. (Photograph by Rob Lewis.)

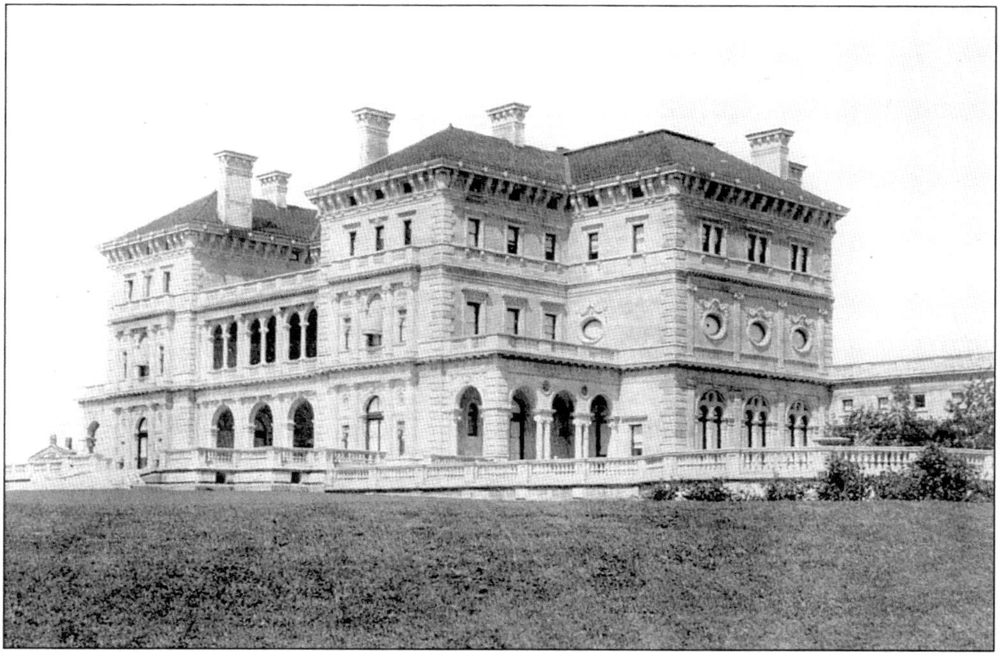

The first Breakers was a wooden structure built for Pierre Lorillard. It burned to the ground in 1892. Cornelius Vanderbuilt purchased the property and, between 1892 and 1895, the second Breakers was built on a Richard Morris Hunt design. The building was designed to be completely fireproof.

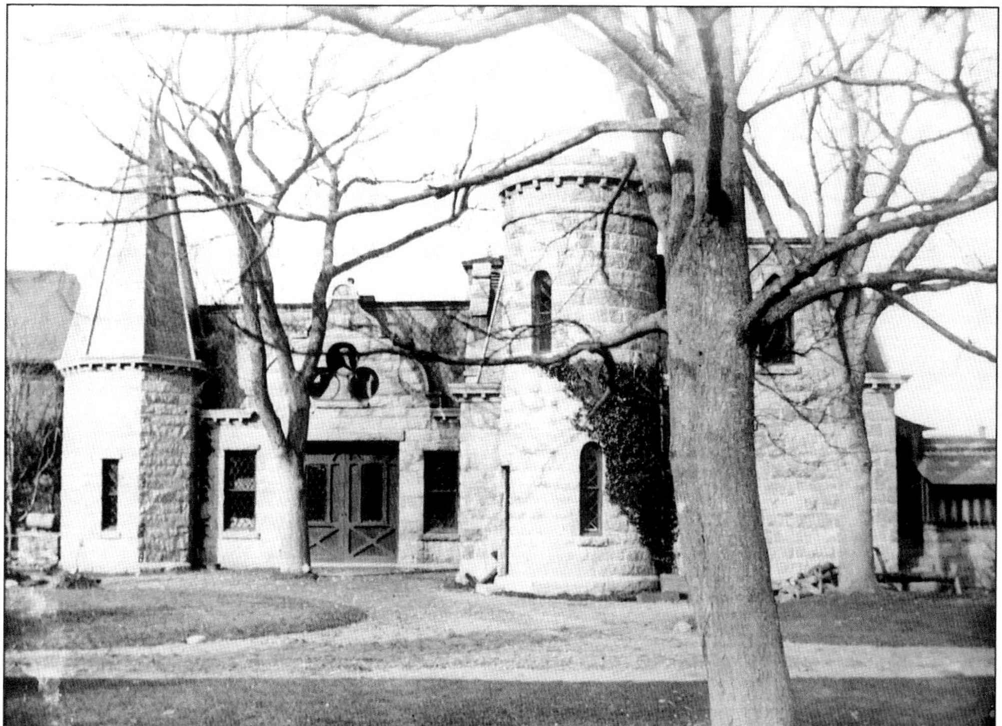

The stable at Belaire, shown *c.* 1890, is on Old Beach Road. It is an early Dudley Newton design.

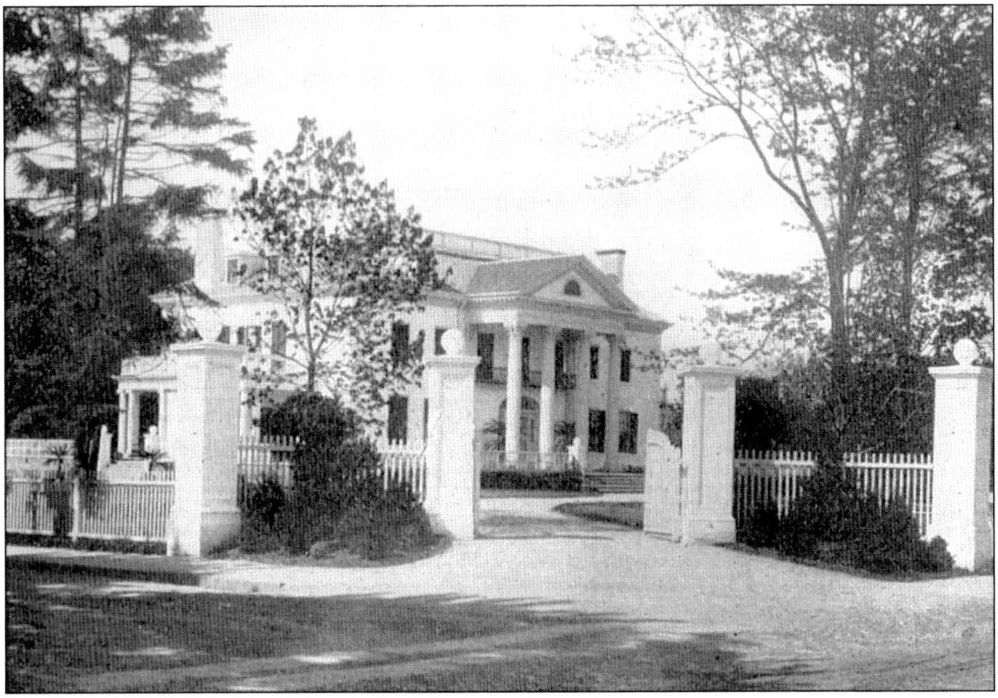

Dexter Bradford built Whitehall in the late 1800s at the corner of Rhode Island Avenue and Catherine Street.

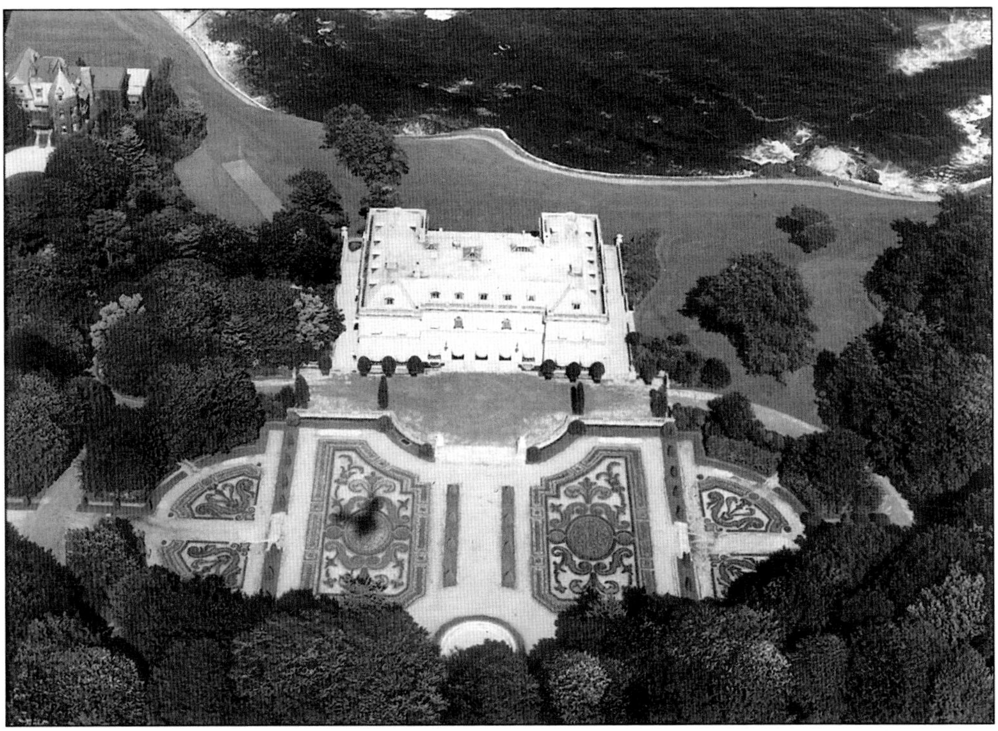

Miramar, designed by Horace Trombauer, was built in 1914 for Dr. Hamilton Rice. The gardens were very elaborate and were said to have been patterned after a favorite Persian rug.

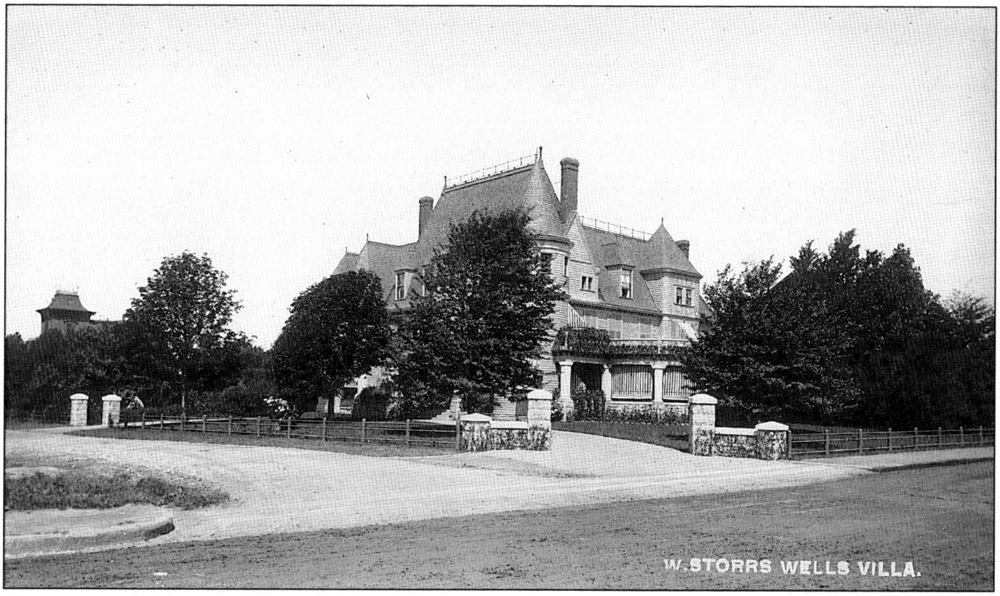

The original Chetwode was built in 1903 on Bellevue Avenue, on the corner of Ruggles Avenue, for William Storrs Wells. J.J. Astor resided in Chetwode between 1934 and 1948.

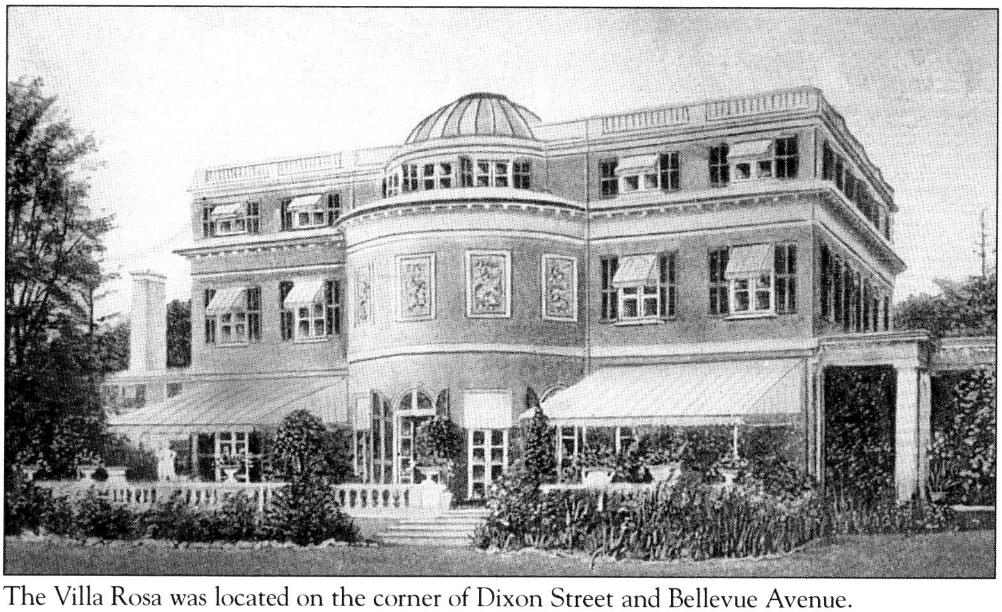

The Villa Rosa was located on the corner of Dixon Street and Bellevue Avenue.

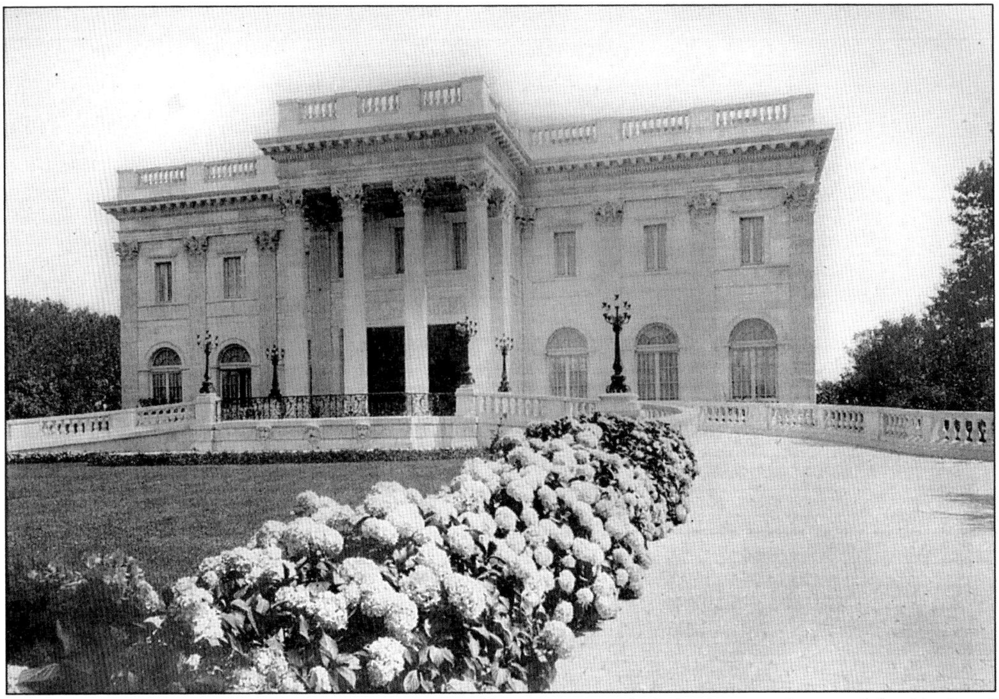

The Marble House was built in 1892 for William K. Vanderbilt. It was designed by Richard Morris Hunt and cost $11 million to build.

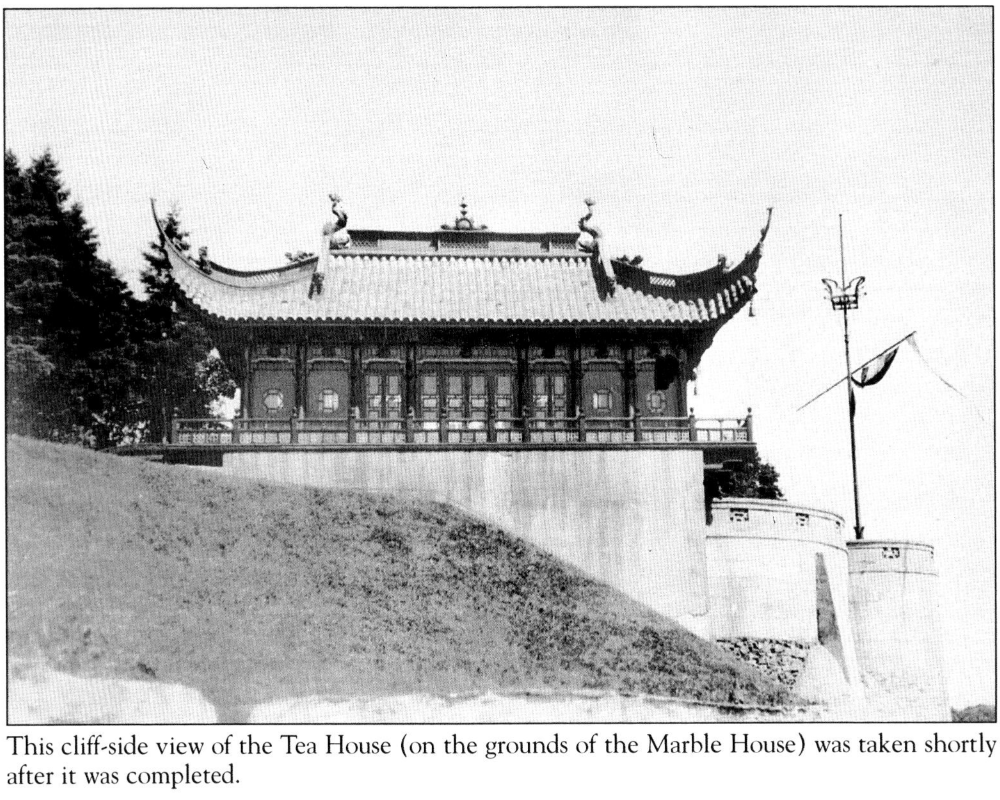

This cliff-side view of the Tea House (on the grounds of the Marble House) was taken shortly after it was completed.

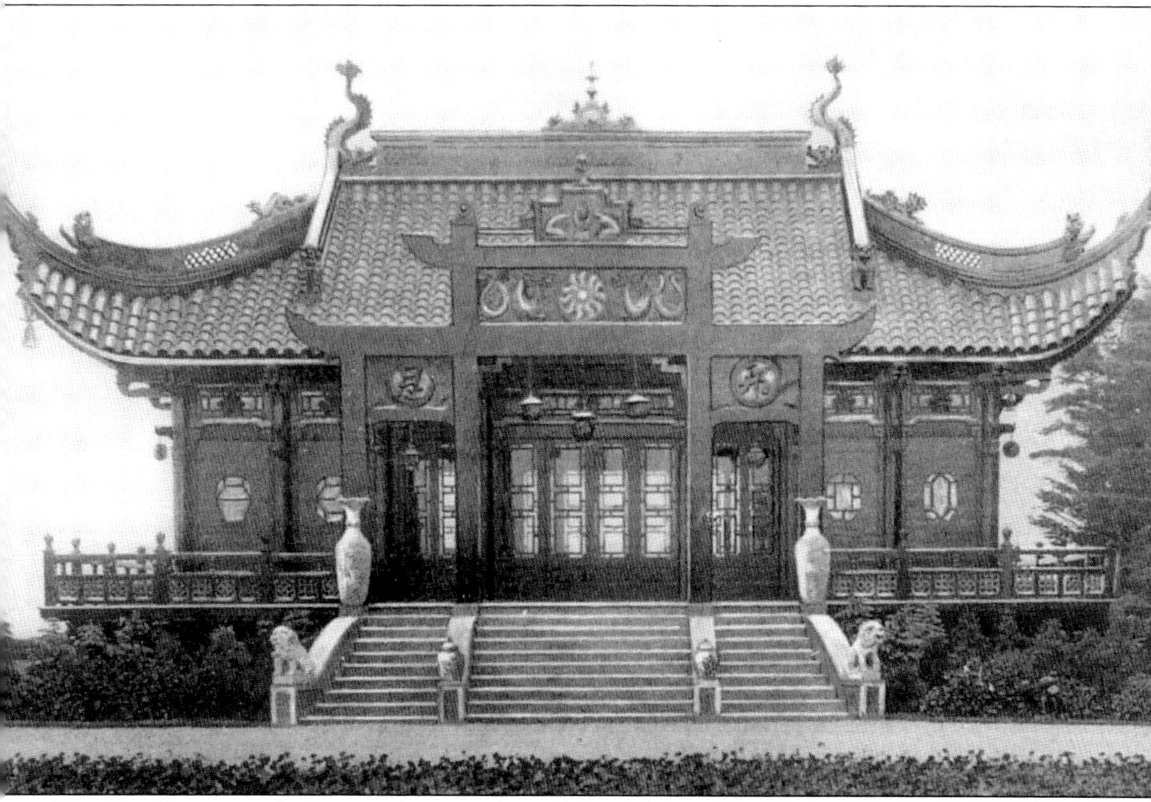

The Tea House was built over the tunnel to Cliff Walk in 1914 for Mrs. O.H. Belmont. In the late 1970s, the structure was moved several feet away from the cliffs and restored by the Newport Preservation Society. This postcard shows the Tea House at its completed state in 1914.

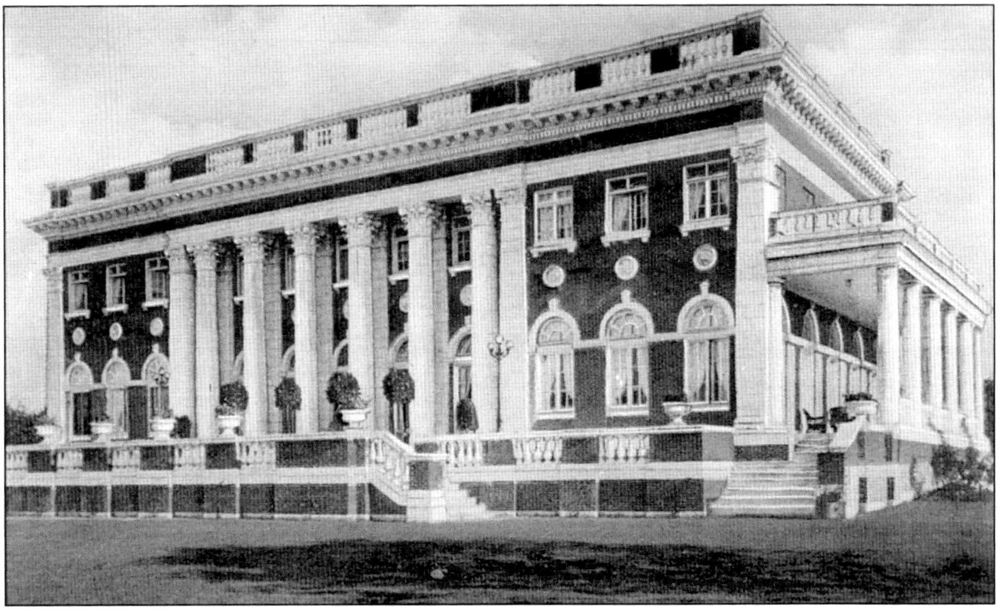

Castlewood was built in the early 20th century at the corner of Girard and Maple Avenues. In 1922, it housed the Mercy Home and School according to the *Newport City Guide*.

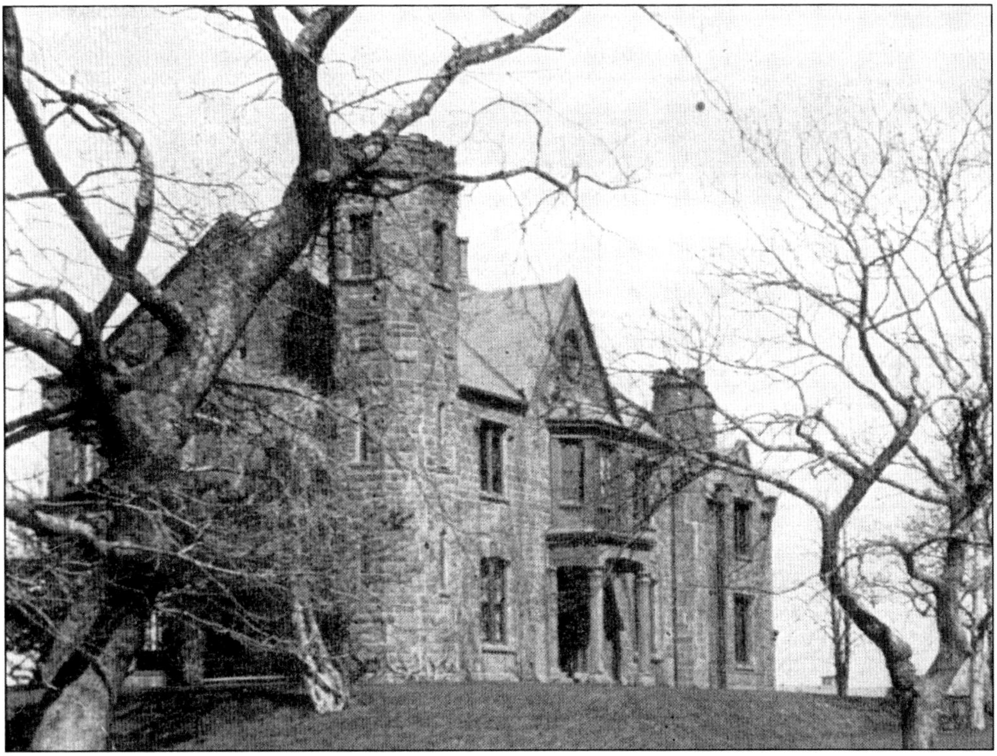

The original Malbone Hall was built on Miantonomi Hill in 1741. On June 7, 1766, it burned to the ground. In 1848, Prescott Hall bought the property and commissioned Alexander Davis to build a new Malbone estate.

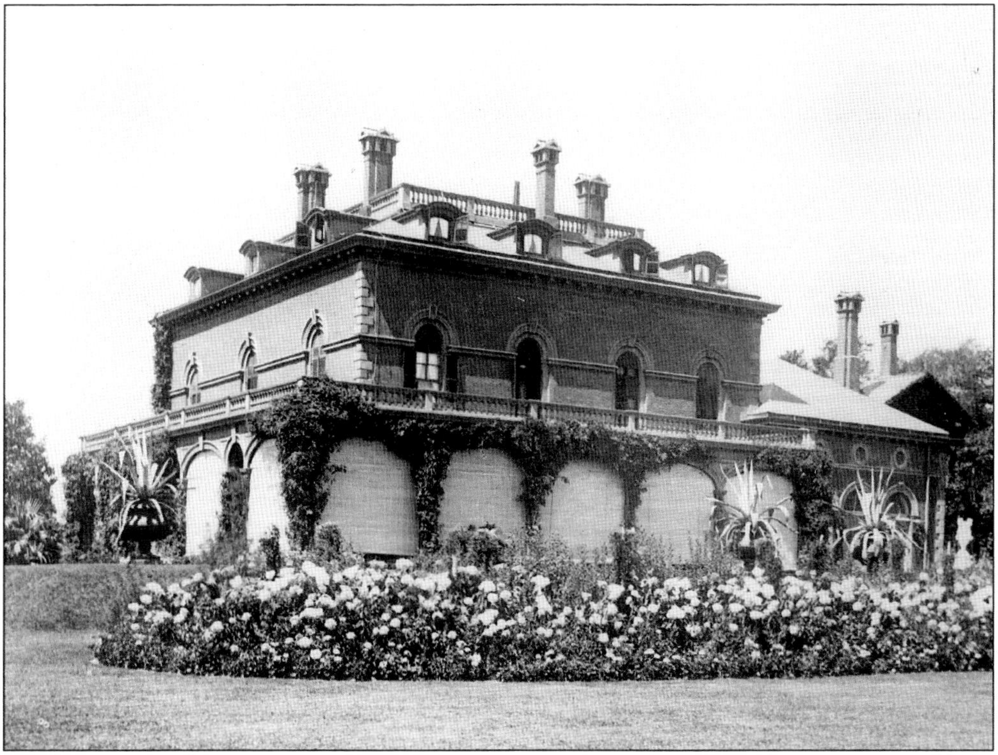

Beechwood was designed and built in 1855 on a Calvert Vaux design. It was first built for Daniel Parish. William Astor Jr. purchased the house in the early 1880s.

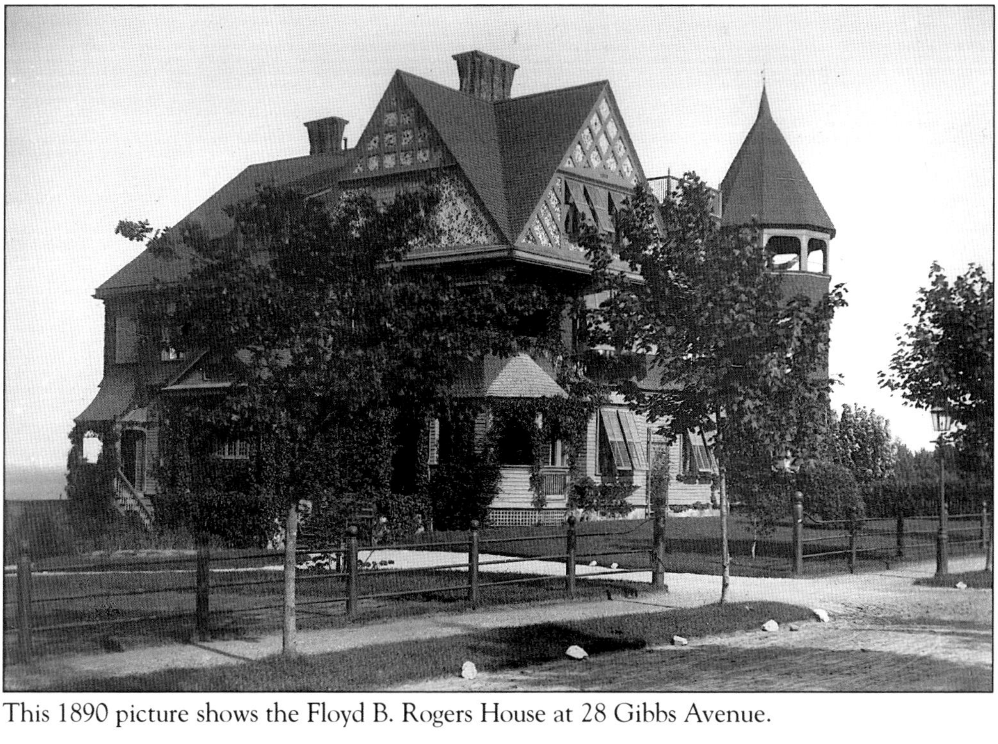

This 1890 picture shows the Floyd B. Rogers House at 28 Gibbs Avenue.

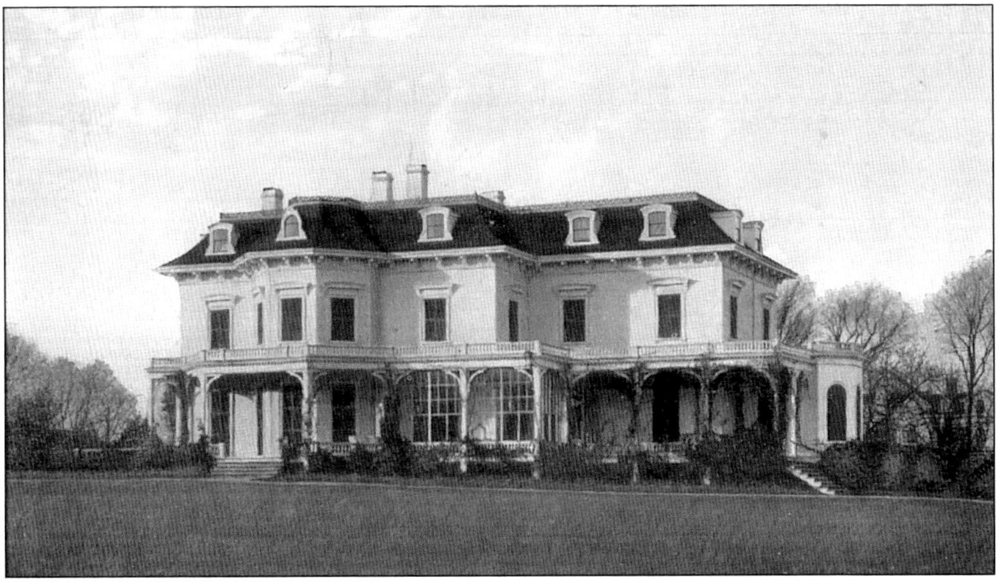

By the Sea was built by Perry Belmont on Bellevue Avenue in 1905. Belmont was a big supporter of the first automobile races to be held in Newport.

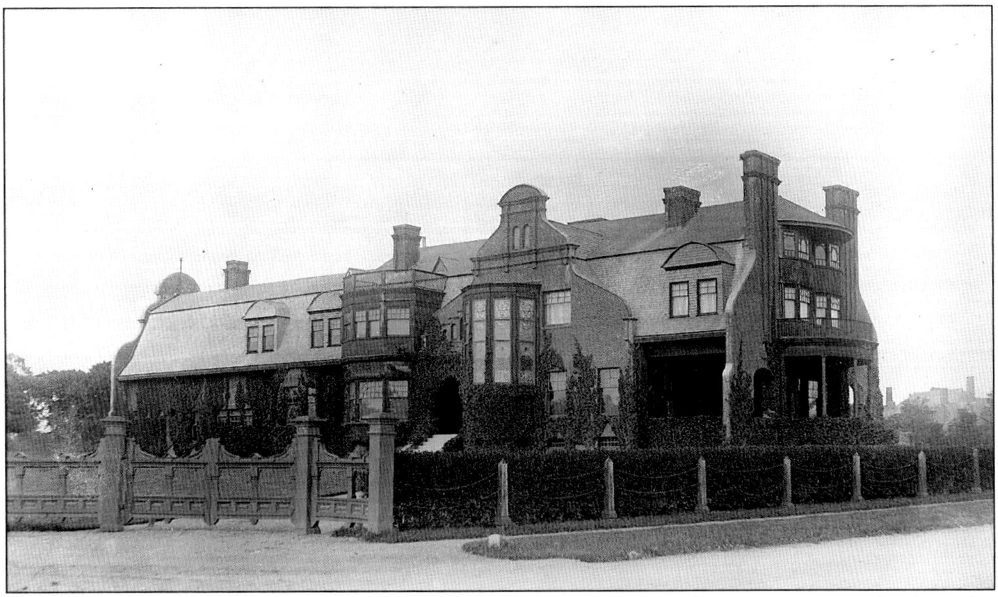

An early Dudley Newton design in the Italian Tuscany style, this house was somewhere in the Gibbs Avenue area.

Seven

THE NAVY IN NEWPORT

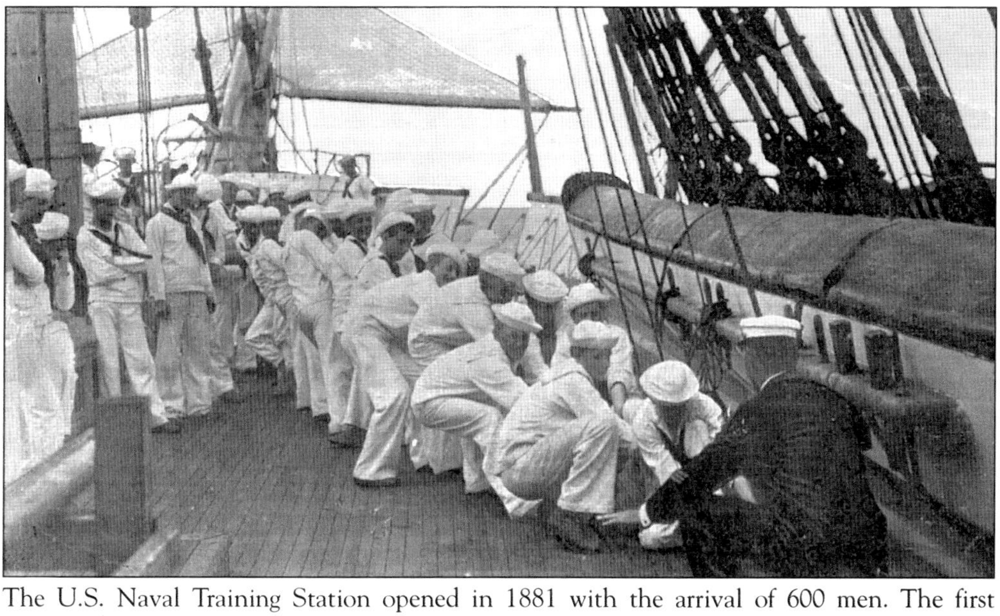

The U.S. Naval Training Station opened in 1881 with the arrival of 600 men. The first commander was Capt. Stephen B. Luce, who would eventually achieve the rank of admiral.

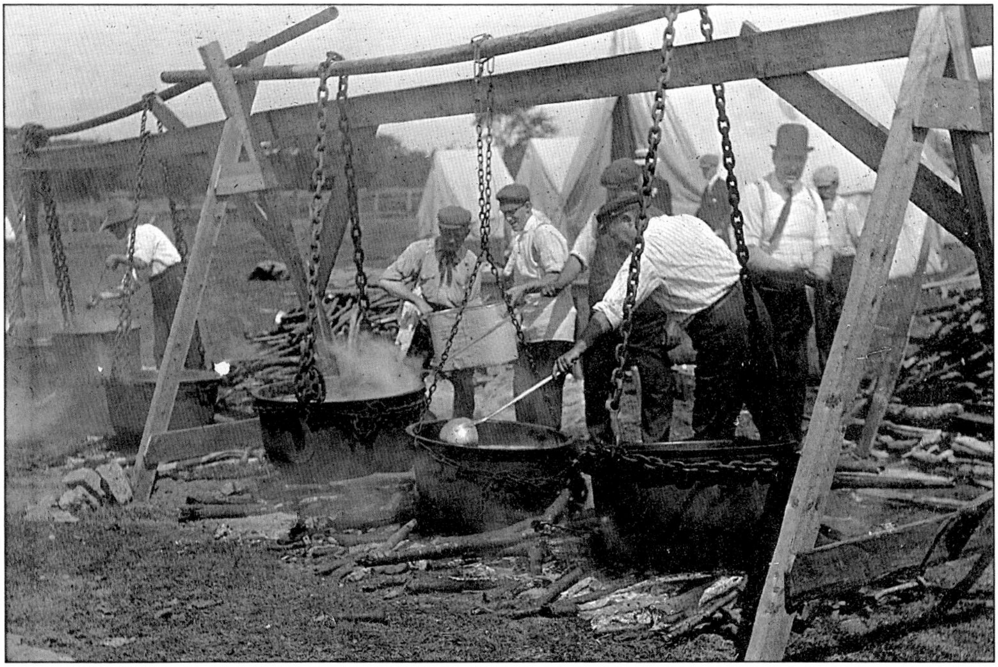

Cooks prepare a New England–style clambake for visiting sailors in 1910. Fleet Week occurred once a year when the North Atlantic Squadron anchored in Newport Harbor. Every year, Newport would mark the celebration with parades, fireworks, and festivities.

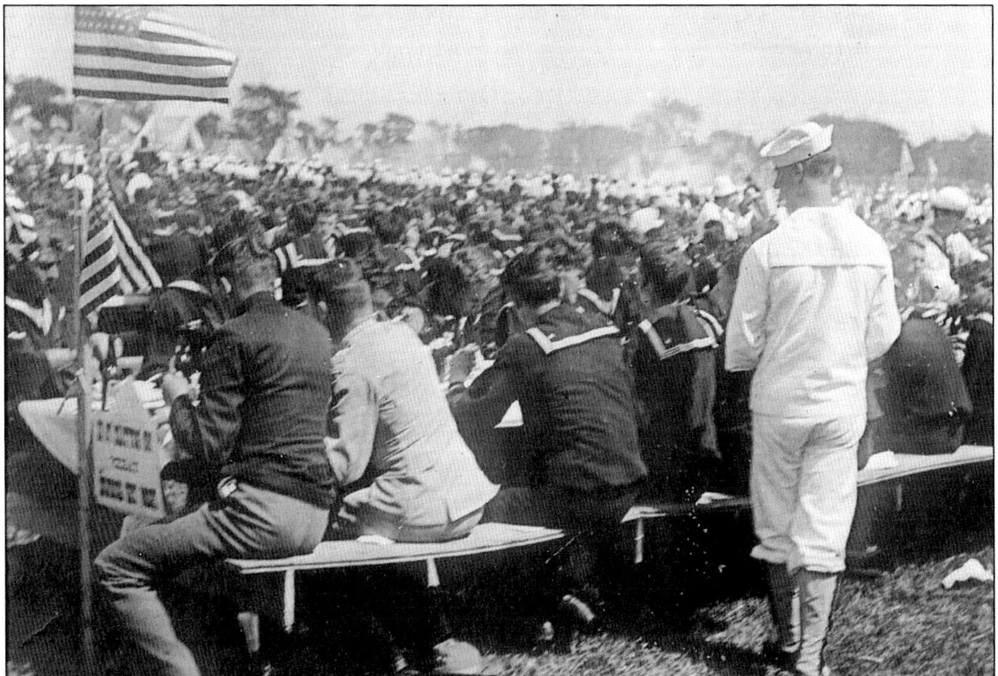

The 1910 celebration was a three-day affair. When it was over, more than 12,000 meals had been served.

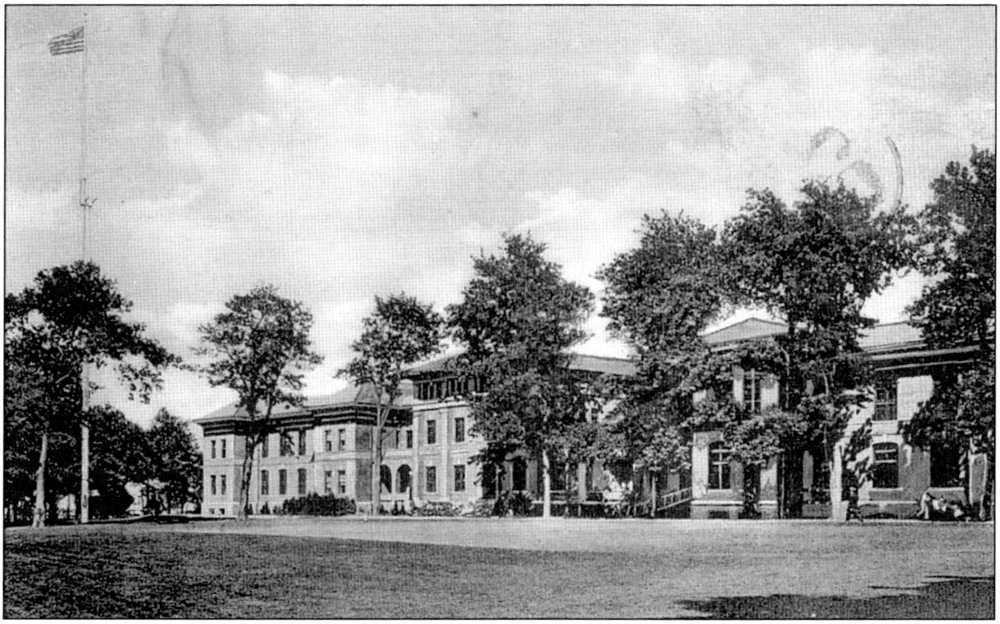

In 1909, the U.S. Navy acquired a 15-acre parcel of land adjacent to Coaster's Island. This hospital was built and admitted its first patients in 1913.

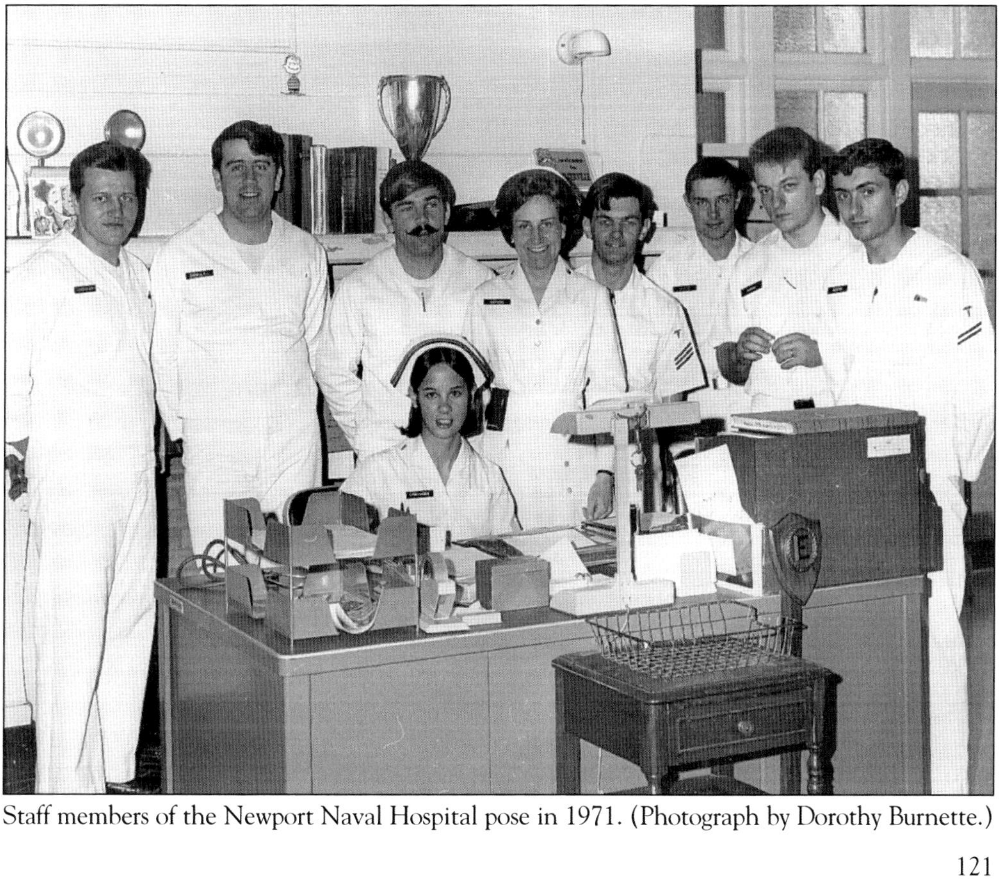

Staff members of the Newport Naval Hospital pose in 1971. (Photograph by Dorothy Burnette.)

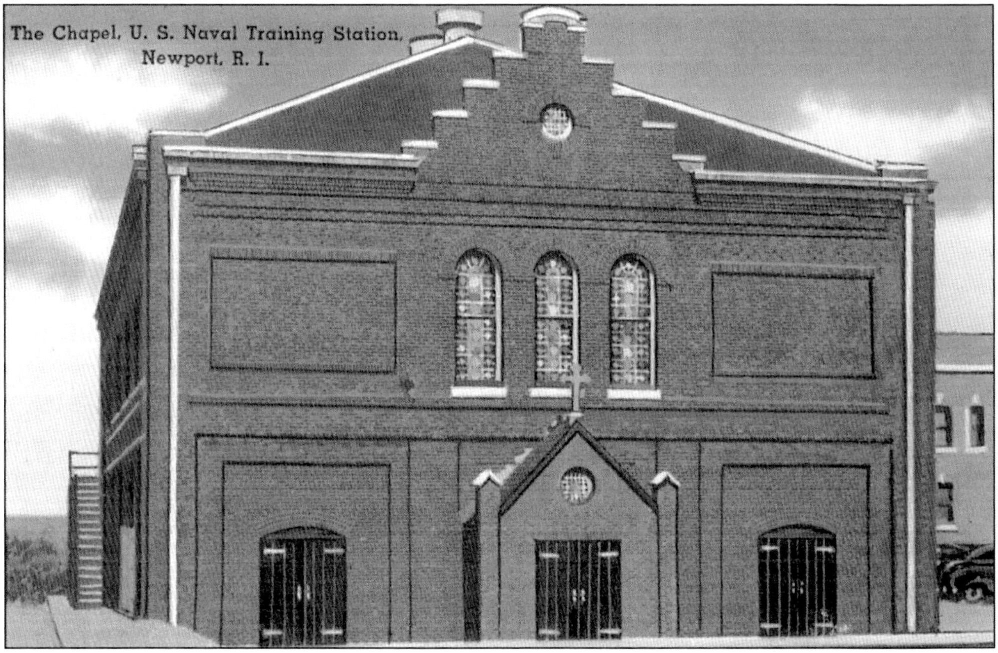

The chapel at the U.S. Naval Training Station is shown c. 1915.

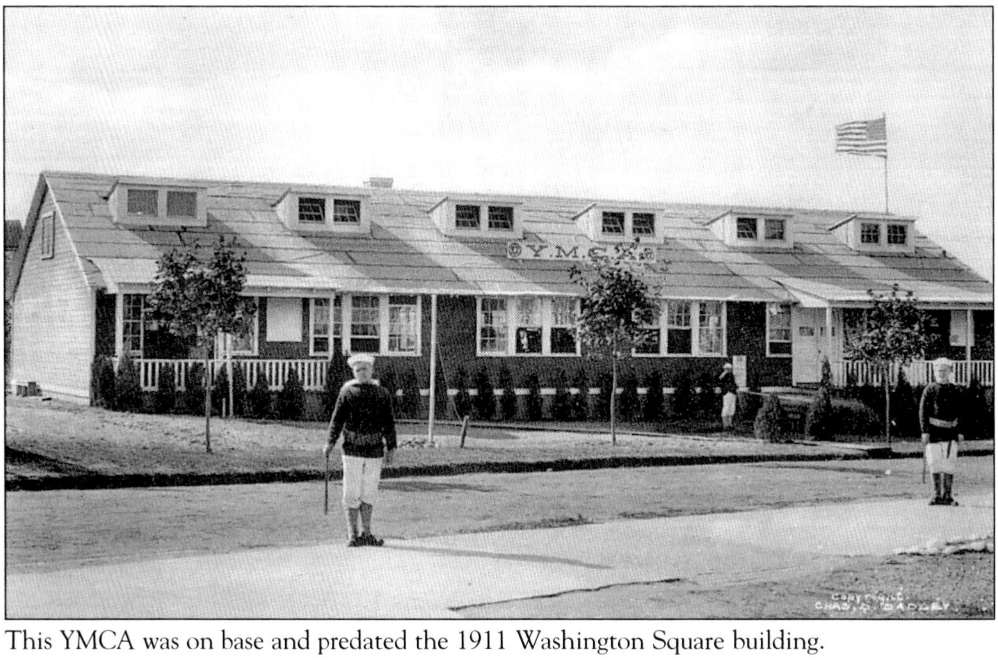

This YMCA was on base and predated the 1911 Washington Square building.

The hospitality of the navy YMCA served as a home-away-from-home to thousands of young men as they passed through Newport.

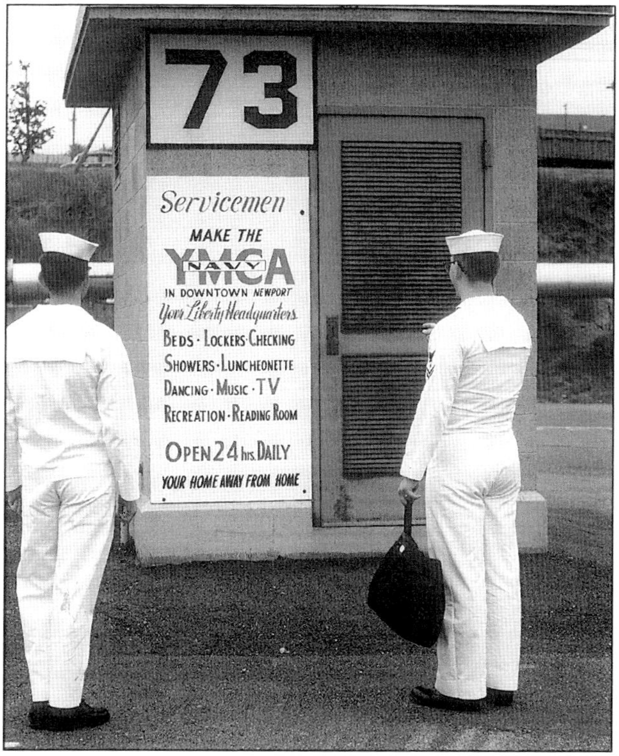

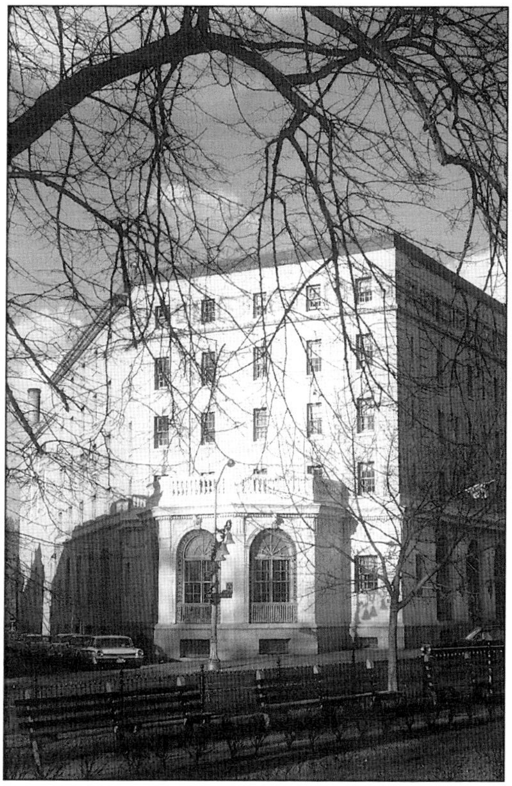

The Washington Square YMCA was built as a gift from Mrs. Thomas J. Emery in memory of her sons. The cornerstone ceremony was held in November 1910. The facility opened in 1911. Among the dignitaries in attendance were Sen. George Peabody and Adm. Stephen B. Luce.

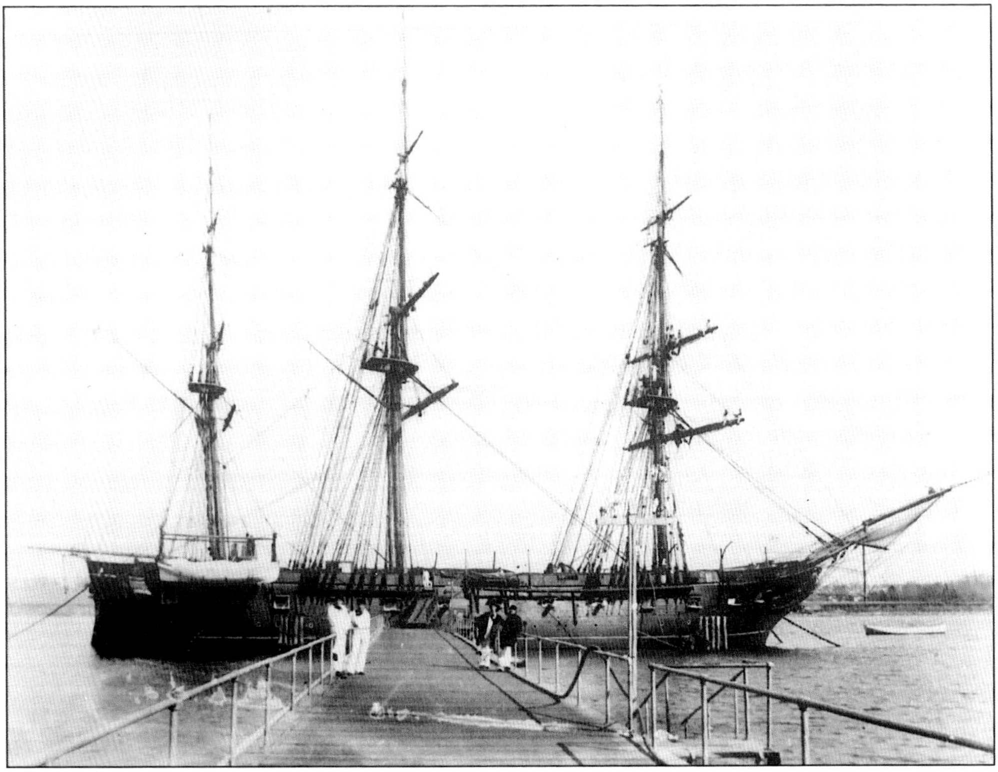

USS *Constellation* is docked at Coasters Island *c.* 1910. The ship was used as a training vessel for naval cadets.

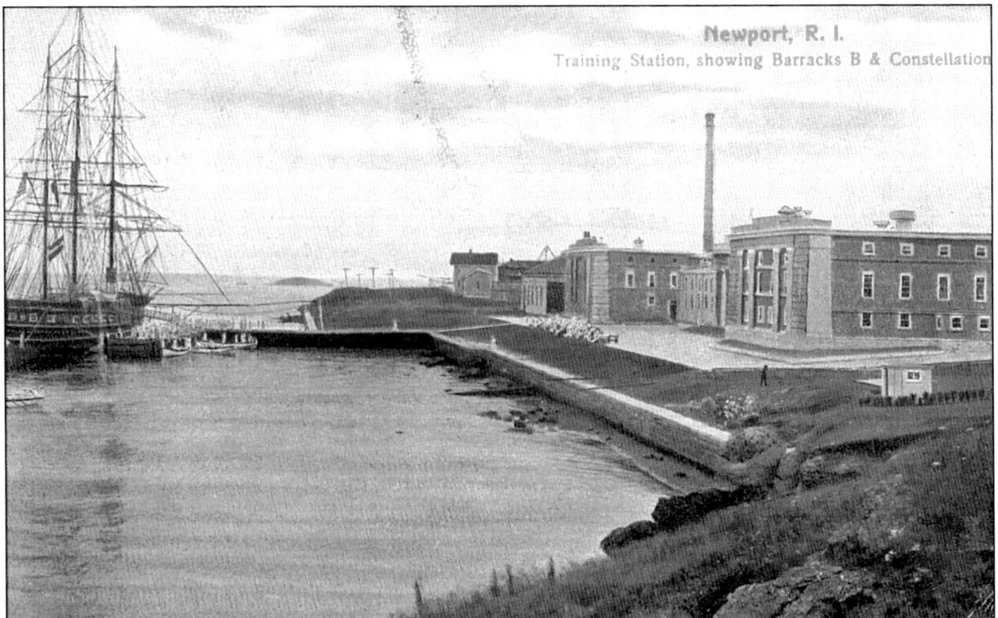

This view shows the USS *Constellation* near Barracks B. The barracks, which were built in 1900, were the first living quarters at the training center.

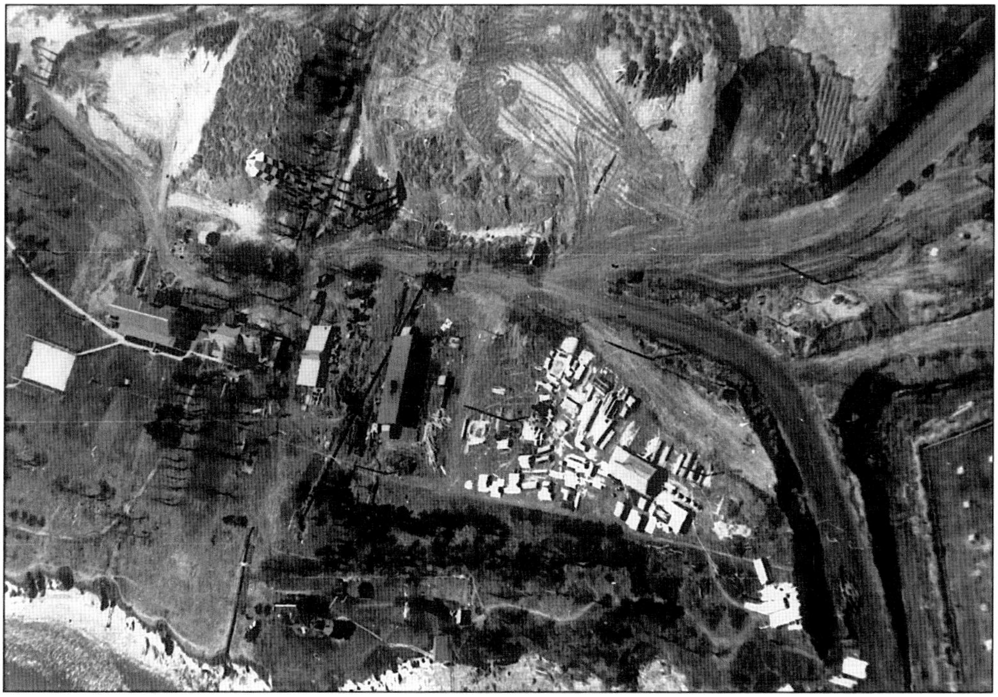

In 1919, the government purchased Gould Island and shortly after built facilities to store explosives. In 1942, machine shops were built on the island to support the war effort. This aerial photograph was taken on April 24, 1942. (Courtesy of the Naval War College Archives.)

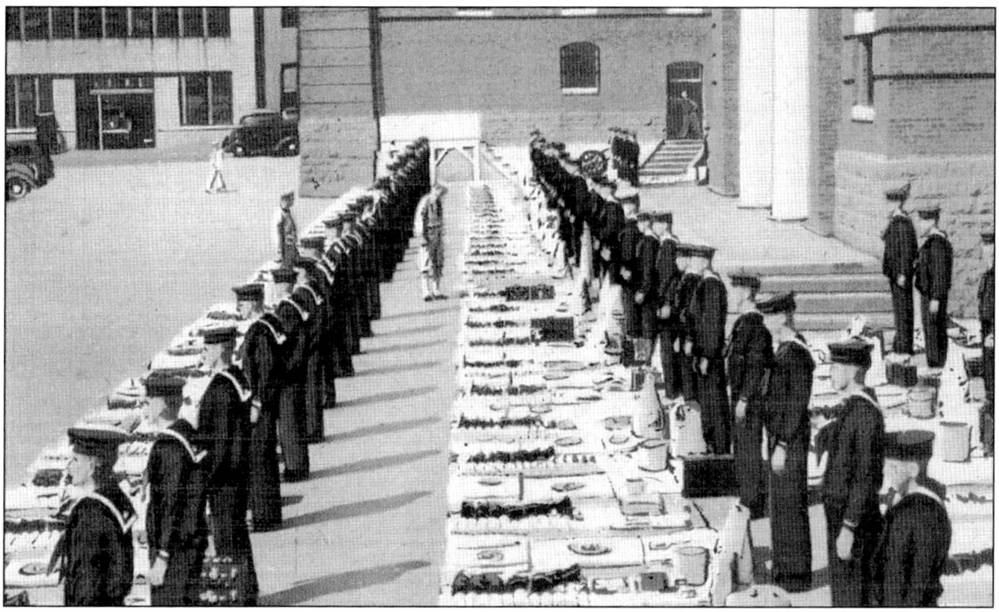

The navy began to develop Coddington Point for uses as the U.S. Naval Training Station c. 1919. The plans called for 365 buildings to be erected and, when completed, they housed more than 14,000 men. In this postcard, trainees line up for gear inspection.

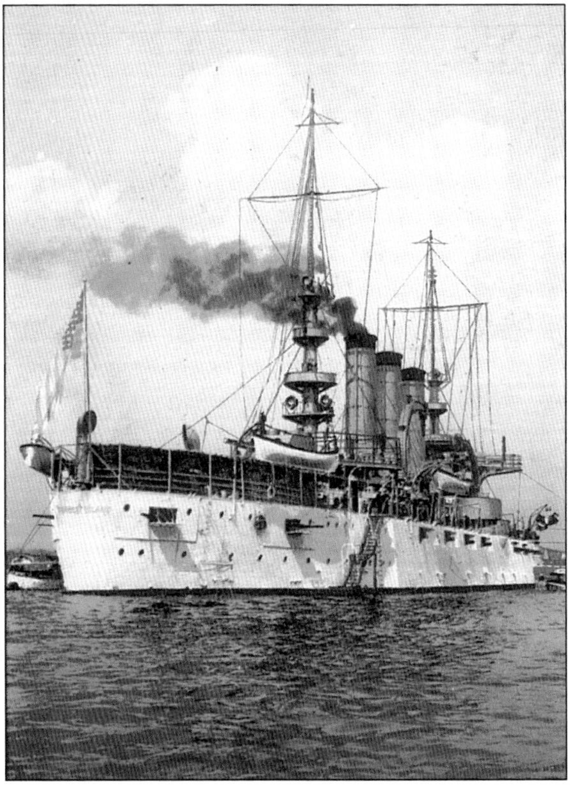

The first ship to bear the name *Rhode Island* was a wooden side-wheel vessel that was built in 1860 and served in the navy until 1867. The ship shown here was the second *Rhode Island* and was launched in May 1904. After becoming part of the Atlantic Fleet and serving in World War I, it was scrapped in November 1923.

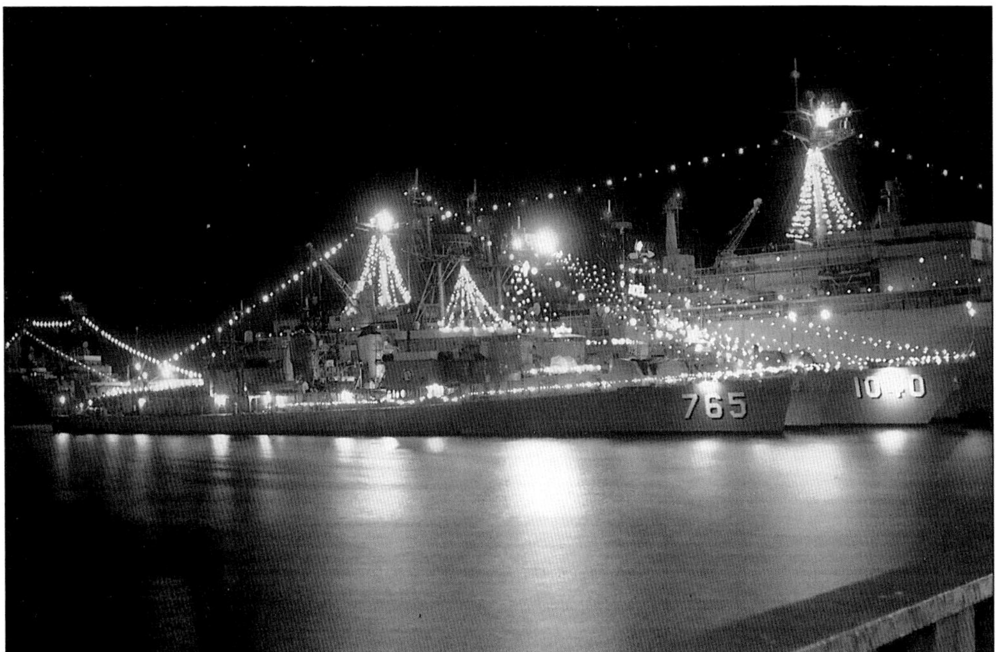

In this view, ships docked at Pier 1 during the Christmas season of 1969 exhibit their holiday dressing.

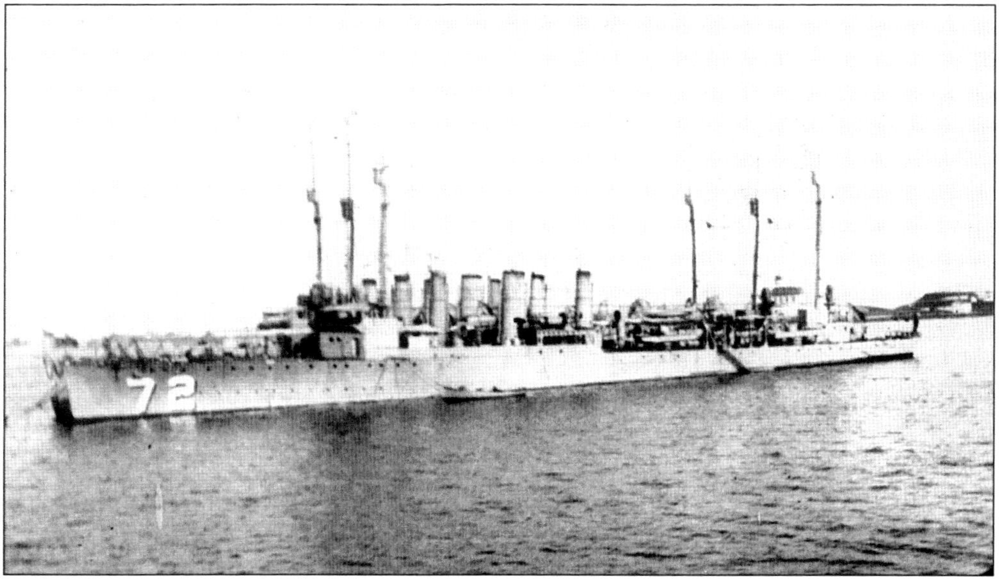

Pods of three or four ships berthed together was a common sight until the massive navy pull-out in 1975. This pod was photographed off Goat Island in 1921.

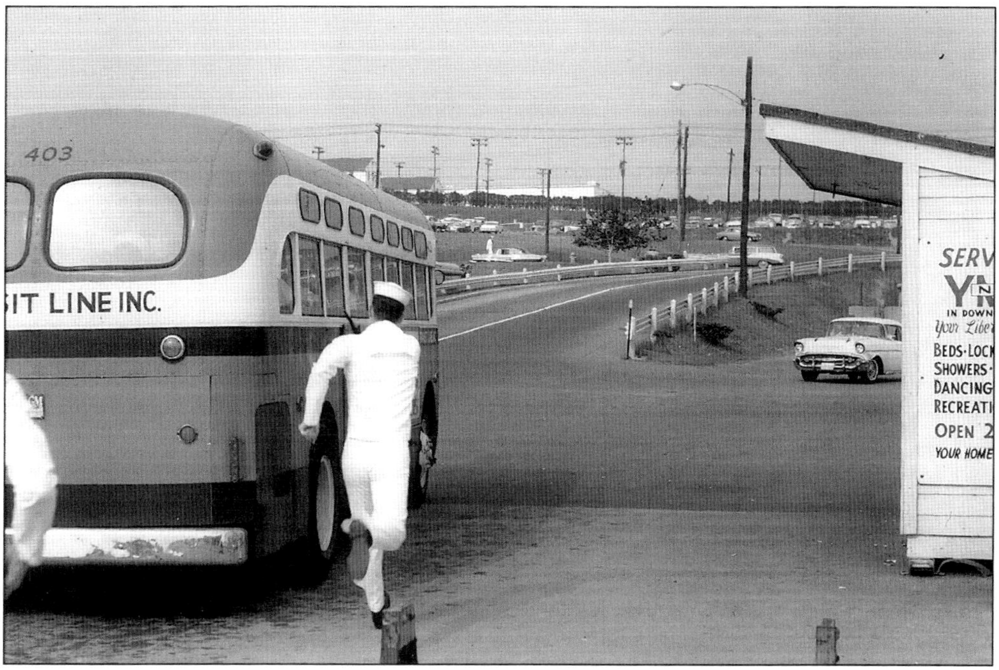

We will end our book with catching the last bus into town.

ACKNOWLEDGMENTS

Again, we must acknowledge the gifted eye of Essig Remington "Doc" Young. He not only documented Newport with his photography from the 1950s through the 1970s but also amassed a collection of antique photographs and ephemera. His strong ties with the navy in Newport is evident in his photography, along with his great love for the community. The Newport Restoration Foundation was again generous with use of images in its archive.

Another pillar of strength for our search for images was Ann Calcutt. Ann has a huge postcard collection, and we left after every visit overwhelmed with data and images. She could not have been more generous and gracious. Thank you, Ann. Again, we are indebted to William Bachus for his help and access to his collection. Thanks also go to Mr. and Mrs. David Sovereign Young, who were in touch with us when we needed them with old slides and information about his father's photography. Thanks are also in order for Dorothy Burnette and the Desilets family. Last but certainly not least, we are grateful to Jennifer Ann Gomes, Bob Lennon, and Rene "Cotton" Charette for their patience and encouragement during the months of grueling research.